All-American
COMFORT
FOOD

Emily Andrae

Egala Anderson Peter

All-American COMFORT FOOD

Recipes for the
Great-Tasting Food
Everyone Loves

EMILY ANDERSON

CONTRIBUTING EDITOR: Elizabeth Anderson

CUMBERLAND HOUSE
Nashville, Tennessee

Published by Cumberland House Publishing, Inc., 431 Harding Industrial Drive,
Nashville, TN 37211.

Distributed to the trade by Andrews & McMeel, 4900 Main Street, Kansas City,
Missouri 64112.

Jacket design by Harriette Bateman.
Interior design by Julie Pitkin.

Library of Congress Cataloging-in-Publication Data

Anderson, Emily, 1948–
    Food for comfort / Emily Anderson ; contributing editor, Elizabeth Anderson.
        p. cm.
    Includes index.
    ISBN 1-888952-32-6 (PBK. : Alk. Paper)
    1. Cookery, American.   I. Anderson, Elizabeth, 1951–   II. Title.
TX715.A56623 1997
641.5973—dc21   96-49095
                                                           CIP

Printed in the United States of America
1 2 3 4 5 6 7 — 02 01 00 99 98 97

To Jana Worley Jones
(1914–1995)

who left us the recipes

How good one feels when one is full—how satisfied with ourselves and with the world! People who have tried it, tell me that a clear conscience makes you very happy and contented; but a full stomach does the business quite as well, and is cheaper, and more easily obtained. One feels so forgiving and generous after a substantial and well-digested meal—so noble-minded, so kindly hearted.

Jerome K. Jerome, 1889

CONTENTS

AUTHOR'S NOTE

All-American Comfort Food is your ticket to a world where life is sweet
and cakes are iced and every Tuesday night is pot roast and mashed
potatoes. Salt, fat, sugar, cream-style corn smothered in bacon drippings and Cheddar cheese, tuna-celery casserole topped with French-
fried onion rings straight from the can. . . . When your spirits are low
and you need a quick lift, this is the place—great-tasting, all-American
comfort food from a time gone by when men were men and women
could fry and all it took to make life grand was a deep-dish apple pie
and a half-pint of vanilla ice cream.

Remember the days when people encouraged you to eat. "Eat up,"
they used to say. "Clean your plate. Enjoy." But somehow, somewhere
along the line, everything changed. Food got to be the enemy. Everyone
started to count calories, calculate fat grams, cut back on sodium.
Every smidgen of chocolate pie, every deep-fried crab cake had to be
weighed against the guilt we'd feel if we ate it. "You're not really going
to eat that?" they say now, snatching away the last of the lamb. "Don't
you think you've had enough?"

Life doesn't have to be like that. Food doesn't have to be like that,
either—and in *All-American Comfort Food*, it's not. My sister Elizabeth
and I wrote this cookbook because we think people should eat what
they want. Food is life, and if a tuna salad sandwich is what it takes to
make you happy, more power to you. Plus, we were lucky. We came by,
upon the death of an elderly cousin in the summer of 1995, fifty years of
American food. Jana Worley Jones was a nutritionist who spent her
career working with women's service clubs, home demonstration
groups, health departments. Her recipes ran the gamut from early con-
venience foods to covered-dish luncheons to prize-winning muffins. It
was all there, tucked inside book covers, scrawled on the backs of
envelopes, copied out neatly on index cards—everything we used to
eat. Remember when you couldn't get through a week without pimiento
cheese? Meat loaf? Lemon chess pie? Remember mandarin orange salad
with English walnuts and whipped topping? Remember Apple Brown
Betty?

Elizabeth and I grouped everything around traditional events: country
breakfast, supper, holidays, dinner on the grounds, buffets. We adapted
old recipes to current products, simplified routines, added favorites of
our own. We made *All-American Comfort Food* as basic a cookbook as
you'll ever need. It tells you how to buy and bake a potato, stuff and
roast a turkey, glaze a ham. It has the only pound cake recipe you'll
ever need, the best scratch cookies, an entire menu you can fix for
Sunday dinner, snacks to see you well into the next millennium, gifts.
There's even a chapter on feeding the multitudes. It's all here—and it's
grand.

The simple truth is good food makes life better. Try this some rainy night when the wind is cold and you need a friend: Soak for a few minutes in cold water 1 pound of thinly sliced waxy potatoes, dry them, layer them in a garlic-rubbed, buttered baking dish with bits of butter and freshly ground white pepper, top with ½ pint of heavy cream, and bake at 325° for 1 hour and 30 minutes. It's Elizabeth David's potatoes *gratin dauphinois*. You'll eat every bite—and you'll sleep till dawn.

Food is, in the final analysis, your own business. So what if health nuts roll their eyes at the mere mention of marshmallows in the sweet potato salad? So what if yours is the last fruitcake on the block still soaking in Jack Daniels? Really, what would life be without Velveeta in the macaroni?

It's a bad world out there, and you have to take your happiness where you find it. Food may well be the last thing you have any control over. So eat up. Clean that plate. Enjoy. *All-American Comfort Food* is just what you need.

Emily Anderson
November, 1996

All-American
COMFORT
FOOD

COUNTRY BREAKFAST

I feel that I will never cease
To hold in admiration grease.
Roy Blount Jr., 1982

The first thing—even before you opened your eyes—was the rooster. The second thing was breakfast. It was daybreak in the country and somebody, somewhere, was hard at work in the kitchen. There was the clean scent of perked coffee rising through the house, the cheerful crack of grease in a hot skillet. An oven door slammed. Someone called out a greeting. You could hear the chink of cutlery on china, the gentle thunk of cups in saucers, the low murmur of early morning conversation. Breakfast was on the table and the quicker you got those lazy bones out of that bed and down the stairs, the quicker you could eat.

Breakfast in the country is no meal for the faint of heart. Fresh coffee with white sugar and clotted cream, bacon, sausage, mushroom casserole, French toast, garlic grits, hash brown potatoes, scrambled eggs, sour cream pancakes, hot curried fruit, jam, butter, jelly, juice. Everyone always says you should start the day like a king. People, after all, have to work, and they need their energy. And there's that long, dry stretch until noon.

Right now the sun is barely up; the air is still; a thin mist cuts lazy curls across the water. Out in the kitchen the biscuits are hot, the butter is sweet, the ham center-cut and fried—and all you have to do is pull up a chair.

◆ APPLE TEA

For some people, the best part of coffee is the smell. What they really want in the morning is hot fruit tea.

2   quarts water, divided
6   individual tea bags
1   6-ounce can frozen apple juice con-
      centrate, thawed and undiluted

¼   cup plus 2 tablespoons firmly
      packed light brown sugar

In a pot bring 1 quart water to a boil and add the tea bags. Remove from the heat, cover, and let steep for 5 minutes. Remove the tea bags. Add the remaining 1 quart of water, the concentrate, and the sugar. Reheat thoroughly. Serve hot.
    Makes 12 servings.

◆ RUSSIAN TEA

2   lemons
3   oranges
12 whole cloves

1   quart water
1½ cups sugar
2   quarts strong tea

Into a small bowl juice the lemons and oranges. In a pot boil the rinds and cloves in 1 quart water for 5 minutes. Strain and add the juices, sugar, and tea.
    Makes 3½ quarts or 15 servings.

◆ PINEAPPLE-GRAPEFRUIT JUICE

⅓   cup water
⅓   cup sugar
1¼ cups grapefruit juice

⅔   cup pineapple juice
¼   cup lemon juice

In a pot boil the water and sugar for 3 minutes. Chill.
    Add the juices. Serve hot or chilled.
    Makes 4 servings.

> The morning stars sang together, and all the sons of
> God shouted for joy.
>
> *Job 38:7*

◆ BUTTERSCOTCH BUNS

It's barely dawn. The morning star is low in the western sky. All the world is peacefully asleep. And you're on the horns of a dilemma. You've got a houseful of relatives you don't see very often with a lot of small children you've never laid eyes on before, and you've got to fix them breakfast. You don't even know if they eat breakfast. It's a dilemma, all right, but the solution is easy: butterscotch buns. It won't matter if they don't eat breakfast. They'll eat butterscotch buns.

½ cup chopped pecans	¼ cup melted butter
½ cup sugar	½ 6-ounce package butterscotch-flavored morsels
1 teaspoon ground cinnamon	
1 10-biscuit package refrigerator biscuits	⅓ cup evaporated milk

Grease and flour a 9-inch cake pan. Sprinkle nuts over the bottom of the pan and set aside.

In a small bowl combine the sugar and cinnamon. Separate the biscuits and dip both sides first into the melted butter, then into the sugar-cinnamon mixture. Place the biscuits close together on top of the nuts in the pan. Bake at 400° for 10 minutes.

In a small saucepan over medium heat combine the butterscotch morsels and evaporated milk, stirring constantly until smooth. Pour over the hot buns. Let cool in the pan 5 minutes.

Makes 6 servings.

> If I can get just a spoonful of Maxwell House, it'll do me as much good as two or three cups of this other coffee.
> *Mississippi John Hurt, 1965*

◆ SOUR CREAM PECAN CAKE

Maybe the smell of fresh coffee isn't enough to get you out of bed in the morning. Maybe you need something a little less subtle. Try this: Repeat over and over to yourself, "coffee cake, coffee cake." Say it long enough that it becomes a chant. Say it longer, and you've got yourself a spiritual experience.

1 18½-ounce package butter-recipe yellow cake mix	4 eggs
½ cup sugar	¼ cup firmly packed dark brown sugar
2 8-ounce cartons sour cream	1 cup chopped pecans
Pinch salt	2 teaspoons ground cinnamon

Grease and flour a 10-inch stem or Bundt pan and set aside.

In a large bowl combine the cake mix, sugar, sour cream, and salt. Add the eggs one at a time, beating well after each addition.

In a separate bowl, mix the brown sugar, pecans, and cinnamon. Into the prepared stem pan pour a thin layer of batter followed by a thin layer of brown sugar mixture. Repeat until you have three layers of batter and two layers of brown sugar. Bake at 300° for 1 hour.

Makes 16 servings.

◆ CORNMEAL PANCAKES

Some people prefer cornmeal pancakes, some prefer flour, but the principles of good pancakes are always the same: (1) Stir the batter as little as possible; (2) grease the skillet lightly; (3) make the oil hot enough to cook a test drop of batter the size of a pea in 10 seconds.

3 cups buttermilk	2 teaspoons salt
3 eggs, beaten	1 teaspoon baking soda
½ cup vegetable oil	½ cup all-purpose flour
2⅔ cups yellow cornmeal	

In a large bowl beat together the buttermilk, eggs, and oil. In a separate bowl mix together the cornmeal, salt, soda, and flour and add to the buttermilk mixture, stirring with a fork only until smooth. Heat a lightly oiled griddle or skillet to 375°. Use ¼ cup batter for each pancake. Cook until the batter rises and the surface is dotted with holes. Turn with a spatula and cook on the other side until lightly browned. Serve with hot maple syrup and butter.

Makes 25 to 30 or 6 servings.

◆ SOUR CREAM PANCAKES

These are very thin and crêpelike. You can serve them with jam and sour cream.

3 eggs, separated	3 tablespoons all-purpose flour
3 tablespoons sour cream	Pinch salt
1 teaspoon baking powder	

In a medium bowl beat the egg yolks and add the sour cream, baking powder, flour, and salt. In a separate bowl beat the egg whites until they form a peak. Fold the egg whites into the sour cream mixture. Heat a lightly oiled griddle or skillet to 375°. Use ¼ cup of batter for each pancake. Cook until the batter rises and the surface is dotted with holes. Turn with a spatula and cook on the other side until lightly brown.

    Makes 12 small pancakes or 2 to 3 servings.

◆ FRENCH TOAST

They don't call it "French toast" for nothing.

2 eggs, beaten	Confectioners' sugar
¼ cup milk	Maple syrup, hot
Pinch salt	Butter
1 teaspoon sugar	
4 slices stale white bread, each cut	
on the diagonal into two pieces	

In a shallow soup bowl combine the eggs, milk, salt, and sugar. Heat a lightly greased skillet to 375°. Dip the bread one piece at a time into the egg mixture to coat, then place in the hot skillet. Cook for 2 to 3 minutes, turn, and cook on the other side for 2 to 3 minutes. Sprinkle with confectioners' sugar and serve with hot maple syrup and butter.

    Makes 2 servings.

◆ ORANGE GLAZED HAM

8 ham slices, fully cooked	¼ cup prepared mustard
1 6-ounce can frozen orange juice	¼ cup firmly packed brown sugar
concentrate, undiluted and	3 heaping tablespoons orange mar-
thawed	malade
3 tablespoons Cognac	

Place the ham in a 9 x 13 x 2-inch baking pan.

    In a medium bowl combine the concentrate, Cognac, mustard, sugar, and marmalade and pour over the ham. Bake uncovered at 350° for 30 to 45 minutes, basting several times.

    Makes 8 servings.

◆ SAUSAGE CASSEROLE

Sausage casseroles are for people who are serious about breakfast. They offer endless possibilities, and generally speaking, the more you add, the better they get.

1 pound bulk pork sausage	2 teaspoons baking powder
1 medium onion, chopped	1/4 teaspoon salt
1 14¾-ounce can whole kernel corn, drained	1 egg, beaten
	1/2 cup milk
1 green bell pepper, chopped	2 tablespoons vegetable oil
Dried red pepper flakes to taste	1 cup grated Cheddar cheese
1 cup cornmeal	

Grease an 8-inch square baking dish and set aside.

In a skillet, sauté the sausage, onion, corn, and peppers until the sausage is done. Pour off the grease. Place the meat mixture into the prepared baking dish.

In a medium bowl mix the cornmeal, baking powder, salt, egg, milk, and oil and pour over the meat. Bake uncovered at 400° for 20 to 25 minutes.

Just before done, sprinkle Cheddar cheese on top.

Makes 6 servings.

◆ EGG-SAUSAGE-MUSHROOM CASSEROLE

A milder cheese, some mushrooms, an easy Hollandaise....

1 pound sausage links	Hollandaise Sauce:
1 pound fresh mushrooms, brushed, stemmed, and thinly sliced	1 0.9-ounce package Hollandaise sauce mix
2 tablespoons butter	1/4 cup butter
1/2 pound Monterey Jack cheese, shredded	1 cup milk
8 eggs, beaten	1 teaspoon lemon juice

In a skillet cook and drain the sausage links.

In a separate skillet sauté the mushrooms in the butter over medium heat until the liquid is reduced.

Grease a 2-quart casserole dish and line with the Monterey Jack cheese. Place the sausage links on top of the cheese and cover with the sautéed mushrooms. Cover with the beaten eggs. Place a shallow pan of boiling water in the oven and place the casserole dish in it. Bake uncovered at 375° for 35 to 40 minutes or until puffed and lightly brown on top.

Meanwhile, prepare the Hollandaise as directed on the package. Serve the casserole with Hollandaise sauce.

Makes 4 to 6 servings.

◆ SAUSAGE-RICE CASSEROLE

Uncooked rice baked in a casserole tastes far better than cooked rice added later. To make certain the uncooked—and slightly translucent—grains absorb enough liquid, you must sauté them until they turn flat white, like the color of milk.

1   pound bulk pork sausage
1   cup uncooked rice
1   large onion, chopped
1   clove garlic, minced
2   stalks celery, chopped

1   green bell pepper, chopped
1   10¾-ounce can cream of mush-
      room soup, undiluted
2   10¾-ounce cans cream of chicken
      soup, undiluted

Grease a 9 x 13 x 2-inch casserole dish and set aside.

In a skillet brown the sausage and pour off the grease. Add the rice and sauté until the rice turns a milky color. Add the chopped onion, garlic, celery, and green bell pepper and simmer until the vegetables are tender. Add the soups. Pour into the prepared casserole dish and bake uncovered at 350° for 1 hour and 30 minutes, stirring occasionally.

Makes 6 servings.

◆ SHRIMP BREAKFAST PIE

3   slices white bread, trimmed of
      crusts and cubed
1   cup milk
2   cups cooked shrimp
2   tablespoons butter, melted

3   eggs, well beaten
½   green bell pepper, chopped
1   stalk celery, chopped
      Salt and pepper to taste

Grease a 1½-quart casserole and set aside. In a bowl soak the bread cubes in milk and mash with a fork. Add the shrimp, butter, eggs, bell pepper, celery, salt, and pepper and pour into the prepared dish. Bake uncovered at 375° for 30 to 40 minutes.

Makes 4 to 6 servings.

We breakfasted luxuriously in an old-fashioned parlor, on tea, toast, eggs, and honey, in the very sight of the beehives from which it had been taken, and a garden full of thyme and wildflowers that had produced it.
William Hazlitt, 1823

◆ VELVEETA EGGS

This half-deviled egg, half-cheese soufflé is big enough to delight a crowd at breakfast. You can, though, eat Velveeta eggs almost any time. Cut the recipe in half for a classy lunch. Cut it in half again for a welcoming supper on a cold night.

2   dozen hard-cooked eggs, halved
    with yolks removed
2   teaspoons lemon juice
1   teaspoon dry mustard
2   teaspoons Worcestershire sauce
2   teaspoons capers
    Salt and pepper to taste

¼   cup butter, melted
½   cup all-purpose flour
½   cup dry sherry
1½ pounds Velveeta cheese, melted
1½ cups milk
    Buttered cracker crumbs

In a medium bowl mash the egg yolks and add the lemon juice, mustard, Worcestershire sauce, capers, salt, and pepper. Stuff the yolk mixture into the egg-white halves and place in a shallow casserole dish.

Into a saucepan pour the melted butter and stir in the flour, sherry, melted Velveeta cheese, and milk. Cook over medium heat, stirring until blended. Pour the mixture on top of the eggs. Sprinkle with buttered cracker crumbs. Bake uncovered at 350° for 15 to 20 minutes.

Makes 12 servings.

◆ QUICHE LORRAINE

Quiche Lorraine is not the province of American fern bars. It comes from an area of northeast France fought over for centuries by neighboring powers. History books will tell you it was strategic location and the lure of mineral rights. Good cooks know it was the whole eggs, cream, bacon, and spinach.

4   eggs, beaten
2   cups half-and-half
    Dash grated nutmeg
    Salt and pepper to taste
1   9-inch uncooked pastry shell

½   pound bacon, cooked and crumbled
8   ounces Swiss cheese, cubed
1   10-ounce package frozen chopped
    spinach, thawed and wrung dry
    by hand

In a medium bowl mix the eggs, cream, nutmeg, salt, and pepper and set aside.

In the bottom of the pastry shell sprinkle the bacon and Swiss cheese. Spread the spinach over the bacon and Swiss cheese. Pour the egg mixture over all. Bake at 400° for 35 to 40 minutes.

Let cool 5 to 10 minutes before cutting.

Makes 4 to 6 servings.

◆ GARLIC GRITS

Some people will seize any opportunity to make garlic grits. It's a dish you can serve to beggars and to kings.

1	cup uncooked grits	2	cups shredded sharp Cheddar cheese
4	cups water		
1	teaspoon salt	⅔	cup milk
½	cup butter	4	large eggs, beaten
3	cloves garlic, pressed		

Grease a 2-quart casserole dish and set aside.

In a large saucepan cook the grits in salted water according to the directions on the package. Add the butter, garlic, Cheddar cheese, and milk and stir until blended. Add the eggs and stir well. The mixture will be like soup. Pour into the prepared casserole dish and bake uncovered at 350° for 1 hour.

Let stand 5 minutes before serving.

Makes 8 to 10 servings.

◆ HASH BROWN POTATOES

2	14½-ounce cans small whole new potatoes, drained and sliced	1	tablespoon paprika
1	teaspoon seasoned salt	⅓	cup vegetable oil

Season the potatoes with the salt and paprika. In a skillet sauté the potatoes in hot oil until brown.

Makes 6 servings.

◆ BACON-CHEESE POTATOES

12	medium new potatoes, cut in ½-inch cubes and cooked	8	slices bacon, cooked and crumbled
1	cup grated yellow cheese	½	cup butter, cut in bits

In a greased 2-quart casserole dish layer the potatoes, then the yellow cheese, then the bacon, then the butter. Repeat until all ingredients are used. Bake uncovered at 350° for 20 to 30 minutes.

Makes 8 servings.

◆ MUSHROOM PIE

2 pounds fresh mushrooms, brushed,
    with stems removed
6 tablespoons butter, divided
    Salt and pepper to taste
    Juice of ½ lemon
3 tablespoons all-purpose flour

1½ cups chicken stock
½ cup Madeira wine
½ cup heavy cream, hot
    Pastry for 1 9-inch pastry shell
1 egg, beaten

Butter a 1-quart baking dish and set aside.

In a large skillet sauté the mushroom caps in 4 tablespoons of butter over medium heat, adding the salt, pepper, and lemon juice. Cover and cook 10 minutes, shaking the skillet frequently to prevent sticking.

Remove the mushrooms to the prepared baking dish, piling them high in the center. To the juices remaining in the skillet add 2 tablespoons butter and stir in the flour. Gradually add the chicken stock and cook, stirring constantly, until thickened. Stir in the wine and cream. Pour the sauce over the mushrooms and cover with the pie dough. Brush with the beaten egg and make slits in the top to allow for escaping steam. Bake at 450° for 15 minutes.

Reduce heat to 350° and bake for 10 to 15 minutes more.

Makes 8 servings.

◆ HOT CURRIED FRUIT

Hot baked fruits make your house smell like the inside of a pie.

½ cup butter
1 cup firmly packed brown sugar
2 tablespoons curry powder
1 1-pound can pears, drained and cut
    into bite-sized pieces
1 1-pound can peaches, drained and
    cut into bite-sized pieces

1 1-pound 4-ounce can pineapple
    chunks
1 1-pound 10-ounce jar mixed fruit for
    salad
1 6-ounce jar maraschino cherries

In a saucepan melt the butter. Dissolve the sugar in the butter and add the curry powder. Into a large casserole pour the fruit. Pour the sauce over the fruit. Bake uncovered at 350° for 1 hour.

Makes 8 servings.

◆ PINEAPPLE PUDDING

3   eggs, well beaten
4   cups cubed white bread, trimmed of
      crusts
1   cup sugar
1   cup firmly packed dark brown
      sugar

1   1-pound 4-ounce can crushed
      pineapple with juice
1   cup butter, cut into small pieces

Grease a 9 x 13 x 2-inch pan and set aside.

In a large bowl beat the eggs until creamy. Add the bread, sugar, brown sugar, pineapple, and butter. Pour into the prepared pan and bake uncovered at 350° for 1 hour.

Makes 8 servings.

◆ APPLE WHIP

1   1/4-ounce envelope unflavored
      gelatin
3   tablespoons sugar
1   cup water

1   15-ounce jar unsweetened apple-
      sauce
1   tablespoon lemon juice
      Ground cinnamon

In a medium saucepan mix the unflavored gelatin with the sugar and water. Let stand 1 minute. Stir over very low heat about 5 minutes or until the gelatin is dissolved. Stir in the applesauce and lemon juice. Pour into a large bowl and chill, stirring occasionally until the mixture is thickened.

With an electric mixer beat at high speed for 10 minutes until light and fluffy. Pour into dessert dishes. Chill until set and sprinkle with cinnamon.

Makes 6 servings.

◆ CREAM CHEESE ASPIC

Any excuse to serve tomato aspic is as good as any other. Call it "fruit" and serve it for breakfast.

1   ¼-ounce envelope unflavored
    gelatin
¼   cup cold water
1   10¾-ounce can cream of tomato
    soup, undiluted
½   can water
1   3-ounce package cream cheese

½   small onion, grated
⅓   cup chopped celery
⅓   cup chopped green bell pepper
⅓   cup chopped pecans
    Salt and pepper to taste
    Dash Worcestershire sauce

Grease a 4-cup mold and set aside.

In a small bowl soften the gelatin in ¼ cup cold water. In a saucepan mix the soup and ½ can water and bring to a boil. Stir in the cream cheese until melted. Add the gelatin and stir until dissolved. Chill until thickened. Add the vegetables, pecans, salt, pepper, and Worcestershire sauce. Pour into the prepared mold. Chill until set.

Makes 4 servings.

BOX LUNCH

Makes you think all the world's a sunny day.
Paul Simon, 1973

Maybe you took one to school or on a bus trip or a cross-country hike with a crowd of people you barely knew, half of whom for reasons you never quite figured out handed over to you outright their giant garlic dills. Maybe it was a long week with elderly aunts in a sleepy resort town during the hottest July on record, and late one morning you decided you'd had it with finger bowls in the hotel dining room, and you sidled over to the front desk and said brightly to the man in charge, "Box lunch."

White cardboard, red ribbon, tiny waxed-paper sacks, cloth napkins wound tightly around someone's second-best cutlery. It didn't matter where you got it or where you took it—inside the box the food was always the same and it was grand: ham biscuits so salty they bit the insides of your mouth, cold batter-baked chicken, pimiento cheese, new potato salad, ripe olives, sweet pickles, carrots, pears, plums, brownies. You could have lived in the woods for a week on the lemon bars alone. Some of us did.

The sun was always brighter when you had a box lunch. The sky was bluer, the breeze breezier. Your feet never hurt then, no one was ever mad at you, and there weren't any bugs. And the shadows under the shade tree where you sat and ate were as cool and sweet as any shadows in any place you've ever been.

◆ BATTER-BAKED CHICKEN

You don't have to be able to fry to make batter-baked chicken. This one works especially well in a box lunch because it's as good cold as hot.

2	cups breadcrumbs	1/2	teaspoon black pepper
3/4	cup grated Parmesan cheese	1/4	cup chopped fresh parsley
2	cloves garlic, pressed	8	chicken breast halves
2	teaspoons salt	2	cups butter, melted

In a large bowl combine the breadcrumbs, Parmesan cheese, garlic, salt, pepper, and parsley.

In a shallow bowl soak the chicken in the melted butter for 3 minutes. Roll and press the crumb mixture onto each piece. Place in a shallow baking dish, pour in the remaining butter, and bake at 325° for 45 minutes to 1 hour. Juices will run clear when chicken is done.

Cool and wrap for box lunch.

Makes 8 servings.

> "Make a remark," said the Red Queen: "It's ridiculous to leave all the conversation to the pudding!"
> Lewis Carroll, 1871

◆ QUICK PIMIENTO CHEESE

If you open your box lunch and there's no pimiento cheese inside, you know you've got the wrong box.

1	5-ounce can evaporated milk	1	teaspoon Worcestershire sauce
3/4	pound sharp Cheddar cheese, diced	1/2	teaspoon onion juice
1	4-ounce jar pimientos, drained		Tabasco sauce and salt to taste

In a medium saucepan heat the milk until steamy. Add the diced Cheddar cheese and stir until melted. Remove from the heat and add the pimientos, Worcestershire sauce, onion juice, Tabasco sauce, and salt. Spread with mayonnaise on bread or stuff into celery sticks.

Makes 12 servings.

◆ HOT PIMIENTO CHEESE

If you're one of those people who eats jalapeño peppers straight from the jar, this is the pimiento cheese for you.

2   cups grated sharp Cheddar cheese
1   4-ounce jar pimientos, drained and
      chopped
¼   teaspoon Tabasco sauce
      Pinch salt

1   teaspoon Worcestershire sauce
½   cup mayonnaise
2   jalapeño peppers, seeded and fine-
      ly chopped (handle with rubber
      gloves)

In a large bowl mix together all the ingredients until well blended. Spread with mayonnaise on bread.
  Makes 2½ cups or 12 sandwiches.

◆ EGG SALAD

Egg salad is a sign of good food. It has to be fresh and it has to be made right, and if you see it in a box lunch, you know you're in the care of a good cook.

2   hard-cooked eggs, chopped
1   teaspoon chopped pimiento,
      drained
½   teaspoon chopped chives

⅛   teaspoon salt
      Dash pepper
2   tablespoons mayonnaise

In a small bowl combine all the ingredients. Chill. Spread with mayonnaise on bread.
  Makes ¾ cup or 3 sandwiches.

◆ BEEF SALAD PITA

A lot of us didn't have pocket bread in the 1950s and life was the poorer for it. Pita is the most practical sandwich bread on earth. You fill it up, hold it with two hands, eat it. No mess, no fuss, no bother. All the first Earl of Sandwich really needed was a Greek cook.

1¼   shredded lettuce
½   cup shredded fresh spinach,
      stemmed
6   Greek olives, pitted and sliced
1   green onion, chopped
1   radish, sliced

3   tablespoons Italian salad dressing
1   3-ounce package cream cheese,
      softened
3   6-inch pita rounds, cut in half
6   ounces roast beef, thinly sliced

In a large bowl combine the lettuce, spinach, olives, onion, radish, and dressing. Toss gently to coat and let stand 5 minutes.
  Spread 1½ tablespoons of cream cheese inside each pita bread half. Fill with one slice of roast beef and ⅓ to ½ cup of salad.
  Makes 6 servings.

◆ HAM SALAD

3 cups cubed cooked ham	½ cup mayonnaise
2 hard-cooked eggs, chopped	2 teaspoons prepared mustard
1 stalk celery, chopped	Dash pepper
½ cup sweet pickle relish	

In a food processor pulse the ham until coarsely ground.

In a large bowl combine the ham with the eggs, celery, relish, mayonnaise, mustard, and pepper and mix well. Cover and chill.

Serve in 1-cup containers or spread with mayonnaise on bread or in pita halves. Makes 4 salads or 8 sandwiches.

◆ CHICKEN SALAD

To make chicken salad, you have to cook the chicken and you have to take it off the bone. It's a time-consuming job and messy, but the rewards are great. Cooks have gone down in history on the strength of a finely chopped, finely seasoned chicken salad. There's no substitute—and no one ever forgets.

5 cups cubed cooked chicken	⅛ teaspoon white pepper
2 teaspoons grated onion	½ teaspoon curry powder
1 cup minced celery	1 tablespoon tarragon vinegar or dry
¼ cup capers	white wine
¼ cup heavy cream	4 hard-cooked eggs, chopped
⅔ cup mayonnaise	½ cup slivered almonds, toasted
1 teaspoon salt	

In a large bowl combine the chicken, onion, celery, and capers.

In a small bowl mix the cream with the mayonnaise, and add the salt, pepper, curry, and vinegar. Pour over the chicken mixture, mix well, and chill.

Just before serving, fold in the eggs and almonds. Serve in 1-cup containers or spread with mayonnaise on bread or in pita halves.

Makes 6 salads or 12 sandwiches.

◆ THREE-BEAN SALAD

Almost always, when you're faced with that all-too-perplexing question of salad, three-bean is your answer. A three-bean salad has structure, balance, style. There's some variation among recipes: wax beans versus limas, red bell peppers versus green, dill versus celery. But two things never change: There are always three beans and there's never any left over. It's one of life's perfect harmonies.

1 15-ounce can red kidney beans, drained and rinsed	½ cup chopped onion
1 1-pound can lima beans, drained and rinsed	¾ cup sugar
	½ cup olive oil
1 1-pound can cut green beans, drained	½ cup cider vinegar
	1 teaspoon salt
½ cup chopped green bell pepper	½ teaspoon black pepper
	½ teaspoon dried dill weed

In a large bowl combine the beans and add the bell pepper and onion.

In a separate bowl stir together the sugar, olive oil, vinegar, salt, pepper, and dill weed until sugar is dissolved and pour over the bean mixture. Toss lightly. Place in a shallow dish so the beans marinate. Cover and chill overnight.

Drain excess dressing before serving. Serve in 1-cup containers.

Makes 6 servings.

> Grown-up people find it very difficult to believe really wonderful things,
> unless they have what they call proof.
> *Edith Nesbit, 1902*

◆ MACARONI SALAD

Macaroni is one of those things, like Italian grand opera and Velcro, that it would be hard to imagine the world without. There's no bad way to fix it. Children gobble it up. Adults get teary-eyed at the very mention of it. All in all, we should be most grateful that Marco Polo made that trip to China.

1 cup uncooked macaroni	¼ teaspoon salt
1 stalk celery, chopped	1 tablespoon chopped onion
¼ cup sweet pickle relish	¾ cup mayonnaise

In a pot cook and drain the macaroni according to the directions on the package. In a large bowl combine the cooked macaroni with the celery, relish, salt, onion, and mayonnaise and toss lightly. Cover and chill.

Serve in 1-cup containers.

Makes 6 servings.

◆ CARROT-RAISIN SALAD

Carrots are vegetables and raisins were at one time fruit, so it only follows that carrot-raisin salad is something your mother would want you to eat. Judging from the taste, though, you'd never know it.

½ cup raisins	1 teaspoon red wine vinegar
2 cups shredded carrots	1 teaspoon sugar
⅓ cup mayonnaise	

In a medium bowl combine the raisins and carrots.

In a small bowl mix the mayonnaise, vinegar, and sugar and stir well. Add to the carrot mixture and mix well. Chill.

Serve in 1-cup containers.

Makes 6 servings.

◆ AMBROSIA

You can spend all morning peeling and sectioning oranges, slicing fruit, bloodying your knuckles on the coconut grater. Or you can open your cabinet and get out the cans. Ambrosia is not called "nectar of the gods" for nothing and there's no rule that says it has to be any trouble.

1 15-ounce can fruit cocktail, undrained	1 tablespoon flaked coconut
1 11-ounce can mandarin oranges, drained	

In a large bowl mix the ingredients and chill.

Serve in 1-cup containers.

Makes 4 servings.

◆ QUICK BROWNIES

You can't have box lunch without brownies—the universe won't permit it. You can buy a mix at the store and stir up a pretty good batch. Or you can make this scratch recipe. Make sure you preheat the oven. It helps to have an electric mixer. And the butter and sugar have to cream until fluffy. Otherwise, you just stir things together.

½	cup butter		¼	cup cocoa
1	cup sugar		½	cup all-purpose flour
2	eggs		¼	teaspoon salt
½	teaspoon vanilla extract			

Grease and flour an 8-inch square pan and set aside.

In a large bowl cream the butter and sugar. Add the eggs one at a time, beating well after each addition. Add the vanilla extract, cocoa, flour, and salt and blend thoroughly. Pour the batter into the prepared pan and bake at 350° for 25 minutes.

Cool in the pan before cutting into squares.

Makes 16 brownies.

◆ BLOND BROWNIES

Brownies are not necessarily chocolate. Some of them are blond. Some people call blond brownies "butterscotch" and prefer them to chocolate.

¼	cup butter		½	cup all-purpose flour
1	cup firmly packed dark brown sugar		1	teaspoon baking powder
			½	teaspoon salt
1	egg, beaten		1	cup chopped pecans
1	teaspoon vanilla extract			

Grease and flour an 8-inch square pan and set aside.

In a saucepan melt the butter. Add the sugar, egg, and vanilla.

In a medium bowl mix the flour, baking powder, and salt and add to the egg mixture. Add the pecans and mix well. Spread into the prepared pan and bake at 350° for 30 minutes. Do not overbake.

Cool slightly in the pan before cutting into squares.

Makes 16 brownies.

> I sit in the melancholy mood that is like cello music and search for
> the answers we shall never know.
> *Ludwig Bemelmans, 1941*

◆ WALNUT-CHOCOLATE BARS

This is an extra-easy, extra-rich layered brownie that stores well and travels well.

½ cup butter	1 cup chopped walnuts
1 cup graham cracker crumbs	1 15-ounce can sweetened condensed milk
1 cup flaked coconut	
1 cup semisweet chocolate morsels	

In a 9-inch square pan melt the butter. Sprinkle into the pan one layer each of crumbs, coconut, chocolate morsels, and nuts. Pour the condensed milk over all. Bake at 350° for 30 minutes.

Cool in the pan before cutting into squares.

Makes 30 bars.

◆ LEMON BARS

A lot of bar cookies are baked in two layers, a little more trouble but well worth the extra step. The bottom layer, here, is a shortbread crust you press into the bottom of the pan. The top is a glorified lemon custard.

BOTTOM LAYER:
- 2 cups all-purpose flour
- ½ cup confectioners' sugar
- 1 cup butter, softened

TOP LAYER:
- 4 eggs, beaten
- 2 cups sugar
- ⅓ cup lemon juice
- ¼ cup all-purpose flour
- ½ teaspoon baking powder

Grease and flour a 9 x 13 x 2-inch baking pan and set aside.

In a medium bowl mix together 2 cups flour and the confectioners' sugar. Cut in the butter with a pastry blender until the mixture clings together. Press into the prepared pan and bake at 350° for 20 to 25 minutes or until lightly browned.

In a medium bowl beat together the eggs, sugar, and lemon juice.

In a separate bowl mix together the flour and baking powder and stir into the egg mixture. Pour over the baked bottom layer. Bake at 350° for 25 minutes.

Sprinkle with additional confectioners' sugar. Cool in the pan. Chill in the refrigerator overnight before cutting into bars.

Makes 36 bars.

◆ COCONUT-PECAN COOKIES

In this simpler double-layer bar, both layers cook at the same time.

½ cup margarine, melted (not
    whipped margarine or butter)
1 18¼-ounce box yellow cake mix,
    without pudding
3 eggs, divided

1 8-ounce package cream cheese,
    softened
1 1-pound box confectioners' sugar
½ cup flaked coconut
½ cup pecan pieces

Grease and flour a 15 x 10 x 1-inch jelly roll pan and set aside.

In a small bowl beat one egg.

In a large bowl combine the margarine, cake mix, and beaten egg and stir together until moist. Pat the mixture into the bottom of the prepared jelly roll pan.

In a large bowl lightly beat the remaining two eggs, then beat in the cream cheese and confectioners' sugar. Stir in the coconut and pecans. Pour over the bottom layer, spreading evenly. Bake at 325° for 45 to 50 minutes or until golden brown.

Cool in the pan before cutting into bars.

Makes 48 bars.

◆ CHOCOLATE CHIP COOKIES

To many people, the words *cookie* and *chocolate chip* are one and the same. You need a couple of good cookie recipes. This is one of them.

¾ cup firmly packed light brown sugar
½ cup sugar
½ cup shortening
½ cup butter, softened
1 egg
1½ teaspoons vanilla extract

1¾ cups all-purpose flour
1 teaspoon baking soda
½ teaspoon salt
1 6-ounce package semisweet chocolate morsels
½ cup chopped walnuts or pecans

In a large bowl cream together the sugars, shortening, and butter. Beat in the egg. Add the vanilla.

In a separate bowl combine the flour, baking soda, and salt and add to the sugar mixture, beating well. Stir in the chocolate morsels and nuts. Drop by rounded spoonfuls 2 inches apart onto an ungreased baking sheet. Bake at 375° for 8 to 10 minutes.

Transfer immediately to a wire rack for cooling.

Makes 48 cookies.

◆ COCONUT-OATMEAL COOKIES

This is your other cookie recipe. These might just be the best scratch cookies you'll ever make. You must use shortening, and all-white sugar is okay, but they're better if you split the sugars half white, half brown.

1 cup firmly packed light brown sugar	1 teaspoon salt
1 cup sugar	1 teaspoon baking soda
1 cup shortening (not butter or margarine)	1 teaspoon baking powder
	1 teaspoon vanilla extract
2 eggs	1 cup flaked coconut
2 cups all-purpose flour	1½ cups regular rolled oats, raw

In a large bowl cream together the sugars and shortening. Beat in the eggs.

In a separate bowl combine the flour, salt, baking soda, and baking powder and add to the sugar mixture. Add the vanilla and beat well. Stir in the coconut and oats. Form the dough into 1-inch balls and place 2 inches apart on an ungreased baking sheet. Bake at 350° for 8 to 10 minutes.

Cool on the pan for 2 minutes and transfer to a wire rack.

Makes 72 cookies.

LUNCH & LUNCHEON

As God is my witness, I'll never be hungry again.
Margaret Mitchell, 1936

Just because you eat it in the middle of the day doesn't mean it's lunch. Lunch is not midday dinner with its ritual courses, polite conversation, and kitchen full of dirty pots and pans at the end. Nor is it any old thing you choke down around noon just to keep body and soul together. There's lunch, and, then of course, luncheon—not exactly the same either but close, and both are essential to civilized well-being. Both take place at midday, both give you something to look forward to throughout an otherwise dull morning, and both serve majestically to renew your spirits.

Luncheon is silk suits and seafood salads. You wouldn't want bacon, lettuce, and tomato dripping down the shirtfronts of the Ladies' Literary Society on Pulitzer Prize Day. You'd want something a little more refined: a nice tomato aspic with parsley mayonnaise, hot curried pineapple, a carrot ring pudding with buttered green peas. Meats at luncheon involve liberal amounts of cream, water chestnuts, melted cheese. Desserts have a simple elegance—gingerbread with hot lemon sauce, fresh apple cake with hard sauce, real fudge pie.

Lunch, on the other hand, is drippy, greasy, crunchy, hot, cold, out of a can—it doesn't matter. You can eat it by yourself or with a renegade band of neighborhood children or a cluster of colleagues AWOL from a morning of sensitivity training and desperate for a chicken pot pie. Cheese soup, tuna-celery casserole, French-fried onion rings—you can put ham and cheese on white bread and eat it with mustard and sweet pickle relish straight from the jar, or you can soak it in egg batter and bake it in cream. Lunch is a meal twice blessed: You almost always get to eat what you want, and you get to leave your dishes in the sink.

— LUNCH —

◆ CHEESE SOUP

Soup is the thing at lunch and you can eat as much as you want. There's no need to save room for the real meal to come. At lunch, soup is the real meal.

2 tablespoons all-purpose flour	Tabasco sauce to taste
2 tablespoons butter	Salt and pepper to taste
1½ cups chicken broth	¼ cup dry white wine
1½ cups milk	1 cup grated sharp Cheddar cheese

In a large pot, brown the flour in melted butter over medium-high heat, stirring briskly with a wire whisk. Add the chicken broth and milk and stir until smooth. Add the Tabasco sauce, salt, pepper, and wine. Bring to a boil and remove from the heat. Add the Cheddar cheese and stir until melted.
    Makes 6 servings.

◆ CAPITOL BEAN SOUP

This is a modified version of the famous U.S. Senate Restaurant Bean Soup that throughout this nation's history has fortified many a public servant in his (mainly) efforts to legislate, filibuster, veto in committee, and otherwise dabble in the lives of those of us who don't have ready access to the senatorial dining room. It's an excellent soup. You'll be glad you have the recipe.

2 15-ounce cans navy beans, drained	mashed potatoes, ⅔ cup water,
1 cup water	¼ cup milk, and 1 tablespoon
½ cup diced cooked ham	butter)
2 cups chopped onion	Dash Tabasco sauce
1 cup chopped celery with leaves	1 teaspoon salt
2 cloves garlic, pressed	⅛ teaspoon white pepper
¼ cup chopped fresh parsley	
1 cup prepared mashed potatoes (made with ⅔ cup instant	

In a covered saucepan simmer all the ingredients for 1 hour.
    Makes 6 servings.

◆ VEGETABLE-BEEF SOUP

1 pound hamburger meat
1 1-pound can tomatoes with juice
1 1-pound can mixed vegetables,
    drained
1 10½-ounce can beef consommé
1 cup water
1 medium onion, chopped

1 bay leaf
1 teaspoon dried oregano
  Salt and pepper to taste
  Dash Tabasco sauce
  Sour cream
  Parmesan cheese, grated

In a skillet brown the hamburger and drain the fat. Add the tomatoes, vegetables, beef consommé, water, onion, bay leaf, oregano, salt, pepper, and Tabasco sauce. Boil for 5 minutes, reduce heat, and simmer covered for 1 hour.

Serve topped with sour cream and grated Parmesan cheese.

Makes 8 servings.

◆ SOUFFLÉ SANDWICH

If you could eat the same thing for lunch day after day for an entire year—and no one says you can't—this would be it.

1 tablespoon butter
8 slices white bread with crusts
    trimmed
4 slices ham
4 slices yellow cheese

2 eggs, beaten
½ teaspoon salt
¼ teaspoon black pepper
2 cups half-and-half

Grease an 8-inch square baking pan and set aside.

Butter the bread slices on both sides. Make four sandwiches using one slice of ham and one slice of cheese for each. In a small bowl mix the eggs, salt, pepper, and half-and-half. Place the sandwiches in the prepared baking pan and cover with the egg mixture. Soak them until they are saturated on both sides, turning once. Bake uncovered at 400° for 45 minutes.

Makes 3 to 4 servings.

> Life's a pudding full of plums.
> W. S. Gilbert, 1889

◆ CHICKEN POT PIE

You can be having the worst day in the history of your life and a chicken pot pie will make it better. Always has, always will.

4 cups cubed cooked chicken	1 cup chicken broth
1 15-ounce can mixed vegetables, drained	2 cups biscuit mix
1 10¾-ounce can cream of chicken soup, undiluted	1 cup milk

Grease a 9 x 13 x 2-inch baking dish. Place the chicken in the dish. In a large bowl mix the vegetables, soup, and chicken broth and pour over the chicken.

In a separate bowl combine the biscuit mix and milk and pour over the vegetable mixture. Bake uncovered at 400° for 35 to 40 minutes.

Cool 15 minutes before serving.

Makes 8 servings.

◆ TUNA-VEGETABLE CASSEROLE

You wouldn't think you could improve on the classic stripped-down, bottom-of-the-line tuna-celery soup casserole—and you certainly don't have to—but the truth is you can. Take advantage of those spare vegetables hanging around the back of your fridge: Chop them up; throw them in.

1 2.8-ounce can French-fried onion rings	¼ teaspoon onion powder
1 6½-ounce can tuna, drained	1 4-ounce can mushrooms, drained
¾ cup chopped celery	1 10¾-ounce can cream of celery soup, undiluted
¼ cup chopped green bell pepper	

Grease a 1-quart casserole dish and set aside.

In a large bowl combine half the can of French-fried onions with the tuna, celery, pepper, onion powder, mushrooms, and soup. Pour into the prepared casserole dish and bake uncovered at 350° for 25 minutes.

Sprinkle with the remaining onions and bake 5 minutes more.

Makes 4 servings.

◆ EASY MACARONI AND CHEESE

This version of the perennial childhood favorite is so easy it makes you wonder why anyone would ever precook the macaroni.

1   cup macaroni, uncooked
2   tablespoons all-purpose flour
¾ teaspoon salt
1   small onion, chopped
1   cup water

1   cup milk
2   tablespoons butter
*   Dash Tabasco sauce*
1   cup grated yellow cheese

Grease a 2-quart casserole dish. In the dish combine the macaroni, flour, salt, onion, water, milk, butter, and Tabasco sauce. Bake covered at 350° for 45 to 50 minutes or until the macaroni is tender, stirring occasionally.

Stir in the yellow cheese and bake uncovered for 5 minutes more.

Makes 3 to 4 servings.

◆ HOT CHICKEN SALAD

Cold chicken salad is elegant and refined. Hot chicken salad means you get to eat in your socks and put your elbows on the table. The difference is in the potato chips on top.

2   cups diced cooked chicken
1   10¾-ounce can cream of chicken
*   soup, undiluted*
1   tablespoon instant minced onion
1   teaspoon salt

1   cup diced celery
1   cup slivered almonds, toasted
1   cup mayonnaise
4   hard-cooked eggs, diced
½ cup crushed potato chips

Grease a 2-quart casserole dish and set aside.

In a large bowl mix the chicken, soup, onion, salt, celery, almonds, mayonnaise, and eggs and pour into the prepared casserole dish. Top with the crushed potato chips. Bake uncovered at 350° for 30 minutes.

Makes 8 servings.

◆ FRENCH-FRIED ONION RINGS

You can get French-fried onion rings out of a can—and don't think we're not grateful. But there is little else on earth like live onion rings French-fried in buttermilk batter.

3 or 4 large Spanish or Bermuda onions	⅔ cup water
2 to 3 cups buttermilk	1 cup all-purpose flour
1 egg, beaten	1 tablespoon vegetable oil
1 teaspoon salt	1 teaspoon lemon juice
1½ teaspoons baking powder	¼ teaspoon cayenne pepper
	Vegetable oil for frying

Slice the onions ⅜-inch thick and separate into rings. Soak in the buttermilk for 30 minutes.

In a medium bowl combine the egg, salt, baking powder, water, flour, 1 tablespoon vegetable oil, lemon juice, and cayenne pepper.

In a heavy skillet or fryer, heat 1 inch of vegetable oil to 375°. Remove the onion rings from the buttermilk and dip into the batter. Fry in the hot oil about 10 minutes until golden brown. Drain on paper towels.

Makes 6 to 8 servings.

◆ FRITTO MISTO

Fritto misto is Italian for "mixed fry," an eclectic collection of vegetables, seafood, and cheese deep-fried in beer batter. In fritto misto, timing is everything. The longer the batter sits at room temperature, the better the texture; the quicker you eat it out of the skillet, the lighter and puffier the misto.

1 cup all-purpose flour	tomatoes, squash, mushrooms,
1 teaspoon salt	diced shrimp, scallops, lobster,
⅛ teaspoon cayenne pepper	fish, or hard cheeses such as
1 cup warm beer	Swiss or fontina
1 pound mixed selection of sliced or chunked onions, okra, eggplant,	Vegetable oil for frying

In a large bowl combine the flour, salt, and pepper and pour in the beer, mixing well. Cover and let stand at room temperature for 2 to 3 hours.

Stir the vegetables, seafood, and/or cheeses into the batter, coating on all sides.

In a heavy skillet or fryer, heat 1½ inches of vegetable oil to 375°. Fry a selection of four or five pieces at a time about 10 minutes until golden brown. Drain on paper towels.

Makes 6 servings.

◆ CHERRY CHEESE PIE

If you eat lunch alone, you could make this on Monday and have a piece for every day of the week. Or you could finish it off by Tuesday and whip up another one.

1   3-ounce package cream cheese,
      softened
1   14-ounce can sweetened condensed
      milk
⅓   cup lemon juice

1   9-inch prepared Vanilla Wafer
      Pastry Shell (recipe follows)
1   21-ounce can cherry pie filling

In a medium bowl beat the cream cheese until light and fluffy. Add the milk and beat again. Stir in the lemon juice. Pour into a Vanilla Wafer Pastry Shell (recipe follows). Spread the cherry filling on top and chill.
    Makes 8 servings.

◆ VANILLA WAFER PASTRY SHELL

2   cups vanilla wafer crumbs
2   tablespoons sugar

¼   cup butter, melted

Mix all the ingredients together and press into a 9-inch pie plate.

◆ EXTRA-EASY LUNCH CAKE

1   16-ounce can sweetened apple-
      sauce
1   16-ounce can crushed pineapple,
      undrained
1   18¼-ounce package yellow cake
      mix

1   cup butter, melted
1½   cups chopped pecans
      Whipped topping, thawed

Grease and flour a 9 x 13 x 2-inch baking pan. In the pan spread without stirring one layer each of applesauce, pineapple, cake mix, butter, and nuts. Bake at 350° for 1 hour. Cool in the pan before cutting into squares. Serve with whipped topping.
    Makes 15 servings.

◆ EASY FUDGE CAKE

1 18¼-ounce package devil's food
   cake mix
2 cups prepared chocolate pudding
1 egg, beaten

½ cup semisweet chocolate morsels
1 cup coarsely chopped pecans
   Whipped topping, thawed

Grease and flour a 9 x 13 x 2-inch baking pan and set aside.

In a large bowl combine the dry cake mix, prepared pudding, and egg, beating well for 2 minutes. Pour the batter into the prepared pan and sprinkle with the chocolate morsels and nuts. Bake at 350° for 30 minutes.

Cool in the pan before cutting into squares. Serve with whipped topping.
Makes 15 servings.

◆ GINGERBREAD

There's really nothing like the smell of hot gingerbread in a cold house. Don't be put off by the long list of ingredients. All it takes is a spoon to stir them together.

1⅓ cups all-purpose flour
¾ teaspoon ground cinnamon
¾ teaspoon ground ginger
½ teaspoon ground allspice
½ teaspoon salt
½ teaspoon baking powder
½ teaspoon baking soda

½ cup firmly packed dark brown
   sugar
½ cup butter, softened
½ cup boiling water
½ cup molasses
1 egg, slightly beaten

Grease a 9-inch square pan on the bottom only and set aside.

In a large bowl combine the flour, spices, salt, baking powder, and soda. Add the brown sugar, butter, water, molasses, and egg. Pour the batter into the prepared pan. Bake at 350° for 30 to 40 minutes.

Serve warm with Lemon Sauce (recipe follows).
Makes 9 servings.

◆ LEMON SAUCE

½ cup sugar
2 tablespoons cornstarch
   Dash salt
1 cup hot water

2 teaspoons grated lemon peel
2 tablespoons lemon juice
2 tablespoons butter

In a medium saucepan combine the sugar with the cornstarch and salt. Blend in the water. Cook over medium heat until the mixture boils and is clear and slightly thickened, stirring constantly. Stir in the lemon peel, juice, and butter. Serve warm or cold.
Makes 1½ cups.

— LUNCHEON —

◆ HOT CRAB DIP

If your luncheon crowd is refined enough, no one is likely to appropriate this crab dip for personal consumption. Serve it at an assertiveness-training seminar graduation ceremony, however, and you'd better look out.

8 ounces cooked crab meat or imitation crab	1½ cups sour cream
1 8-ounce package cream cheese	2 tablespoons mayonnaise
1 teaspoon Worcestershire sauce	1 tablespoon chopped onion
	½ cup grated Cheddar cheese

Grease a 1½-quart casserole dish and set aside.

In a large bowl mix the crab, cream cheese, Worcestershire sauce, sour cream, mayonnaise, and onion. Pour into the prepared casserole dish and top with the Cheddar cheese. Bake uncovered at 350° for 20 minutes.

Serve on crackers or with potato chips.

Makes 3½ cups or 10 servings.

◆ CURRIED CHEESE ROUNDS

¾ cup grated Cheddar cheese	⅓ cup mayonnaise
⅓ cup chopped scallions	½ teaspoon curry powder
¾ cup pitted and chopped ripe olives	

In a medium bowl mix all the ingredients. Spread on rounds of bread. Run under broiler for 2 to 3 minutes.

Makes 2 cups.

◆ MARINATED MUSHROOMS

Very small button mushrooms work best in this recipe. Large mushroom caps have an embarrassing way of dripping down chins. You could make it with canned mushrooms if you can find whole caps. You can also chop up an avocado and add it at the last minute.

1 pound fresh mushrooms, brushed and trimmed of stems	2 bay leaves
½ teaspoon salt	1 clove garlic, minced
Freshly ground white pepper	½ cup vegetable oil
1 teaspoon dried tarragon	1 tablespoon chopped fresh parsley
	2 tablespoons lemon juice

In a large bowl toss the mushrooms, salt, pepper, tarragon, bay leaves, garlic, oil, and parsley. Cover and chill overnight.

Transfer to a saucepan and simmer 10 minutes. Add the lemon juice and chill thoroughly.

Drain and serve in a bowl with toothpicks.

Makes 15 servings.

◆ QUICK CORN LIGHT BREAD

There's something about corn light bread that elevates the tone of a social occasion. Maybe it's the white cornmeal; maybe it's the sugar. Maybe it's one of those philological confluences where the whole becomes greater than the sum of its parts. If you have any left over—which isn't likely—you can toast it and have it with soup the next day. It will also do wonders for your tone.

2 cups white cornmeal	½ teaspoon baking soda
½ cup all-purpose flour	1 teaspoon salt
¾ cup sugar	1 teaspoon baking powder
2 cups buttermilk	2 tablespoons shortening, melted

Grease a 9 x 5-inch loaf pan.

In a large bowl mix together all the ingredients and pour into the prepared pan. Bake at 350° for 1 hour.

Cool 10 minutes, then remove from pan.

Makes 10 servings.

◆ EASY PROCESSOR BISCUITS

2½ cups self-rising flour
½ cup cold butter, cut into 1-inch
    pieces

¾ cup buttermilk

In a food processor pulse the flour and butter until the mixture resembles coarse meal. With the processor running, slowly add the buttermilk until the dough forms a ball and leaves the sides of the bowl. Turn out onto a floured surface and knead three or four times. Roll out to ½-inch thickness and cut into rounds with a 2½-inch biscuit cutter. Place the biscuits on an ungreased baking sheet and bake at 450° for 10 minutes.
    Makes 12 biscuits.

◆ DEVILED CRAB

Whether or not you use real crab meat, you can stuff this elegant deviled crab into real shells. It's the same principle by which the French stuff gussied-up cream cheese into snail shells they buy by the pack at their neighborhood grocery. Allusion makes all the difference.

1 pound crab meat, picked and
    flaked, or 1 pound imitation crab
    meat
1 10¾-ounce can cream of mush-
    room soup, undiluted
¼ cup breadcrumbs
1 egg, beaten
2 hard-cooked eggs, chopped
½ cup grated sharp Cheddar cheese

¼ cup dry sherry
¼ cup butter, melted
½ teaspoon salt
    Freshly ground black pepper
6 prepared individual pastry shells or
    crab shells
    Additional breadcrumbs
    Additional butter

In a large bowl mix together the crab, soup, breadcrumbs, eggs, Cheddar cheese, sherry, butter, salt, and pepper. Place in the shells. Sprinkle with breadcrumbs and dot with butter. Bake at 375° for 30 minutes.
    Makes 6 servings.

◆ TUNA-NOODLE CASSEROLE

You might think a bunch of women in hats and dress gloves wouldn't be all that hungry. But that's one of the reasons they have luncheons. They need something to tide them over until afternoon tea.

1   10¾-ounce can cream of mush-
    room soup, undiluted
1   8-ounce carton sour cream
¼   cup dry white wine
¼   cup chopped celery
½   teaspoon garlic salt
1   teaspoon onion salt

½   teaspoon lemon juice
1   6½-ounce can tuna, drained
1   5-ounce package egg noodles,
    cooked and drained
   Breadcrumbs
   Parmesan cheese, grated

Grease a 2-quart casserole dish. In the dish combine the soup, sour cream, wine, celery, garlic salt, onion salt, and lemon juice. Stir well and add the tuna. Add the noodles and mix well. Top with breadcrumbs and Parmesan cheese. Bake at 400° for 20 minutes.

Makes 4 to 6 servings.

◆ SHRIMP PIE

2   cups breadcrumbs
1   cup half-and-half
2   cups cooked small shrimp, peeled
    and deveined
1   tablespoon chopped celery

2   tablespoons dry sherry
½   teaspoon salt
   Freshly ground white pepper
1   teaspoon Worcestershire sauce
2   tablespoons butter

Grease an 8-inch square baking dish and set aside.

In a large bowl soak the breadcrumbs in the half-and-half. Add the shrimp, celery, sherry, salt, pepper, Worcestershire sauce, and butter. Place in the prepared baking dish and bake uncovered at 375° for 30 minutes.

Makes 6 servings.

◆ CHICKEN CORDON BLEU

This is a stripped-down version of a famous recipe from French grand cuisine. Buy chicken already boned, ham and cheese already sliced, breadcrumbs in a box. All you have to do is flatten the breasts.

8   *chicken breast halves, boned and skinned*
8   *slices luncheon ham*
8   *4-inch-square slices Swiss cheese*
1   *cup breadcrumbs, toasted*

1   *teaspoon salt*
1   *teaspoon white pepper*
1   *teaspoon paprika*
½   *cup butter, melted*

Grease a 9 x 13 x 2-inch baking dish and set aside.

Wash and dry chicken breasts and flatten them with a rolling pin or meat hammer. Place one slice of ham and one slice of Swiss cheese on each breast, roll up, and secure with wooden picks. In a medium bowl mix the breadcrumbs, salt, pepper, and paprika. Roll the chicken in the melted butter and then in the breadcrumb mixture. Place in the prepared baking dish and chill overnight.

Bake uncovered at 400° for 40 minutes.

Makes 8 servings.

◆ CARROT PUDDING

Puddings have been greatly neglected in this century. They are not dishes exclusive to schoolchildren, nor are they dull and weighty and hard to digest. This one will brighten your eyes.

1   *cup shortening*
½   *cup firmly packed brown sugar*
1   *egg, beaten*
1¼   *cups grated carrots*
    Juice and grated rind of ½ lemon
1¼   *cups all-purpose flour*

1   *teaspoon salt*
1   *teaspoon baking powder*
½   *teaspoon baking soda*
1   *10-ounce package frozen broccoli, green peas, or Chinese pea pods, cooked and buttered*

Grease a 1½-quart casserole dish or ring mold and set aside. In a large bowl cream the shortening and sugar. Add the egg, carrots, lemon juice, and rind. In a separate bowl mix the dry ingredients and add to the carrot mixture. Pour into the prepared dish and bake at 375° for 30 to 45 minutes. Cool in the pan before turning out. Pile the cooked broccoli, green peas, or Chinese pea pods around the pudding or in the center of ring before serving.

Makes 6 servings.

> I say it's spinach, and I say the hell with it.
> *E. B. White, 1928*

◆ BAKED ASPARAGUS

1½ cups cracker crumbs
½ cup chopped almonds, toasted
1 10¾-ounce can cream of mush-
    room soup, undiluted
2 15-ounce cans asparagus tips,
    drained with liquid reserved

⅓ pound Cheddar cheese, grated
6 tablespoons butter
1 tablespoon Worcestershire sauce

Grease a 2-quart casserole dish and set aside.

In a medium bowl mix the cracker crumbs and almonds. In a saucepan combine the soup, ¾ cup reserved asparagus liquid, Cheddar cheese, butter, and Worcestershire sauce and heat until blended. In the prepared casserole dish alternate layers of asparagus, soup mixture, and cracker crumbs. Bake at 350° for 30 minutes.

Makes 8 servings.

◆ CHIVE-MUSTARD SAUCE FOR VEGETABLES

⅓ cup sour cream
¼ cup mayonnaise
¼ teaspoon salt

1½ tablespoons chopped fresh chives
¼ teaspoon dry mustard
1 teaspoon lemon juice

In the top of a double boiler combine all ingredients. Heat over hot water until warm, not hot. Serve over asparagus or green beans.

Makes ⅔ cup or 4 servings.

◆ FROZEN FRUIT SALAD

People at luncheons expect to be indulged. It would be cruel to disappoint them.

1 cup mayonnaise
1 8-ounce package cream cheese,
    softened
1 13½-ounce can pineapple tidbits,
    drained
1 13½-ounce can apricot halves,
    drained and chopped

½ cup maraschino cherries, drained
2 tablespoons confectioners' sugar
    Red food coloring as desired
2 cups miniature marshmallows
1 cup heavy cream, whipped, or 2
    cups whipped topping, thawed

Grease a 9 x 5-inch loaf pan and set aside.

In a large bowl gradually add the mayonnaise to the cream cheese, mixing until well blended. Stir in the fruit, sugar, and food coloring. Fold in the marshmallows and whipped cream. Pour into the prepared pan and freeze. Leave in the freezer until just before ready to serve, as salad melts quickly.

Makes 10 servings.

◆ MANDARIN ORANGE MOLD

2   11-ounce cans mandarin oranges,
      drained, with syrup reserved
    Water
2   3-ounce packages orange-flavored
      gelatin

1   pint orange sherbet
1   13½-ounce can crushed pineapple,
      undrained

Grease a 2-quart mold and set aside

In a saucepan bring the reserved syrup and enough water to make 1½ cups of liquid to a boil. Remove from the heat, and add the gelatin, stirring until dissolved. Add the orange sherbet and stir until melted. Chill until the mixture is the consistency of uncooked egg whites.

Fold in the oranges and pineapple. Pour into the prepared mold and chill several hours until set.

Makes 8 servings.

◆ CURRIED PEACHES

Don't be deceived by the simplicity of this dish. It goes beautifully with old silver and nasturtiums.

1   29-ounce can peach halves, drained
2   tablespoons butter

2   teaspoons hot curry powder

In a baking dish arrange the peach halves skin-side down. Place 1 teaspoon of butter and a pinch of curry powder in the center of each. Run under the broiler for 2 to 3 minutes. Watch carefully, as they burn easily.

Makes 6 servings.

◆ LEMONADE MOLD

1   3-ounce package lemon-flavored
      gelatin
1   cup boiling water
⅛   teaspoon salt
1   6-ounce can frozen lemonade con-
      centrate, undiluted

2   cups whipped topping, thawed
    Fresh fruit
    Fresh mint leaves
    Grated rind of 1 lemon

Grease a 4-cup ring mold and set aside.

In a large bowl dissolve the gelatin in the boiling salted water. Stir in the lemonade. Chill until the gelatin is the consistency of uncooked egg whites. Fold in the whipped topping. Pour into the prepared ring mold and chill.

Unmold on a plate and fill the center with fresh fruit. Garnish with mint leaves and lemon rind.

Makes 6 servings.

◆ CARROT CAKE

If you're going to have two or three cakes you make from scratch—and everyone should—carrot cake has got to be one of them. You can make them with or without pineapple. This one is without. Try both kinds and settle on the one you like best.

3 cups all-purpose flour
2 teaspoons baking powder
2 teaspoons baking soda
½ teaspoon salt
2¼ cups sugar
2 teaspoons ground cinnamon
1 teaspoon ground nutmeg
½ teaspoon ground allspice
1½ cups vegetable oil
2 cups grated carrots
4 eggs, beaten

1 teaspoon vanilla extract
1 cup chopped pecans or walnuts

ICING:

2 3-ounce packages cream cheese, softened
3 cups confectioners' sugar
1 teaspoon butter
1 teaspoon vanilla extract
Chopped pecans or walnuts

Grease and flour a 10-inch stem pan and set aside.

In a large bowl mix the flour, baking powder, soda, and salt. In a separate bowl mix the sugar and spices and add to the dry ingredients.

In a separate bowl mix the oil, carrots, eggs, vanilla, and nuts and add to the dry mixture. Pour into the prepared stem pan and bake at 350° for 1 hour.

Let cool 10 minutes before removing from the pan. Cool completely and ice with a blended mixture of cream cheese, confectioners' sugar, butter, and vanilla. Sprinkle with additional chopped nuts.

Makes 16 servings.

◆ REAL FUDGE PIE

The fact that this wonderfully indulgent dessert is not baked in a crust furthers the illusion that it's fudge. Be careful of two things: (1) Chocolate burns easily, so melt it in the top of a double boiler over hot water; and (2) you have to warm the beaten eggs with a small amount of melted chocolate before adding them to the whole mixture. If you don't, they'll curdle.

2 squares unsweetened baking chocolate
½ cup butter
1 cup sugar
½ cup all-purpose flour

Pinch of salt
2 eggs, beaten
1 cup chopped walnuts or pecans
1 teaspoon vanilla extract

In the top of a double boiler melt the chocolate and butter over hot water. Add the sugar, flour, and salt and mix well. Stir a small amount of chocolate mixture into the eggs; then add the eggs to the remaining chocolate mixture. Add the nuts and vanilla. Pour into a 9-inch pie plate and bake at 350° for 30 minutes.

Serve with whipped topping or ice cream while still warm.

Makes 8 servings.

◆ FRESH APPLE CAKE

This is another cake for your short list of scratch cakes. It's made with oil, which makes it easy to stir together. You don't have to ice it. The apples make lovely spots of cooked fruit in a moist and spicy batter. This recipe is for one loaf pan, but it doubles for a 10-inch stem or Bundt pan. It's even better the second day. Use tart apples like Granny Smith or fall Winesap.

1 egg, beaten	1 teaspoon baking soda
½ cup sugar	½ teaspoon ground cinnamon
½ cup firmly packed dark brown sugar	½ teaspoon ground ginger
⅔ cup vegetable oil	2 cups chopped tart fresh apples
1½ cups all-purpose flour	1 cup chopped walnuts or pecans
	1 teaspoon vanilla extract

Grease and flour a 9 x 5-inch loaf pan and set aside.

In a large bowl combine the egg, sugars, and vegetable oil.

In a separate bowl mix together the flour, soda, and spices and add to the egg mixture alternately with the apples. The batter will be very stiff. Stir in the nuts and vanilla and spoon into the prepared pan. Bake at 350° for 1 hour.

Cool in the pan for 15 minutes. Serve with vanilla ice cream or Hard Sauce (recipe follows).

Makes 16 servings.

◆ HARD SAUCE

Hard sauce livens up just about anything. Maybe not toast, but it would be great on carrot pudding.

½ cup butter	⅛ teaspoon salt
1 cup confectioners' sugar	1 tablespoon brandy

In a medium bowl cream the butter until very soft. Add the sugar gradually, then the salt, and beat until smooth. Add the brandy. Chill well.

Makes 1½ cups.

◆ IRISH COFFEE

Do not serve Irish coffee to luncheon guests who have anything they have to do before dark.

1 teaspoon sugar	5 ounces hot coffee
1½ ounces Irish whiskey	1 tablespoon whipped cream

Into a large wine or Irish coffee glass place sugar, whiskey, and coffee and stir well. Top with whipped cream.
    Makes 1 serving.

◆ COFFEE PUNCH

2 quarts strong coffee	2 quarts vanilla ice cream
1 pint cold milk	½ pint whipping cream, whipped, or 1
2 teaspoons vanilla extract	½ cups whipped topping, thawed
½ cup sugar	Grated nutmeg

In a large container combine the coffee, milk, vanilla, and sugar. Chill.
    Place the ice cream in large spoonfuls in a punch bowl. Pour the chilled coffee over ice cream. Spoon mounds of whipped cream on top of punch. Sprinkle with nutmeg.
    Makes 15 servings.

◆ FROSTED MINT TEA

3 quarts boiling water	Additional sugar
24 regular tea bags	3 quarts lemon-lime carbonated drink
¼ cup mint jelly	or ginger ale, well chilled
¼ cup sugar	Lemon or lime slices
Lemon juice	Fresh mint sprigs

In a large container pour boiling water over the tea bags, cover, and let steep 5 minutes.
    Remove the tea bags. Add the jelly and sugar, stirring until dissolved. Chill.
    Dip rims of glasses in the lemon juice, then in the sugar, and freeze. To serve, and pour over ice in glasses. Garnish with lemon slices and mint.
    Makes 6 quarts or 30 servings.

SUNDAY DINNER

A tourist stopped at a roadside diner that claimed on tacky signs up and down the highway to have the world's best fried chicken, guaranteed. The man was dubious, but he tried it. It was the best. Flabbergasted, he called the cook out from the back and said, "Tell me, how do you prepare your chickens?" The cook replied, "Nothing special—we just tell 'em they're gonna die."

Mary Hood quoting Reynolds Price, 1996

It was always after church, noon or one o'clock, generally involved company—a distant relative, a couple of old friends, somebody's in-laws just passing through town—and everyone was there to eat: two meats, three starches, a random assortment of cooked vegetables, salads, breads, jams, jellies, pickles, cakes, pies, the more the better. Conversation was lively and no one had any place they'd rather be, and besides, people had to eat to keep up their strength. It was important.

The cooking started at daybreak and by church time the house smelled divine and it seemed like noon would never come. But finally, there it was, Sunday dinner, spread out in all its glory before God and everyone: cut-glass bowls brimming with ambrosia, china platters piled high with chicken, plates of biscuits, pitchers of iced tea, carving knives, silver servers, ladles dripping with meat juices and grease. You passed to the right and to take seconds, even thirds, was considered extra complimentary to the cook who, after all, liked nothing better than to see a hearty eater tossing down her three-bean salad.

It was a time of the week devoted solely to food and we ate as much as we wanted, every one of us. All we had before us was a long, idle Sunday afternoon stretching out to supper and cold leftovers, and if we got sleepy we could always take a nap.

◆ QUICK ROLLS

If a reputation for not being able to make dinner rolls has gotten you out of a lot of work through the years, snip out this recipe right now and hide it away where no one will find it. Even a child could make these rolls.

2¼ cups biscuit mix, divided   ½ cup butter, melted
1   8-ounce carton sour cream

Grease twelve 2½-inch muffin cups and set aside.

In a large bowl combine 2 cups biscuit mix, the sour cream, and the butter. Stir well. Sprinkle the remaining ¼ cup biscuit mix on a flat surface. Drop the dough by tablespoons onto the surface and roll into balls. Place three balls in each of the prepared muffin cups. Bake at 350° for 15 to 20 minutes.

Makes 12 rolls.

◆ SOUR CREAM CORN BREAD

Corn bread made with canned creamed corn is almost as custardlike as spoon bread. You can make the regular version of this for Sunday dinner or add green chilies and Cheddar cheese for a Mexican variation.

1   cup self-rising cornmeal   1   4-ounce can green chilies with
1   8¾-ounce can cream-style corn   jalapeños, drained and chopped
1   8-ounce carton sour cream   (optional)
3   large eggs, lightly beaten   ½ cup grated Cheddar cheese (option-
¼   cup vegetable oil   al)

Heat a lightly greased 8-inch cast-iron skillet in a 400° oven for 10 minutes.

In a large bowl combine the cornmeal, corn, sour cream, eggs, and oil, stirring just until moistened. Remove the skillet from the oven and fill with the batter. For a Mexican variation, pour half the batter into the skillet, cover with chilies and Cheddar cheese, and pour the remaining batter on top. Bake for 20 to 25 minutes or until golden.

Makes 6 servings.

◆ FRY BREAD

1 25-ounce package frozen roll dough, thawed Vegetable oil for frying	¼ cup sugar 1 tablespoon ground cinnamon

Flatten each roll to a 3½-inch diameter. In a heavy skillet or deep-fat fryer heat 2 inches of oil to 375°. Drop the rolls a few at a time into the hot oil and fry 2 minutes or until golden brown. Drain on paper towels and toss with the combined sugar and cinnamon. Serve immediately.

Makes 24 rolls.

◆ SUNDAY PECAN MUFFINS

Be careful with these muffins. Once they've had them a couple of times, people start demanding them: "Are you losing your grip?" they gasp, hand to heaving bosom. "It's Sunday, isn't it? What do you mean we're not having pecan muffins?"

1⅓ cups all-purpose flour 1 cup chopped pecans ½ cup firmly packed dark brown sugar 2 teaspoons baking powder	Pinch salt ½ cup milk ¼ cup butter, melted 2 eggs, beaten ½ teaspoon vanilla extract

Grease and flour fifteen 2½-inch muffin cups and set aside.

In a large bowl combine the flour, pecans, brown sugar, baking powder, and salt, making a well in the center.

In a separate bowl combine the milk, butter, eggs, and vanilla and pour into the well, stirring until just moistened. Spoon the batter into the prepared muffin tins, filling each cup halfway. Bake at 350° for 20 to 25 minutes. Remove immediately from the tins.

Makes 15 muffins.

◆ REFRIGERATOR PICKLES

You don't have to can and process to make great pickles. Refrigerator pickles are so crisp and sweet that people have been known to eat a whole jar at one sitting. No processing or sealing, no boiling water: All you do is slice, mix, put them in the refrigerator, and resist for a couple of weeks the temptation to eat them.

2 teaspoons kosher salt, divided	1 green bell pepper, thinly sliced
1 teaspoon celery seed, divided	1 medium onion, finely chopped
7 cups thinly sliced small cucumbers, very fresh	2 cups sugar
	1 cup cider vinegar

In a large bowl sprinkle half the salt and celery seed over the cucumbers. Top with the pepper and onion and sprinkle with the remaining salt and celery seed. Mix well and chill.

In a saucepan combine the sugar and vinegar and simmer over medium heat, stirring until the sugar is dissolved. Do not boil. Cool and chill for 2 hours.

Pour over the cucumber mixture, mixing gently. Place in two sterilized quart jars and refrigerate 2 to 3 weeks before serving. Will keep in the refrigerator 6 months.

Makes 2 quarts.

◆ REFRIGERATOR RELISH

1 large red onion, coarsely chopped	2 tablespoons raspberry preserves
2 tablespoons water	2 teaspoons lemon juice
½ teaspoon dried dill weed	Salt and pepper to taste
½ teaspoon dried marjoram	

In a saucepan place the onion, water, dill, and marjoram. Heat to boiling, reduce heat, cover, and simmer for 10 to 15 minutes or until the onion is tender.

Stir in the preserves, lemon juice, salt, and pepper. Serve warm with meats, fish, or poultry. May be stored in the refrigerator for 1 week.

Makes 1 cup.

◆ BASIC POT ROAST

2½ pounds chuck or rump roast	1 medium carrot, chopped
Salt and pepper to taste	1 celery stalk, chopped
1 medium onion, finely chopped	1 14½-ounce can stewed tomatoes
2 tablespoons olive oil	with juice
½ cup boiling water	1 tablespoon all-purpose flour
2 bay leaves	Cold water

Season the meat with salt and pepper.

In a covered Dutch oven sauté the onion in oil over low heat until translucent, not brown. Increase the heat to medium, add the meat, and brown on all sides. Add the boiling water, bay leaves, carrot, and celery. Cover tightly, reduce the heat, and simmer slowly for 2 hours and 30 minutes.

Thirty minutes before serving add the tomatoes and season to taste. Thicken the gravy with flour mixed with a little cold water.

Makes 4 servings.

> The custom of saying grace at meals had, probably, its origin in the early times of the world...when dinners were precarious things, and a full meal was something more than a common blessing!
>
> *Charles Lamb, 1823*

◆ BAKED PORK CHOPS

8 pork chops, cut 1-inch thick	2 onions, thickly sliced
1 cup catsup	2 lemons, thickly sliced
½ cup firmly packed dark brown sugar	

In a shallow baking dish place the pork chops. On top of each place the following: 2 tablespoons catsup, 1 tablespoon brown sugar, one slice onion, one slice lemon. Bake covered at 350° for 45 minutes.

Uncover and bake 45 minutes more.

Makes 8 servings.

◆ FRIED CHICKEN

Some people can fry and some can't. It's a cruel twist of fate that singles out a chosen few and leaves the rest of us wondering how on earth we'll ever manage to come by a decent fritter. Frying takes an understanding of temperature and grease, an impeccable sense of timing, and a healthy disregard for spatters and clean-up. Immortality through the ages has rested on far less than a crisp, batter-coated drumstick hot from the stove or cold from the refrigerator the next day. If you happen to be one of those cooks who know their way around a skillet, you are rare indeed.

4 to 5 pounds chicken pieces with skin	1 teaspoon baking powder
Buttermilk	½ teaspoon dry mustard
2 cups all-purpose flour	½ cup butter
Salt and pepper to taste	½ cup vegetable oil
Dash cayenne pepper	Milk

Soak the chicken in buttermilk 1 to 2 hours.

In a plastic bag combine the flour, salt, pepper, cayenne, baking powder, and dry mustard. Drain and pat dry the chicken, drop a few pieces at a time into the bag, and shake to coat well. In a heavy iron or electric skillet place the butter and oil and heat to 375°. Place the chicken pieces skin-side down in the skillet. Cook until dark golden brown on one side. Turn carefully with tongs and brown on the other side. Cover the skillet, reduce the heat to low, and cook until juices run clear, 30 to 40 minutes.

Remove the lid for the last 15 minutes for crisp chicken. Transfer to a warm plate in a warm oven to keep crisp and hot. Drain the fat from the skillet and add a little flour to the drippings still in the pan. Stir until light brown. Add the milk slowly, stirring constantly with a wire whisk until thickened. Season with salt and pepper.

Makes 6 to 8 servings.

◆ COUNTRY STEWED CHICKEN

This is a variation of an Indian curry called Country Captain. *Captain* is thought to be a corruption of the word *capon*. It's especially good with hot, sweet chutney.

1 cup all-purpose flour	1 14½-ounce can stewed tomatoes with juice
1 teaspoon salt	1 cup beer, room temperature
1 teaspoon white pepper	1 tablespoon salt
5 pounds chicken pieces	1 teaspoon curry powder
2 tablespoons olive oil	¼ cup golden raisins
3 large onions, sliced	4 cups cooked rice
2 cloves garlic, minced	
1 green bell pepper, diced	

In a bag combine the flour, 1 teaspoon salt, and white pepper. Drop the chicken pieces into the bag to coat.

In a Dutch oven heat the olive oil and brown the chicken on all sides. Remove the chicken, add the onions, garlic, and bell pepper, and cook until soft, not brown. Return the chicken to the Dutch oven and add the tomatoes, beer, 1 tablespoon salt, and the curry powder. Cover and simmer 1 hour. Add the raisins and cook 10 minutes longer.

Serve over rice.

Makes 8 servings.

> But, Atticus, he's gone and drowned his dinner in syrup!
> *Harper Lee, 1960*

 EASY MEAT LOAF

1 10¾-ounce can tomato soup, undiluted and divided	½ cup breadcrumbs
	1 egg, beaten
2 pounds ground beef	¼ cup water
1 1-ounce envelope onion soup mix	

Grease a 2-quart baking dish and set aside.

In a large bowl mix thoroughly ½ cup tomato soup, the beef, onion soup mix, breadcrumbs, and egg. In the prepared baking dish shape the meat mixture into an 8 x 4-inch loaf. Bake at 350° for 1 hour and 15 minutes or until the meat is no longer pink.

Drain the drippings, reserving 2 tablespoons. In a saucepan over medium heat combine the remaining tomato soup, water, and 2 tablespoons drippings. Heat thoroughly and serve over slices of meat loaf.

Makes 8 servings.

◆ SALMON-MUSHROOM CASSEROLE

2   cups egg noodles, uncooked
1   10¾-ounce can cream of mushroom
    soup, undiluted
½   cup half-and-half
1   cup frozen peas, thawed
2   tablespoons chopped pimiento,
    drained

1   14¾-ounce can salmon, drained
    and flaked
¼   cup shredded yellow cheese
2   tablespoons breadcrumbs
1   tablespoon butter, melted

Cook and drain the noodles according to the directions on the package. In a 1½-quart casserole combine the soup and half-and-half. Stir in the noodles, peas, pimiento, and salmon. Bake at 400° for 20 minutes. Stir.

In a medium bowl combine the yellow cheese, breadcrumbs, and butter and spread on top. Bake 5 minutes more.

Makes 4 servings.

◆ BAKED SHRIMP

Shrimp baked in sherry and cream is a hymn to civilized living. Children who eat this at Sunday dinner at a big table surrounded by people who love them can't go far wrong.

1   tablespoon butter
1   4-ounce can chopped mushrooms,
    drained
1   onion, minced
2   tomatoes, peeled and diced
½   cup half-and-half
2   tablespoons all-purpose flour

¼   cup dry sherry
1   tablespoon Worcestershire sauce
    Salt and pepper to taste
3   pounds cooked shrimp, peeled and
    deveined (use small or medium)
½   cup buttered breadcrumbs

Grease a 2-quart casserole dish and set aside.

In a large skillet combine the butter, mushrooms, onion, and tomatoes, and simmer for 10 minutes. Blend in the half-and-half, flour, sherry, Worcestershire sauce, salt, and pepper. Add the shrimp. Pour into the prepared casserole dish, top with breadcrumbs, and bake at 350° for 20 minutes or until browned.

Makes 8 servings.

> One might think there wouldn't be a next course,
> but one would be mistaken.
> *Elizabeth David, 1960*

◆ BROCCOLI CASSEROLE

1   cup mayonnaise
1   10¾-ounce can cream of celery
    soup, undiluted
2   eggs, beaten
2   10-ounce packages frozen, chopped
    broccoli, cooked and drained
2   tablespoons minced onion

1   cup grated sharp Cheddar cheese
1   tablespoon Worcestershire sauce
1   teaspoon seasoned salt
    Freshly ground black pepper
1   cup herb-seasoned stuffing mix
2   tablespoons butter

Grease a 2-quart casserole dish and set aside.

In a large bowl combine the mayonnaise and soup, mixing well. Stir in the eggs and broccoli. Add the onion, Cheddar cheese, Worcestershire sauce, salt, and pepper. Place in the prepared casserole dish and top with the stuffing mix. Dot with butter. Bake at 325° for 45 minutes.

Makes 8 servings.

◆ SPINACH SOUFFLÉ

½   cup chopped onion
¼   cup butter plus 2 tablespoons, divid-
    ed
2   10-ounce packages frozen, chopped
    spinach, thawed and wrung dry
    by hand

1   teaspoon salt
1   10¾-ounce can cream of mushroom
    soup, undiluted
½   cup grated Cheddar cheese
2   eggs, beaten
    Breadcrumbs

Grease a 2-quart casserole dish and set aside.

In a skillet sauté the onion in ¼ cup butter covered over low heat until translucent, not brown.

In a bowl mix the spinach, salt, onion, soup, and Cheddar cheese. Fold the eggs into the mixture. Pour into the prepared casserole dish and sprinkle with breadcrumbs. Dot top with 2 tablespoons butter. Bake at 350° for 30 minutes.

Makes 6 servings.

◆ STEWED TOMATOES

Canned tomatoes, oddly enough, stew better than fresh ones. That means you can make this elegant side dish any season of the year.

4 slices white bread, toasted	1 tablespoon sugar
6 tablespoons butter	½ teaspoon salt
¼ cup chopped onion	⅛ teaspoon white pepper
1 1-pound 12-ounce can tomatoes with juice	2 tablespoons grated Parmesan cheese

Grease a 1½-quart casserole dish and set aside.

Cut three slices of toast into ½-inch cubes; cut the remaining slice into strips for top. Place the cubes in the prepared casserole dish.

In a medium skillet melt the butter and sauté the onion covered over low heat until translucent, not brown. Add the tomatoes, sugar, salt, and pepper and pour on top of the toast cubes in the casserole. Arrange the toast strips on top and sprinkle with the Parmesan cheese. Bake at 350° for 45 minutes.

Makes 6 servings.

◆ OKRA CREOLE

If you've got some poor, misguided soul in your family who gags at the mere thought of okra, just put a little zydeco on the stereo and neglect to mention what's in with the corn and the bacon fat. By the time they figure it out, they'll be halfway to Opelousas.

¼ cup chopped onion	1 cup cut fresh corn or 1 15-ounce can whole kernel corn, drained
1 green bell pepper, chopped	Salt and pepper to taste
3 tablespoons bacon fat	
2 cups sliced okra	
1 1-pound 12-ounce can stewed tomatoes with juice	

In a skillet sauté the onion and bell pepper in the bacon fat until soft. Add the okra and cook 5 minutes. Add the tomatoes and corn. Simmer 15 minutes.

Season with salt and pepper. Serve over rice.

Makes 8 servings.

◆ FRESH CUCUMBER SALAD

The smaller the cucumbers and the thinner the slices, the crisper these will be. You should score the skins of larger cucumbers with the tines of a fork or peel them. Slice the onion, also, as thinly as possible, and try to get a sweet one like a Vidalia or a Texas Sweet. These are great to munch on. Keep your eye on the bowl or they'll be gone before dinner.

7 cups thinly sliced cucumbers	1½ cups sugar
1 large onion, thinly sliced and separated into rings	¾ teaspoon celery seed
1½ cups water	½ teaspoon garlic salt
1½ cups cider vinegar	½ teaspoon onion salt
	½ teaspoon celery salt

In a large bowl layer the cucumber and onion slices. In a small bowl combine the remaining ingredients, blend thoroughly, and pour over the vegetables. Cover and chill at least 2 hours.

Makes 12 servings.

◆ SPAGHETTI SALAD

You wouldn't think the shape of pasta would have any effect on taste, but it does. Shells taste different from fusilli; penne is nothing like angel hair. Spaghetti is one of the more amazing ones. Sure, it's great with meatballs and marinara sauce, but you can also make a cold salad with it.

1 16-ounce package spaghetti, cooked and drained	2 tomatoes, peeled and diced
1 medium red onion, finely chopped	1 cucumber, scored and diced
4 green onions, finely chopped	2 tablespoons salad seasoning
1 cup prepared Italian salad dressing	Fresh parsley, chopped

In a large bowl combine the spaghetti, red onion, green onions, and salad dressing, tossing gently. Cover and chill overnight. Just before serving, add the tomatoes, cucumber, and salad seasoning. Sprinkle with chopped parsley.

Makes 10 servings.

◆ EGG-MACARONI SALAD

This recipe is for anyone with fond memories of macaroni and cheese from a box. You could stop at the first step, but if you do, come back sometime and add the rest. You might find you have a new favorite.

1 7¼-ounce box macaroni and cheese dinner mix	½ cup sliced celery
1 10-ounce package frozen peas	½ cup chopped onion
1 medium tomato, peeled and chopped	½ teaspoon salt
	Dash pepper
¾ cup mayonnaise	6 hard-cooked eggs, 5 chopped and 1 sliced

In a pot prepare the macaroni and cheese as directed on the package. Add the peas, tomato, mayonnaise, celery, onion, seasonings, plus five chopped eggs. Mix lightly and chill. Garnish with the remaining egg, sliced.

Makes 8 servings.

◆ PERFECTION SALAD

This molded salad is a serious combination of vegetables and dressing—none of that whipped cream-marshmallow froufrou people like to call salad when we all know it's really dessert. You're eating salad with this one, no doubt about it, and you'll want seconds.

1 ¼-ounce envelope unflavored gelatin	2 cups diced celery
½ cup cold water	1 cup shredded cabbage
½ cup boiling water	1 cup canned peas, drained
½ cup sugar	1 cup diced cucumber
½ cup cider vinegar	1 cup pecan pieces
Juice of 1 lemon	1 7-ounce bottle pimiento-stuffed green olives, sliced
2 teaspoons salt	

Grease a 6-cup mold or 12 individual molds and set aside.

In a medium bowl soak the gelatin in the cold water for 5 minutes, then dissolve in the boiling water. Add the sugar, vinegar, lemon juice, and salt. Chill in the refrigerator until the mixture is the consistency of uncooked egg whites. Add the vegetables, pecans, and olives. Pour into the prepared mold or molds.

Makes 12 servings.

◆ HEAVENLY HASH

1 3-ounce package lemon-flavored
    gelatin
1 3-ounce package lime-flavored
    gelatin
1½ cups hot water
1 8-ounce package cream cheese,
    softened

½ cup mayonnaise
1 16-ounce can crushed pineapple
    with juice
1 cup miniature marshmallows
1 cup chopped pecans

Grease a 6-cup mold and set aside.

In a large bowl dissolve the gelatins in hot water. Add the cream cheese, stirring well. Add the mayonnaise, pineapple, marshmallows, and pecans. Pour into the prepared mold and chill to set.

Makes 8 to 10 servings.

◆ RUM FRUIT SALAD

Rum on Sunday is okay because it's mixed up with all this fruit and fruit is good for your complexion.

6 cups watermelon balls
4 cups strawberries, stemmed
4 cups honeydew melon balls
1 fresh pineapple, peeled and cubed
½ pound green or red seedless grapes

2 bananas, sliced
2 large oranges, peeled and sec-
    tioned
½ cup sugar
1 cup light rum

In a large bowl combine the fruit and add the sugar and rum. Toss gently. Cover and chill 1 to 2 hours.

Makes 15 servings.

◆ HEAVENLY CHOCOLATE CAKE

Chocolate cake and cold milk is one of life's perfect combinations. If you're lucky and there's a piece of this left over from dinner, you can have it at bedtime.

1 18¼-ounce package chocolate cake
    mix
½ cup unsweetened cocoa
3 eggs, beaten

1⅓ cups water
1 cup mayonnaise
    Prepared cake icing

Grease and flour a 9 x 13 x 2-inch baking pan and set aside.

In a large bowl mix together the cake mix and cocoa. Add the eggs, water, and mayonnaise. Beat at medium speed with an electric mixer until blended. Pour into the prepared pan and bake at 350° for 30 to 40 minutes or until a toothpick inserted in the center comes out clean.

Cool in the pan and frost as desired.

Makes 12 servings.

◆ CHERRY PECAN PIE

This is just about as easy as dessert gets and just about as good. You can put it together in five minutes, wow a table full of people with your culinary skills, and still have some left for yourself the next day.

1   14-ounce can sweetened condensed
   milk
1   8-ounce container whipped topping,
   thawed
¼   cup lemon juice

1   cup chopped pecans
1   21-ounce can cherry pie filling
2   9-inch prepared graham cracker
   pastry shells

In a large bowl combine the condensed milk and whipped topping. Gradually stir in the lemon juice and fold in the pecans and pie filling. Spoon into the crusts and chill 2 hours.

Makes 2 pies or 12 servings.

◆ FRESH PEACH COBBLER

Write yourself a note and put it on your refrigerator: This July, when the peach crop comes in, make yourself a fresh peach cobbler.

5   cups peeled and sliced fresh
   peaches
1   tablespoon lemon juice
1   cup all-purpose flour
1   cup sugar

½   teaspoon salt
1   egg, beaten
6   tablespoons butter, melted
   Vanilla ice cream

Grease a 10 x 6 x 2½-inch baking dish. Spread the peaches on the bottom of the dish. Sprinkle with lemon juice. In a medium bowl mix the flour, sugar, and salt and add the egg, tossing with a fork until crumbly. Sprinkle over the peaches and drizzle with the butter. Bake at 375° for 35 to 40 minutes. Serve with vanilla ice cream.

Makes 6 servings.

◆ APPLE CRISP

1   1-pound 6-ounce can apple pie fill-
       ing
¼   cup firmly packed light brown sugar
½   teaspoon ground cinnamon
¼   teaspoon ground nutmeg

2   tablespoons lemon juice
½   18¼-ounce package white cake mix
6   tablespoons butter, thinly sliced
     Whipped topping, thawed

Grease a 9-inch pie pan. Pour the apple pie filling into the pan. In a medium bowl mix the brown sugar, cinnamon, and nutmeg and sprinkle over pie filling. Sprinkle lemon juice over the pie filling. Top with the cake mix and completely cover with thin slices of butter. Bake at 350° for 45 minutes.

Serve warm with whipped topping.

Makes 8 servings.

◆ ORANGE ANGEL CAKE

This sounds like one of those healthy desserts people keep bugging you to try. But it doesn't taste like it.

1   16-ounce package angel food cake
       mix
¾   cup frozen orange juice concen-
       trate, thawed and divided

1   8-ounce carton whipped topping,
       thawed
½   cup vanilla yogurt

In a large bowl prepare the cake as directed on the package, except substitute ⅓ cup of thawed orange juice concentrate for an equal amount of the liquid called for. Bake in a 10-inch stem pan, according to directions.

When the cake is done, invert immediately, leaving in the pan to cool complete-ly. When cool, loosen from the sides of the pan and remove.

For the icing, in a large bowl combine the whipped topping, yogurt, and remain-ing orange juice concentrate. Spread the mixture on the top and sides of the cake. Store in the refrigerator.

Makes 16 servings.

◆ ICED LEMON-MINT TEA

6 cups water, divided	2 46-ounce cans pineapple juice
6 regular tea bags	1 cup sugar
3 lemons, cut into ½-inch slices	1½ teaspoons vanilla extract
1 cup crushed fresh mint leaves	1½ teaspoons almond extract

In a pot bring 2 cups water to a boil and pour over the tea bags. Add lemons and mint. Cover and let steep for 20 minutes. Strain. Combine the tea mixture with the pineapple juice, sugar, vanilla extract, almond extract, and 4 cups water. Serve over ice.
Makes 3 quarts.

◆ HOT CITRUS TEA

2 cups water	½ cup lemon juice
6 whole cloves	⅔ cup orange juice
1½ quarts water	1½ cups sugar
8 regular tea bags	

In a saucepan combine 2 cups of water and the cloves and bring to a boil. Remove from the heat, cover, and let steep for 2 hours.

In a large saucepan bring 1½ quarts of water to a boil and add the tea bags. Remove from the heat, cover, let steep for 5 minutes, and remove the tea bags.

Strain the clove mixture and add to the tea. Add the fruit juices and sugar, stirring until the sugar dissolves. Cover and let steep for 1 hour more.

Reheat before serving.
Makes 2 quarts.

DINNER ON THE GROUNDS

Thus mortals ate the bread of angels.
Psalm 78:25

They still do it on hot summer Sundays when the sky is a washed-out blue and thunderheads are massing on the horizon and the light is so bright it gets in behind your eyes and makes all the world seem hazy. After the midday service they set up gingham-covered tables underneath the shade trees by the parking lot, and someone brings in a truckload of folding chairs from the funeral home and a box of paper fans on wooden sticks with a picture of the River Jordan on the front and the dove descending. And people open up their trunks and pull out covered baskets of vegetable casseroles and cardboard boxes crammed with crushed newspapers and lemon chess pies. There are platters of cold sliced ham, molded salads with marshmallows and mandarin oranges, great pots of hot dogs and baked beans, raw onion rings.

Dinner on the grounds is an astonishing variety. Children, strollers, dogs, young people, old people, pickup softball, horseshoes, conversation, more friends than you see in a month, more food than you can imagine. Someone always brings lasagna; the sweetened iced tea never runs out; and if you're first in line for dessert you can have funeral pie. The person who can't find something good to eat just isn't trying.

◆ ROLLED SAUSAGE BISCUITS

1   10-biscuit can refrigerator biscuits   1   pound hot bulk sausage

On a floured board roll out each biscuit to ¼-inch thickness. Cover with the raw sausage and roll tightly. Chill 2 to 3 hours.

Cut the rolled biscuits crosswise into ⅜-inch slices and place flat on an ungreased baking sheet. Bake at 375° for 8 to 10 minutes or until brown and crisp.

Makes 60 to 72 biscuits.

◆ SWEET-AND-EASY CORN BREAD

1   18½-ounce package yellow cake   1   15-ounce package corn bread mix
    mix, without pudding

Grease two 9-inch square baking pans and place them in the oven to heat.

Make the cake and corn bread batters according to the directions on the package. Blend the batters together and pour into the hot pans. Bake at 350° for 30 to 35 minutes or until the center of the corn bread springs back when lightly touched.

Makes 24 servings.

◆ PARSLEY-HERB BREAD

1   egg, beaten   1   cup grated sharp Cheddar cheese,
½   cup milk   divided
1½   cups biscuit mix   2   tablespoons chopped fresh parsley
½   cup chopped onion   1   teaspoon dried dill weed
3   tablespoons butter, melted and
    divided

Grease an 8-inch square pan and set aside.

In a medium bowl add the egg and milk to the biscuit mix, stirring only until moistened.

In a skillet sauté the onion in 1 tablespoon butter and add to the biscuit mixture with a ½ cup Cheddar cheese, the parsley, and the dill. Stir lightly to combine. Pat the dough into the prepared pan. Sprinkle the remaining Cheddar cheese on top and drizzle with the remaining butter. Bake at 400° for 20 minutes.

Cut into 2-inch squares.

Makes 8 servings.

◆ CORNMEAL BISCUITS

2 cups all-purpose flour
¾ cup white cornmeal
1 tablespoon baking powder
1 teaspoon salt

½ teaspoon baking soda
½ cup butter
1 cup buttermilk

In a large bowl combine the flour, cornmeal, baking powder, salt, and soda. Stir well. Cut in the butter with a pastry blender until the mixture resembles coarse meal. Add the buttermilk, stirring only until moistened. Turn the dough out onto a floured surface and knead lightly 3 or 4 times. Roll out the dough to ½-inch thickness. Cut with a 2½-inch biscuit cutter. Place the biscuits on an ungreased baking sheet and bake at 450° for 10 to 12 minutes.

Makes 24 biscuits.

> Human beings dream of life everlasting....
> But most of them want it on earth.
> *Tennessee Williams, 1955*

◆ SWEET-AND-SOUR SPARERIBS

Marriages have been founded on ribs. When you're facing that big decision, wondering what life might be like down through the years with a certain someone at your side, and he turns suddenly and hands you a plate of ribs, it all becomes clear. It was not for naught that Adam gave Eve one of his.

1 teaspoon salt
3 to 4 pounds spareribs, cut in pieces
3 tablespoons cider vinegar
½ cup orange juice

½ cup firmly packed dark brown
    sugar
1 tablespoon cornstarch
1 tablespoon water

Salt the ribs. Place them in a shallow roasting pan and roast at 450° for 45 minutes.

Drain the excess fat from the pan. Make a basting sauce from the remaining ingredients and pour over the ribs. Reduce the heat to 350° and bake 1 hour and 30 minutes more, basting frequently.

Makes 4 servings.

◆ EASY CHICKEN

So you can't fry. So what? Fried chicken isn't the only chicken in the world.

6   chicken breast halves
¼   cup mayonnaise

Parmesan cheese, grated

Place the chicken in a shallow baking pan. Spread with the mayonnaise and sprinkle with the Parmesan cheese. Bake uncovered at 350° for 1 hour.
   Makes 4 servings.

◆ EASY LASAGNA

The lasagna noodles, amazingly enough, cook themselves in this recipe. It will spoil you for any other.

¾   pound ground beef
3   cups spaghetti sauce
6   lasagna noodles, uncooked
1   15-ounce container ricotta cheese

2   cups shredded mozzarella cheese
    Parmesan cheese, grated
¼   cup water

Grease a 9 x 13 x 2-inch baking dish and set aside.
   In a 10-inch skillet over medium-high heat brown the beef. Drain the fat, add the spaghetti sauce, and stir until heated.
   In the prepared baking dish spread 1½ cups of the meat mixture. Top with three uncooked lasagna noodles, half the ricotta cheese, and half the mozzarella cheese. Repeat the layers, ending with the meat mixture. Sprinkle with Parmesan cheese. Slowly pour water around the edges and cover tightly with heavy foil. Bake at 375° for 45 minutes.
   Uncover and bake 10 minutes more. Let stand 10 minutes before serving.
   Makes 8 servings.

◆ BEEF-BEAN-BACON BAKE

If you're eating dinner on a paper plate, it's a foregone conclusion that you're eating baked beans.

1   pound ground beef
½   pound bacon
1   cup chopped onion
2   tablespoons Dijon-style mustard
2   tablespoons molasses
½   cup tomato catsup
1   cup firmly packed dark brown
    sugar

1   16-ounce can green lima beans,
    drained
1   16-ounce can red kidney beans,
    drained
1   16-ounce can pork and beans
    Extra catsup
1   small onion, cut in rings

In a skillet brown the beef and pour off the excess fat.

In a separate skillet brown the bacon, pour off the excess fat, and add the chopped onions, cooking until tender, not brown. Add the bacon and onions to the beef. Add the mustard, molasses, catsup, and brown sugar. Add the beans. Pour into a large casserole dish, top with the extra catsup and onion rings, and bake uncovered at 350° for 35 to 40 minutes.

Makes 6 servings.

◆ CHEDDAR SOUP MACARONI

3 cups corkscrew macaroni, uncooked	1 soup can milk
½ teaspoon salt	2 teaspoons prepared mustard
2 10¾-ounce cans Cheddar cheese soup, undiluted	¼ teaspoon black pepper
	2 tablespoons seasoned breadcrumbs
	2 tablespoons butter, melted

In a pot cook and drain the macaroni according to the directions on the package. In a large bowl combine the soup, milk, mustard, and pepper and mix with the macaroni.

In a separate bowl combine the breadcrumbs and melted butter and sprinkle over the macaroni mixture. Bake at 400° for 25 minutes.

Makes 6 to 8 servings.

An intellectual carrot. The mind boggles.
Robert Cornthwaite in The Thing, 1951

◆ CHEDDAR POTATOES

A perfectly cooked vegetable by itself is a fine thing, but never at dinner on the grounds. When you sign up in the church basement to bring a vegetable, that means a vegetable cooked with lots of other stuff. It's what people expect. It's one of the reasons they eat dinner on the grounds.

1 10¾-ounce can cream of mushroom soup, undiluted	4 medium baking potatoes (about 1 ½ pounds), cut into ½-inch slices
½ teaspoon paprika	1 cup shredded Cheddar cheese
½ teaspoon black pepper	

Grease a 2-quart oblong baking dish and set aside.

In a medium bowl combine the soup, paprika, and pepper. Arrange the potatoes in over-lapping rows in the prepared baking dish. Sprinkle with the Cheddar cheese. Spoon the soup mixture over the Cheddar cheese. Cover with heavy foil and bake at 400° for 45 minutes. Uncover and bake 10 minutes more.

Makes 6 servings.

◆ SHERRIED SWEET POTATOES

2	15-ounce cans sweet potatoes, drained	2	tablespoons orange juice
½	cup butter, cut up	2	tablespoons dry sherry
½	cup firmly packed dark brown sugar	3	marshmallows
		½	cup pecan pieces
			Additional butter

Grease an 8-inch square baking dish and set aside.

In a large bowl combine the sweet potatoes, butter, brown sugar, orange juice, sherry, marshmallows, and pecans. Pour into the prepared baking dish and dot with butter. Bake at 350° for 20 to 30 minutes.

Makes 8 servings.

◆ LAYERED DINNER SALAD

Salads at dinner on the grounds, like vegetables, have a lot going for them. Anywhere else, this one would be a meal in itself.

1	cup small pasta shells, uncooked	½	pound cooked ham, cut into ½-inch cubes
4	cups shredded romaine lettuce	½	cup shredded Swiss cheese
4	carrots, pared and cut into 2-inch sticks	1½	cups mayonnaise
1	10-ounce package frozen green peas, thawed	2	tablespoons snipped fresh dill or 1 ½ teaspoons dried dill weed
1	small red onion, cut into rings	2	hard-cooked eggs, cut into wedges

In a pot cook and drain the pasta according to the directions on the package. Place the lettuce in an even layer in the bottom of a 3-quart glass bowl. Layer the carrots over the lettuce. Cover with the macaroni, then the peas, then the onion, then the ham. Sprinkle the top with Swiss cheese.

In a small bowl combine the mayonnaise and dill. Mound the dill dressing in the center of the salad surrounded by egg wedges. Cover and chill several hours.

Just before serving, toss well.

Makes 8 servings.

 ## PICKLED SLAW

The boiling oil really does pickle this slaw, and it only gets better the longer it stays in the fridge.

1 large head cabbage, shredded	½ cup cider vinegar
1 large onion, thinly sliced	½ cup vegetable oil
1 large green bell pepper, chopped	1 tablespoon salt
½ cup sugar plus 1 tablespoon, divid-ed	1 teaspoon dry mustard
	1 teaspoon celery seed

In a bowl layer the cabbage, onion, and bell pepper. Stir in ½ cup sugar.

In a saucepan boil together the vinegar, vegetable oil, salt, dry mustard, celery seed, and 1 tablespoon sugar. Pour the boiling mixture over the cabbage mixture. Cover tightly and chill.

The slaw will keep for several weeks in the refrigerator.

Makes 8 servings.

RICE SALAD

½ cup prepared Italian dressing, divid-ed	¼ cup sliced pimiento-stuffed green olives
¾ cup water	¼ cup diced cucumber
1 cup instant rice, uncooked	1 cup shredded Cheddar cheese
1 17-ounce can English peas, drained	Lettuce leaves
4 green onions with tops, chopped	1 hard-cooked egg, sliced

In a medium saucepan combine ¼ cup of dressing and the water and bring to a boil. Stir in the rice, cover, and remove from heat. Let stand 5 minutes.

In a large bowl combine the rice, remaining ¼ cup dressing, peas, onions, olives, cucumber, and Cheddar cheese. Cover and chill.

Serve on lettuce leaves garnished with egg slices.

Makes 4 servings.

◆ TWENTY-FOUR-HOUR SALAD

1 head iceberg lettuce, shredded	2 cups mayonnaise
½ cup chopped celery	2 tablespoons sugar
¼ cup chopped green bell pepper	1 cup grated Parmesan cheese
½ cup chopped onion	½ cup cooked and crumbled bacon, or
2 cups chopped fresh spinach, stemmed	½ cup imitation bacon bits
1 10-ounce package frozen peas, thawed	

Grease a 9 x 13 x 2-inch pan. In the pan arrange the lettuce, celery, bell pepper, onion, spinach, and peas in layers. Do not stir. Spread the mayonnaise evenly over all. Layer the sugar, Parmesan cheese, and bacon over the mayonnaise. Cover tightly and refrigerate 24 hours. Cut into squares.

Makes 16 servings.

◆ CARROT-PINEAPPLE CAKE

1½ cups vegetable oil	**FROSTING:**
2 cups sugar	1 3-ounce package cream cheese
3 eggs, beaten	1¼ cups confectioners' sugar
2 cups all-purpose flour	½ cup butter
2 teaspoons baking soda	2 tablespoons crushed pineapple, drained
2 teaspoons vanilla extract	¼ cup chopped walnuts
1 teaspoon salt	
2 teaspoons ground cinnamon	
2 cups grated carrots	
1 cup chopped walnuts	
½ cup crushed pineapple, drained	

Grease and flour a 9 x 13 x 2-inch baking pan and set aside.

In a large bowl combine the cake ingredients and mix until blended. Pour into the prepared pan and bake at 350° for 1 hour. Cool in the pan.

For frosting, in a medium bowl cream the cream cheese, confectioners' sugar, and butter until fluffy. Add the pineapple and nuts, mixing well. Spread over the top of the cooled cake. Serve in squares from pan.

Makes 16 servings.

◆ GLAZED LEMON CAKE

1   18¼-ounce package lemon supreme
        cake mix
1   3-ounce package lemon-flavored
        gelatin
¾   cup vegetable oil
4   eggs

½   teaspoon lemon extract
¾   cup cold water.

GLAZE:
1   cup confectioners' sugar
¼   cup lemon juice

Grease and flour a 10-inch stem pan and set aside.

In the bowl of electric mixer combine the cake mix and gelatin. Stir in the oil. Beat at slow speed. Add the eggs one at a time, beating well after each addition. Add the lemon extract and cold water and beat 2 minutes longer. Pour into the prepared stem pan and bake at 350° for 45 minutes.

Let stand 10 minutes and punch holes from top to bottom with a wooden pick.

In a small bowl mix the sugar and juice for the glaze and pour over the hot cake in the pan. Let cool in the pan and turn out onto a cake plate or stand.

Makes 16 servings.

◆ COCA-COLA CAKE

2   cups all-purpose flour
2   cups sugar
3   tablespoons cocoa
1   cup Coca-Cola
1   cup butter
1½ cups miniature marshmallows
2   eggs, beaten
½   cup buttermilk
1   teaspoon baking soda
1   teaspoon vanilla extract

FROSTING:
½   cup butter
1   tablespoon cocoa
6   tablespoons Coca-Cola
1   1-pound box confectioners' sugar
½   cup chopped pecans

Grease and flour a 9 x 13 x 2-inch pan and set aside.

In a large bowl mix the flour and sugar. In a saucepan bring to a boil the cocoa, Coca-Cola, butter, and marshmallows. Combine the boiled mixture with the flour mixture.

In a separate bowl mix the eggs, buttermilk, baking soda, and vanilla extract and add to the first mixture. Pour into the prepared pan and bake at 350° for 35 minutes.

For frosting, in a saucepan bring to a boil the butter, cocoa, and Coca-Cola. Stir in the sugar and mix well. Stir in the nuts. Spread over the cake while both the cake and icing are still warm. Serve from the pan.

Makes 16 servings.

◆ CHOCOLATE POUND CAKE

8	1.2-ounce Hershey bars	1	cup butter
1	5½-ounce can Hershey's chocolate syrup	2	cups sugar
		4	eggs
½	teaspoon baking soda	2½	cups all-purpose flour
1	cup buttermilk	1	teaspoon vanilla extract

Grease and flour a 10-inch stem pan and set aside.

In a heavy saucepan melt the candy bars in the syrup over low heat. In a small bowl add the soda to the buttermilk.

In a separate bowl cream the butter and sugar. Add the eggs one at a time, beating well after each addition. Add the buttermilk and flour alternately. Add the chocolate mixture and the vanilla. Bake in the prepared stem pan at 350° for 1 hour and 15 minutes.

Cool in the pan for 10 to 15 minutes on a wire rack before removing.
Makes 16 servings.

◆ RAISIN-NUT PIE

This used to be called "funeral pie." People always brought especially good food to funerals. It was a great comfort.

½	cup sugar	½	teaspoon ground nutmeg
½	cup firmly packed light brown sugar	½	teaspoon ground cinnamon
½	cup butter, melted	1	tablespoon cider vinegar
1	cup golden raisins	2	eggs, beaten
1	cup chopped pecans	1	9-inch prepared pastry shell

In a large bowl combine all the ingredients and pour into the pastry shell. Bake at 325° for 40 minutes.

Makes 8 servings.

◆ OATMEAL-RAISIN-NUT COOKIES

1 cup sugar	1 cup dark raisins
¾ cup butter, softened	1 cup chopped pecans or walnuts
2 eggs	1 teaspoon ground cinnamon
2 cups regular rolled oats, raw	1 teaspoon ground nutmeg
2 cups all-purpose flour	1 teaspoon vanilla extract
1 teaspoon salt	

In the bowl of an electric mixer cream the sugar and butter. Add the eggs one at a time, beating well after each addition. Add the oats, flour, salt, raisins, nuts, cinnamon, nutmeg, and vanilla extract. Drop the dough by spoonfuls onto an ungreased baking sheets and bake at 350° for 8 to 10 minutes. Transfer to a wire rack and cool.

Makes 48 cookies.

◆ SWEETENED ICED TEA

If you're expecting two hundred people, multiply this recipe by twenty.

6 cups water, heated to just below boiling point	6 tea bags
	1 cup sugar

Just before the water boils, in a glass pitcher pour the water over the tea bags. Cover and let steep for 10 minutes.

Remove the tea bags. Add the sugar and stir. Pour the tea into a ½-gallon container. Fill to the top with cold water.

Makes ½ gallon or 10 servings.

◆ FRUIT PUNCH

1 46-ounce can grapefruit juice, unsweetened	1 12-ounce can frozen lemonade concentrate plus 2 cans water
1 46-ounce can pineapple juice	1 16-ounce can Hawaiian Punch

Make ice cubes of combined grapefruit and pineapple juices. Place in a punch bowl, and add the remaining ingredients.

Makes 30 servings.

◆ LEMONADE TEA

6 cups water, heated just to boiling
¾ cup sugar
4 tea bags

6 sprigs fresh mint
1 6-ounce can frozen lemonade concentrate, thawed

In a large container combine the water, sugar, tea bags, and mint. Cover and let steep for 1 hour.

Remove the tea bags and mint and add the lemonade.

Makes 12 servings.

◆ LEMONADE FOR 100

4 cups boiling water
8 cups sugar

7½ cups lemon juice
4 gallons cold water

In a large pot boil the water with the sugar for 10 minutes. Cool.

Add the lemon juice and cold water. Chill.

Makes 100 servings.

AFTERNOON TEA

I would eat sawdust if you put Cool Whip on it.
Elizabeth Blake, 1973

People don't get invited to tea in the afternoon like they used to. For one thing, afternoon tea is for women only—no man has ever set foot in one and lived to tell about it. And women now are so tied to family, work, and community that it's hard to imagine a pace of life where two or three hours smack in the middle of the afternoon were set aside solely for them. No car pools, no deadlines, no meetings, no crises, just a living room full of old friends and neighbors, maybe an out-of-town guest or two as the excuse for being there in the first place—not that we needed one. Out in the dining room with the freshly cut flowers were tray after tray of tiny crustless sandwiches, fudge brownies, amaretto cake, minted fruit, a chafing dish of seafood and cream bubbling on a sideboard that lured us back time after time, fat chunks of French bread clutched in our well-fed little hands.

You could actually drink tea at an afternoon tea, but most people didn't. Sherry was more often the beverage of choice, especially as the neighborhood aged and there really wasn't anyone waiting at home anymore. That or the milk punch that had buckled so many knees in our grandmothers' day.

Afternoons were the high point of the day. Men never bothered you; children didn't need you; it was too early to start supper. You could take a nap if you wanted to. Or, you could put on your best sprigged dress and your pearl choker and join twenty of your closest friends for gossip and goodies. It was far and away the better choice.

◆ ALMOND TEA

It is, after all, called "tea," and even if no one drinks them, spiced teas will lend a festive touch to your house.

2 tablespoons lemon-flavored iced
    tea mix
2 cups water, heated just to boiling
1½ cups sugar
10 cups cold water, divided

1 12-ounce can frozen lemonade concentrate, thawed and undiluted
1 tablespoon almond extract
2 teaspoons vanilla extract

In a medium bowl dissolve the iced tea mix in the hot water and set aside.

In a Dutch oven combine the sugar and 2 cups cold water, bring to a boil, and boil 5 minutes.

Add the tea mixture, remaining water, lemonade concentrate, and extracts. Heat thoroughly. Serve hot or iced.

Makes 3 quarts.

◆ ORANGE-SPICE PERCOLATOR TEA

Perked spiced tea is as easy as perked coffee. If you entertain often, you might want to dedicate a percolator just to tea.

11 cups water, divided
9 small tea bags
12 to 14 whole allspice
8 whole cloves
    Peel from ½ orange, cut into narrow strips

1 12-ounce can frozen orange juice concentrate, thawed and undiluted
½ cup lemon juice
½ cup sugar
½ cup honey

Into a 12-cup percolator pour 9 cups water.

In the percolator basket combine the tea bags, allspice, cloves, and orange peel. Perk through a complete cycle, removing the basket when completed. Add the concentrate, lemon juice, sugar, and honey to the tea mixture. Stir. Heat thoroughly.

Makes 13 servings.

I have measured out my life with coffee spoons.
T. S. Eliot, 1907

◆ CAFÉ MOCHA CRÈME

> 1   *10-cup pot freshly brewed coffee*
> 2   *tablespoons chocolate syrup*
> ½ *cup Crème de Cacao liqueur*
>
> *Sweetened whipped cream or*
>   *whipped topping*
> *Grated chocolate*

Into six 6-ounce cups pour the brewed coffee. To each cup add 1 teaspoon chocolate syrup and 1 tablespoon liqueur. Stir. Top with whipped cream and grated chocolate.
    Makes 6 servings.

◆ SPICED COFFEE

You can flavor any coffee just by adding spices and extracts to the coffee grounds in the basket of your coffee maker.

> 4   *to 5 tablespoons coffee grounds for*
>   *automatic drip coffee maker*
> ½ *teaspoon ground cardamom*
>
> ½ *teaspoon almond extract*
> ½ *teaspoon vanilla extract*
> 4½ *cups water*

In a coffee pot basket place the coffee. Sprinkle the cardamom and extracts and flavorings on top. Add the water to the coffee maker and brew as usual. Serve with cream and sugar if desired.
    Makes 6 servings.

◆ MILK PUNCH

Milk punch is smooth and full of memories and perfect for a neighborhood tea because, afterward, everyone can walk home.

> ½ *gallon milk*
> 1½ *cups bourbon*
>
> 5 *tablespoons sugar*

In a pitcher mix all the ingredients, stirring well to dissolve the sugar. Pour over ice in 8-ounce glasses.
    Makes 12 servings.

— PARTY SANDWICHES —

Mark this section. It will see you through years of parties. Buy bread sliced very thinly, cut off the crusts, and freeze for easier handling. To prevent sogginess, spread bread with soft butter or mayonnaise before spreading with filling. Use sharp cookie cutters to cut sandwiches into desired shapes. Sandwiches can be made a day ahead, placed on serving plates, wrapped in plastic wrap, then wrapped in damp towels and kept in the refrigerator.

◆ TUNA AND CHEESE

1 cup grated sharp Cheddar cheese
½ cup canned tuna, drained

2 tablespoons dry vermouth
   Freshly ground black pepper

Mix well.
   Makes 60 appetizer sandwiches.

◆ EGG SALAD

3 hard-cooked eggs, chopped
2 tablespoons butter, melted
½ teaspoon prepared mustard

   Freshly ground black pepper
½ teaspoon grated onion
½ teaspoon lemon juice

Mix well.
   Makes 24 appetizer sandwiches.

◆ CURRIED CHEESE

1 3-ounce package cream cheese,
      softened
8 ripe olives, pitted and chopped

¼ teaspoon curry powder
1 teaspoon chopped fresh chives

Mix well.
   Makes 24 appetizer sandwiches.

◆ CUCUMBER

1 cucumber, scored and thinly sliced
1 cup cider vinegar

   Salt and pepper to taste

Soak cucumber slices in vinegar for 30 minutes. Drain. Season liberally with salt and pepper. Place on bread that has been spread with mayonnaise.
   Makes 24 appetizer sandwiches.

◆ CREAMY PIMIENTO SPREAD

This is a fancier pimiento cheese than the kind you find in lunches. It spreads nicely on thin, crustless bread or party crackers. You can even stuff it into pitted ripe olives.

1   8-ounce package cream cheese, softened
2   tablespoons cream
¼   teaspoon Worcestershire sauce

½   cup shredded Cheddar cheese
2   tablespoons chopped pimiento, drained

In a small bowl combine the cream cheese, cream, and Worcestershire sauce and beat with an electric mixer until light and fluffy. Fold in the Cheddar cheese and pimiento.
    Makes 1½ cups or 60 appetizers.

> A woman's work, from the time she gets up to the time she goes to bed, is as hard as a day at war.
> *Marguerite Duras, 1987*

◆ CHICKEN OR TURKEY

2   cups finely chopped cooked chicken or turkey
¼   cup sweet pickle relish, drained
2   tablespoons chopped pimiento, drained

¼   teaspoon salt
    Dash pepper
1   stalk celery, finely chopped
¼   cup mayonnaise

In a medium bowl combine all the ingredients. Mix well and chill.
    Makes 2½ cups or 24 half-sandwiches.

◆ SEAFOOD

1   6½-ounce can crab meat, tuna, or shrimp, drained and flaked
2   tablespoons chopped dill pickle

2   tablespoons mayonnaise
½   teaspoon lemon juice

In a medium bowl combine all the ingredients. Mix well and chill.
    Makes 1 cup or 12 half-sandwiches.

◆ PINEAPPLE-CHEESE

1   5-ounce jar pasteurized processed cheese spread

¼   cup crushed pineapple, drained

In a small bowl combine the cheese and pineapple. Mix well and chill.
    Makes ¾ cup or 10 half-sandwiches.

◆ CRAB SALAD

Salads at teas should be luxurious and beautiful. This one is red, white, and green, and in a chili sauce ring (recipe follows) could be the centerpiece of a sideboard.

1 pound cooked crab meat, flaked, or imitation crab meat	2 to 3 ounces feta cheese, finely crumbled
1 medium tomato, peeled and chopped	1/4 cup chopped fresh cilantro leaves
1/2 cup finely chopped red onion	1/4 cup mayonnaise
1/2 cup chopped green bell pepper	1 clove garlic, minced
1/2 cup plain yogurt	Freshly ground white pepper

In a large bowl combine all the ingredients. Mix well and chill. Serve as a salad or in pita bread halves or in a molded chili sauce ring.

Makes 6 servings.

◆ CHILI SAUCE RING

1 1/4-ounce envelope unflavored gelatin	1 cup ricotta cheese
1/4 cup cold water	1 cup mayonnaise
1 cup chili sauce	1/2 cup whipping cream, whipped, or 1 cup whipped topping, thawed

Grease a 4-cup ring mold and set aside.

In a large bowl dissolve the gelatin in the water. In a saucepan heat the chili sauce to boiling, pour over the gelatin, stir, and cool. Add the ricotta and mayonnaise. Fold in the whipped cream. Pour into the prepared ring mold. Refrigerate until set.

Unmold onto crisp salad greens. Fill the center with crab, seafood, or chicken salad.

Makes 8 to 10 servings.

◆ CHICKEN SALAD WITH GRAPES

Chicken salad with green grapes and almonds is very refined. And if you've got a houseful of women drinking milk punch, you're going to need a little refinement.

3 cups diced cooked chicken	DRESSING:
1 1/2 cups diced celery	1 cup mayonnaise
3 tablespoons lemon juice	1/4 cup half-and-half
1 1/2 cups halved seedless green grapes	1 1/2 teaspoons salt
3/4 cup slivered almonds, toasted	Freshly ground white pepper
	1 teaspoon dry mustard

In a large bowl combine the chicken, celery, and lemon juice and chill for at least 1 hour. Add the grapes and almonds.

In a separate bowl mix the dressing ingredients and combine with the chicken mixture.

Makes 8 to 10 servings.

◆ SEAFOOD MOUSSE

2   ¼-ounce envelopes unflavored
      gelatin
½   cup water
1   10¾-ounce can cream of tomato
      soup, undiluted
1   8-ounce package cream cheese,
      softened
1   cup mayonnaise
½   cup chopped celery

1   teaspoon onion salt
1   tablespoon Worcestershire sauce
2   tablespoons grated onion
½   pound cooked small shrimp, peeled
      and deveined
7½   ounces cooked lobster, shredded
6½   ounces cooked crab meat, flaked
      Dash cayenne pepper

Grease a 6-cup salad mold and set aside.

In a large bowl dissolve gelatin in the water. In a saucepan heat the soup to boiling and add to the gelatin. Stir in the cream cheese and cool. Fold in the mayonnaise, celery, onion salt, Worcestershire sauce, onion, shrimp, lobster, crab, and cayenne pepper. Pour into the prepared salad mold. Chill until set.

Makes 6 servings.

◆ CURRIED TURKEY SALAD

2   quarts coarsely chopped cooked
      white-meat turkey
1   20-ounce can water chestnuts,
      drained and diced
2   pounds seedless green grapes,
      halved
2   cups chopped celery
2   cups slivered almonds, toasted and
      divided

3   cups mayonnaise
1   tablespoon curry powder
2   tablespoons soy sauce
      Lettuce leaves
1   15½-ounce can pineapple chunks,
      drained

In a large bowl mix the turkey, water chestnuts, grapes, celery, and 1½ cups almonds.

In a separate bowl mix the mayonnaise with the curry and soy sauce and combine with the turkey mixture. Chill for several hours.

Serve on lettuce garnished with the remaining almonds and pineapple chunks.

Makes 18 servings.

◆ PINEAPPLE-PIMIENTO SALAD

1 8-ounce can crushed pineapple,
   drained
1 5-ounce jar cheese spread with
   pimiento

½ cup whipping cream, whipped, or 1
   cup whipped topping, thawed
¼ cup mayonnaise
3 cups miniature marshmallows

Grease an 8-inch square pan or serving bowl and set aside.

In a medium bowl combine all the ingredients, mixing well. Pour into the prepared pan or serving bowl. Cover and refrigerate at least 3 hours.

Makes 8 servings.

◆ OVERNIGHT FRUIT SALAD

1 15½-ounce can pineapple chunks,
   drained, with syrup reserved and
   divided
   Water
1 3-ounce package lemon-flavored
   gelatin

1½ cups whipped topping, thawed
4 cups miniature marshmallows
1¼ cups halved seedless green grapes
1 11-ounce can mandarin oranges,
   drained

In a measuring cup measure the pineapple syrup and add enough water to make 1¾ cups. In a small saucepan heat 1 cup of the syrup mixture to boiling and pour into a large bowl with the gelatin. Stir to dissolve. Add the remaining syrup mixture. Chill until the mixture is the consistency of uncooked egg whites.

Fold in the whipped topping. Add the marshmallows, grapes, and mandarin oranges and blend well. Cover and refrigerate overnight.

Makes 8 servings.

◆ WALDORF SALAD

The classic Waldorf Salad is named, of course, after the Waldorf-Astoria Hotel in New York City—diced apples, celery, walnuts, and mayonnaise. It's so simple it's easy to mess up. Somewhere along the line raisins were added, and it used to show up in school cafeterias so heavy on the mayonnaise and sugar that the mere sight of it could gag an entire class. It's really quite nice, however, when done right. This version calls for dates instead of raisins. Be sure to use a good quality mayonnaise.

¼ cup chopped English walnuts
¼ cup chopped dates
2 tablespoons sugar
4 medium apples, cored and cubed

1 stalk celery, chopped
⅔ cup mayonnaise
1 teaspoon lemon juice

In a large bowl combine all the ingredients. Mix well. Cover and chill.

Makes 6 servings.

◆ MINTED FRUIT

2 cups honeydew melon balls
1 cup whole seedless green grapes
1 8-ounce can pineapple chunks,
   drained

1 cup cubed fresh or canned pears
   (canned pears should be
   drained)
1/4 cup apple-mint or mint jelly

In a salad bowl combine the melon balls, grapes, pineapple, and pears. In a saucepan melt the jelly over low heat and pour over the fruit. Toss lightly. Cover and chill.
    Garnish with fresh mint leaves.
    Makes 6 servings.

◆ AMARETTO-ALMOND CAKE

If you're going to serve fancy cakes, you have to serve something with almonds. Amaretto is even better. This is one of those easy oil cakes, especially moist because of the pudding and the soaked glaze.

1 1/2 cups chopped almonds, toasted and
      divided
1 18 1/2-ounce box yellow cake mix,
      without pudding
1 3 1/2-ounce box vanilla instant pud-
      ding mix
4 eggs, beaten
1/2 cup vegetable oil
1/2 cup water

1/2 cup amaretto liqueur
1 teaspoon almond extract

GLAZE:
1/2 cup sugar
1/4 cup water
2 tablespoons butter
1/4 cup amaretto
1/2 teaspoon almond extract

Grease and flour a 10-inch stem pan, sprinkle 1 cup almonds over the bottom, and set aside.
    In a mixing bowl combine the cake mix, pudding mix, eggs, oil, water, amaretto, and almond extract. Beat on low speed with an electric mixer about 30 seconds until dry ingredients are moistened. Increase the speed to medium and beat 4 minutes. Stir in the remaining 1/2 cup almonds. Pour the batter into the prepared stem pan and bake at 325° for 1 hour.
    Cool in the pan for 10 to 15 minutes before removing. Cool completely and place on a cake plate.
    For glaze, in a small saucepan combine the sugar, water, and butter and bring to a boil. Reduce heat to medium, and gently boil for 4 to 5 minutes, stirring occasionally, until the sugar dissolves. Remove from heat and cool 15 minutes.
    Stir in the amaretto and almond extract. Punch holes in the cake from top to bottom with a wooden pick. Slowly spoon the glaze over top until entirely absorbed.
    Makes 16 servings.

If Eve had had a spade in Paradise and known what to do with it, we
should not have had all that sad business of the apple.
Elizabeth von Arnim, 1898

◆ ICED LEMON COOKIES

These are light and delicate and fit nicely in the saucer of a tea cup. You can ice them or sprinkle them with confectioners' sugar.

1 cup butter, softened	**ICING:**
1/3 cup confectioners' sugar	1/4 cup butter, softened
1 1/4 cups all-purpose flour	1 1/2 cups confectioners' sugar
1/2 cup cornstarch	2 tablespoons lemon juice
	1 tablespoon grated lemon rind

In a medium bowl cream the butter and add the sugar gradually, beating well. Gradually add the flour and cornstarch, beating until smooth. Drop the mixture by level teaspoonfuls onto ungreased baking sheets. Bake at 350° for 10 to 12 minutes. Do not overbake. Cookies will not brown on top.

Cool slightly on baking sheets, then remove to wire racks to cool completely. Ice when cool.

For icing, in a small bowl cream the butter and gradually add the confectioners' sugar and lemon juice, beating until smooth. Stir in the lemon rind.

Makes 84 cookies.

I knew a woman, lovely in her bones.
Theodore Roethke, 1960

◆ COCOA KISSES

1 cup butter, softened	1/4 cup cocoa
2/3 cup sugar	1 cup coarsely ground walnuts
1 teaspoon vanilla extract	1 9-ounce package chocolate kisses,
1 2/3 cups all-purpose flour	unwrapped

In a large bowl cream the butter and sugar, beating until fluffy. Add the vanilla, mixing well. Add the flour and cocoa, mixing well. Stir in the walnuts. Chill the dough 2 hours or until firm.

Wrap 1 tablespoon of dough around each chocolate kiss and roll to form a ball. Place on ungreased baking sheets and bake at 375° for 12 minutes. Cool slightly on the baking sheets and remove to wire racks to cool completely.

Makes 48 cookies.

◆ COCONUT-PECAN BARS

BOTTOM LAYER:
1½ cups all-purpose flour
½ cup firmly packed light brown sugar
½ cup butter, softened

TOP LAYER:
2 eggs, beaten

1 cup firmly packed light brown sugar
2 tablespoons all-purpose flour
½ teaspoon baking powder
¼ teaspoon salt
½ teaspoon vanilla extract
1¼ cups flaked coconut
½ cup chopped pecans

Grease and flour a 9-inch square pan and set aside.

For the bottom layer, in a medium bowl combine the flour and brown sugar. With a pastry blender cut in the butter until the mixture resembles coarse meal. Press the mixture into the prepared pan. Bake at 350° for 15 minutes.

For the top layer, in a medium bowl combine the eggs, brown sugar, flour, baking powder, salt, and vanilla, mixing well. Stir in the flaked coconut and chopped pecans. Pour the egg mixture over the baked bottom layer. Bake for an additional 20 minutes.

Let cool completely in the pan before cutting into bars.

Makes 24 bars.

◆ SNICKERDOODLES

Snickerdoodles are some people's favorite childhood cookie. You should mark this recipe. You never know when you might run into someone who's been wanting one for years.

1 cup shortening (not butter or mar-
      garine)
1½ cups sugar
2 eggs
2¾ cups all-purpose flour
2 teaspoons cream of tartar

1 teaspoon baking soda
½ teaspoon salt

TOPPING:
2 tablespoons sugar
2 teaspoons ground cinnamon

Grease a baking sheet and set aside.

In the bowl of an electric mixer cream the shortening with the sugar, and add the eggs one at a time, beating well after each addition.

In a separate bowl sift together the flour, cream of tartar, soda, and salt and add to the shortening-egg mixture, beating until smooth. Chill the dough for several hours or overnight.

Shape the dough into 1-inch balls. For the topping, in a small bowl mix together the sugar and cinnamon. Roll the balls in the sugar-cinnamon mixture and place about 2 inches apart on the prepared baking sheet. Bake at 400° for 8 to 10 minutes. Cookies will puff up at first and then flatten out.

Immediately transfer to wire racks to cool.

Makes 48 cookies.

◆ HOMEMADE BROWNIES

These are the real thing. With a batch of homemade brownies and a tableful of old friends, you can while away an entire afternoon. It really won't matter what the rest of the world is up to.

4 *1-ounce squares unsweetened bak-* *ing chocolate*	2 *teaspoons vanilla extract*
½ *cup butter*	1 *cup all-purpose flour*
2 *cups sugar*	1 *teaspoon baking powder*
4 *eggs*	½ *teaspoon salt*
	1 *cup chopped walnuts*

Grease and flour a 9 x 13 x 2-inch pan and set aside.

In the top of a double boiler melt the chocolate and butter over hot water. Remove from the heat and stir in the sugar, eggs, and vanilla and mix well.

In a medium bowl stir together the flour, baking powder, and salt and add to the chocolate mixture. Stir in the nuts. Spread the batter in the prepared pan. Bake at 325° for 35 to 40 minutes. Do not overbake.

Let cool completely in the pan before cutting into bars.

Makes 24 brownies.

SUPPER

There is not so much virginity in the world that one can
afford not to love it when one finds it.
Graham Greene, 1936

Supper is not lunch and it's not dinner and it's a good thing. Supper
is what you eat at the end of a long day when you're too tired to
dress up and you only want to be with people you like. Lentil soup,
New England clam chowder, lasagna, sweet onion pie, zucchini-nut
bread, apple-crumb pie—supper is something you can make in one
dish, serve on one plate, eat at a gingham-covered table with
asters in a blue vase. Or you can kick off your shoes and settle
back on the sofa in front of the television set while a cold rain
slashes the windowpanes and your toes dry out in front of the fire.

Some people talk while they eat supper and some people don't.
No one notices—no one cares. All they really care about is the
bean soup with hot sausage and thyme, the two sticks of butter in
the mushroom-rice casserole, the scalloped new potatoes. The
lemon-lime salad brings to mind someone you dated years ago but
you can't quite place the name and on a night like this it doesn't
much matter.

You've got it all right here. Velveeta in the macaroni, garlic
bread in tinfoil on the hearth, strawberry tea, and if you save room
for dessert there's apple pie with vanilla ice cream. It's a wonder
people go out at all.

◆ GARLIC BREAD

The better the French bread, the better this will be, although given the combination itself—garlic, butter, bread—however you fix it, it's going to be good.

1 clove garlic, minced, or 2 teaspoons canned minced garlic

½ cup butter, melted
1 loaf French bread, uncut

In a small bowl mix the garlic with the melted butter. Slice the bread ½-inch thick, leaving the loaf uncut at bottom. Brush the sides and tops of the slices with the garlic butter. Heat at 350° for 15 minutes.
 Makes 6 servings.

◆ ZUCCHINI-NUT BREAD

People used to make this in the middle of the summer when the sun was high and every afternoon meant another thunderstorm and the squash was growing three inches a day. You had no choice. You had to do something with all that zucchini. It's called "bread," but it's really grated squash added to a basic cake recipe, and it's a treat. Be sure to let the grated zucchini stand in a colander for a couple of hours and then wring out the liquid by hand. Otherwise, the bread will be soggy.

3 cups sifted all-purpose flour
1½ teaspoons ground cinnamon
1 teaspoon baking soda
1 teaspoon salt
¼ teaspoon baking powder
3 eggs, beaten
2 cups sugar

1 cup vegetable oil
2 teaspoons vanilla extract
2 cups grated zucchini, wrung dry by
 hand
½ cup chopped walnuts, plus 1 teaspoon all-purpose flour

Grease and flour two 9 x 5-inch loaf pans and set aside.
 In a large bowl combine the flour, cinnamon, baking soda, salt, and baking powder.
 In a separate bowl combine the eggs, sugar, and oil. Add the vanilla and the dry ingredients. Add the zucchini and walnuts. Pour the batter into the prepared pans. Bake at 350° for 1 hour. Cool in the pans on wire racks for 10 minutes.
 Remove from the pans and cool on racks.
 Makes 2 loaves.

◆ HOT SUMMER SALAD

5 large tomatoes, peeled and sliced
1 large green bell pepper, thinly
    sliced
1 large sweet onion, thinly sliced
¾ cup cider vinegar
¼ cup water
1½ teaspoons celery salt

1½ teaspoons whole mustard seed
½ teaspoon salt
4½ teaspoons sugar
¼ teaspoon red pepper flakes
    Cucumber for garnish, scored and
    sliced

In a large bowl combine the tomatoes, bell pepper, and onion.

In a separate bowl make a dressing of the vinegar, water, celery salt, mustard seed, salt, sugar, and pepper flakes and boil furiously for 5 minutes. Pour the dressing over the tomato mixture, cool, and chill overnight.

When ready to serve, stir and garnish with cucumber slices.

Makes 8 servings.

◆ PERPETUAL SALAD

Do you ever have those long stretches when your house seems like a magnet for foot-loose relatives—retired aunts, grandnieces, second cousins once removed with four stepchildren and someone you're quite sure has never been anyone's husband? If you're one of those people who never knows how many there'll be for supper on any given night, fix this salad and put it in the fridge. It lasts for weeks. All you have to do is spoon it on the plates.

1 1-pound can French-style green
    beans, drained
1 1-pound can small English peas,
    drained
1 1-pound can fancy Chinese vegeta-
    bles, drained
1 8-ounce can water chestnuts,
    drained and thinly sliced

1½ cups thinly sliced celery
1 cup sugar
¾ cup cider vinegar
1 teaspoon salt
    Pepper to taste
3 medium onions, thinly sliced

In a large bowl mix all the ingredients. Cover and refrigerate overnight.

The salad will keep in the refrigerator for several weeks.

Makes 10 servings.

◆ COLD PASTA SALAD

This is also a salad you can fix ahead. With garlic bread and dessert, it makes a fine light supper.

4   *cups shell macaroni, uncooked*
2   *cups peeled and diced tomatoes*
1   *cup grated sharp Cheddar cheese*
1   *cup mayonnaise*
¼   *cup sliced pimiento-stuffed green olives*

2   *tablespoons grated onion*
½   *clove garlic, minced*
1½   *teaspoons Worcestershire sauce*
    Cayenne pepper to taste
    Salt to taste

In a pot cook and drain the pasta according to the directions on the package and mix with the remaining ingredients. Chill 3 to 4 hours.
    Makes 16 servings.

> There was pleasure in eating strawberries, before they became quite common—in the first dish of peas, while they were yet dear—to have them for a nice supper, a treat. What treat can we have now?
> *Charles Lamb, 1823*

◆ LEBANESE SALAD

1   *15-ounce can garbanzo beans, drained*
¼   *cup minced fresh mint*
1   *cup torn fresh spinach, stemmed*

⅔   *cup grated Parmesan cheese*
½   *cup grated carrots*
½   *cup lemon juice*

In a large bowl combine all the ingredients and chill for 1 hour.
    Makes 6 servings.

◆ FRIDAY LENTIL SOUP

You can make this soup with canned lentils, but dried lentils are no trouble at all and the truth is—and please don't take this as a tiresome lecture on your personal health, which is, after all, entirely your business—canned beans are chock-full of salt and will make your ankles swell.

1	pound lentils	1	tablespoon red wine vinegar
2	carrots, chopped	1	bay leaf
1	large onion, diced	2	teaspoons salt
2	stalks celery, chopped	¼	teaspoon black pepper
1	clove garlic, minced	8	cups water
1	6-ounce can tomato paste		

Rinse the lentils and pour into a deep pot with the carrots, onion, celery, garlic, tomato paste, vinegar, bay leaf, salt, pepper, and water. Bring to a boil, reduce heat, and simmer covered about 1 hour and 30 minutes.

Makes 10 servings.

◆ SPICY SAUSAGE-BEAN SOUP

The very thought of a big pot of sausage-bean soup simmering on the stove is enough to make anyone sprint for home.

1	pound bulk pork sausage	1	bay leaf
2	16-ounce cans red kidney beans, undrained	1½	teaspoons seasoned salt
		½	teaspoon garlic salt
1	28-ounce can tomatoes, undrained and coarsely chopped	½	teaspoon dried thyme
		½	teaspoon black pepper
1	quart water	1	green bell pepper, chopped
1	large onion, chopped	1	cup peeled and diced potatoes

In a large Dutch oven brown the sausage, stirring to crumble the meat. Drain the drippings. Stir in the kidney beans, tomatoes, water, onion, bay leaf, seasoned salt, garlic salt, thyme, and black pepper. Cover and simmer 1 hour, stirring occasionally. Add the bell pepper and potatoes. Cover and simmer 20 minutes more.

Remove the bay leaf before serving.

Makes 11 servings.

◆ EASY NEW ENGLAND CLAM CHOWDER

¼ cup finely chopped celery
2 tablespoons finely chopped onion
1 tablespoon butter
1 10¾-ounce can cream of potato
　　soup, undiluted

1 6½-ounce can minced clams,
　　undrained
2 teaspoons minced fresh parsley
1 cup milk

In a medium saucepan cook the celery and onion in the butter until tender. Add the soup, clams, and parsley. Heat just to boiling, reduce the heat, and simmer covered 5 to 10 minutes.

　　Add the milk and heat but do not boil.

　　Makes 4 servings.

◆ HAM AND SPLIT PEA SOUP

1 16-ounce package dried split peas
½ cup diced cooked ham
2 teaspoons salt
½ teaspoon dried basil
1 small onion, chopped

　　Freshly ground white pepper
2 quarts water
2 medium stalks celery, sliced
1 medium carrot, chopped

In a large saucepan combine all the ingredients. Simmer covered for 1 hour and 30 minutes until the peas are tender and the soup thickens.

　　Makes 6 to 9 servings.

◆ EASY CURRIED CHICKEN BISQUE

Plagued with drop-in supper guests you have a life-and-death obligation to impress? Look no farther. This soup is your salvation. Ten minutes after the entire board of directors of a major national corporation bursts through your door, you can be passing out bowls of creamy bisque, hot or cold. They'll think you knew all along they were coming, and they'll be very, very nervous.

1 10¾-ounce can cream of chicken
　　soup, undiluted
1 14½-ounce can chicken broth
1 cup half-and-half

2 tablespoons curry powder
1 4-ounce can sliced mushrooms,
　　drained

In a pot combine all the ingredients. Heat thoroughly but do not boil. Serve hot or cold.

　　Makes 4 servings.

◆ LASAGNA

1   pound ground beef
2   8-ounce cans tomato sauce
1   beef bouillon cube
1   small onion, chopped
1   teaspoon dried oregano
    Salt and pepper to taste
1   8-ounce carton sour cream

1   16-ounce carton cottage cheese
6   ounces Parmesan cheese, grated
6   lasagna noodles, cooked
6   ounces mozzarella cheese, grated
    or sliced
6   ounces Swiss cheese, grated or
    sliced

In a large skillet brown the beef and drain off the fat. Add the tomato sauce, bouillon cube, onion, oregano, and salt and pepper, and simmer uncovered for 30 minutes.

In a large bowl combine the sour cream, cottage cheese, and Parmesan cheese.

Fill a 9 x 13 x 2-inch pan with two repetitions of the following layers: half the ground beef mixture, three lasagna noodles, half the cottage cheese mixture, half the mozzarella cheese, and half the Swiss cheese. Bake at 350° for 30 minutes.

Makes 8 servings.

> A house means a family house, a place specially meant for putting children and men in so as to restrict their waywardness and distract them from the longing for adventure and escape they've had since time began.
> *Marguerite Duras, 1987*

◆ EASY SUPPER CHILI

1   pound ground beef or ground turkey
    Olive oil for browning turkey
1   14½-ounce can stewed tomatoes,
    undrained
1   16-ounce can red kidney beans,
    undrained

1   1¾-ounce envelope chili seasoning
    mix
    Cheddar cheese, grated
    Sour cream

In a skillet brown the beef or turkey (use olive oil when browning turkey) and drain. Add the tomatoes, beans, and chili seasoning. Bring to a boil, reduce heat, cover, and simmer for 15 to 20 minutes.

Serve topped with grated Cheddar cheese and/or sour cream.

Makes 4 servings.

◆ MUSHROOM-BEEF SKILLET SUPPER

Stir this together on top of the stove and all you'll have to wash is one skillet. If you're really, really tired, you can stand at the stove and eat it.

4 ounces noodles, uncooked
1 pound ground beef
1 10¾-ounce can cream of mushroom
  soup, undiluted
¼ cup milk

1 4-ounce can sliced mushrooms,
  drained
½ cup chopped onion
1 8-ounce carton sour cream

In a pot cook and drain the noodles according to the directions on the package. In a medium skillet brown the beef and drain off the grease. Add the soup, milk, mushrooms, onion, sour cream, and noodles. Simmer covered for 5 to 8 minutes.
    Makes 4 servings.

◆ MEAT LOAF

There is no national recipe for meat loaf. It is, rather, a dish of infinite variety. You could have meat loaf once a week for a year and never repeat yourself. Of course, sooner or later you're going to run into one you think is the best. This might be it.

1 pound ground beef
2 tablespoons dry onion soup mix
1 5-ounce can evaporated milk
2 tablespoons firmly packed light
  brown sugar

½ teaspoon dry mustard
2 tablespoons catsup

Grease a 9 x 5-inch loaf pan. In the pan combine the ground beef, soup mix, and evaporated milk. The mixture will be very moist. Press evenly into the pan.
    In a small bowl combine the sugar, mustard, and catsup and spoon over the meat. Bake at 350° for 45 minutes.
    Makes 4 servings.

◆ VELVEETA MACARONI

Scoffers can scoff. Naysayers can say nay. The fact is an entire generation of Americans automatically salutes whenever they pass a grocery store cheese display. It's not often that one product so completely captures the childhood of so many.

1	7-ounce package elbow macaroni	12	ounces Velveeta cheese, cut in cubes
2	tablespoons butter		

In a pot cook the macaroni according to the directions on the package. Drain and toss with the butter until melted. Stir in the Velveeta cheese until melted.
    Makes 4 servings.

◆ SCALLOPED HAM AND POTATOES

2	large potatoes, scrubbed and cubed	1	cup grated yellow cheese
1	large onion, chopped	1	cup cubed cooked ham
2	cups boiling water, salted	4	slices bread, toasted
1	10¾-ounce can cream of mushroom soup, undiluted		

In a pot boil the potatoes and onion in salted water until tender. Drain and set aside.
    In a saucepan combine the soup and yellow cheese and simmer until the cheese melts. Add the ham. Stir in the potatoes and onion and heat thoroughly. Serve over toast.
    Makes 4 servings.

◆ ITALIAN EGGPLANT

1	medium eggplant, thinly sliced		Freshly ground black pepper
1	tablespoon salt	½	cup olive oil
2	large onions, thinly sliced		Buttered breadcrumbs
1	green bell pepper, thinly sliced		

Salt eggplant and place in a colander in the sink under a heavily weighted plate for 1 to 2 hours until bitter juices drip out.
    Grease a 1-quart casserole dish. In the dish layer the vegetables in the order given. Season with pepper. Pour the olive oil on top and bake uncovered at 350° for 1 hour.
    Sprinkle with breadcrumbs and run under the broiler for 3 or 4 minutes until brown.
    Makes 4 servings.

◆ EASY MUSHROOM-RICE CASSEROLE

2 cups long grained white rice,
   uncooked
1 pound fresh mushrooms, brushed
   and sliced

1 cup butter, melted
3 10¾-ounce cans cream of mushroom soup, undiluted
   Parmesan cheese, grated

Grease a 2-quart casserole dish and set aside.

In a saucepan cook the rice according to the directions on the package. In a skillet sauté the mushrooms over medium heat in the melted butter about 15 minutes until the liquid is reduced.

Combine the mushrooms, rice, and soup. Pour into the prepared casserole dish. Sprinkle with Parmesan cheese. Bake covered at 350° for 1 hour.

Makes 12 servings.

◆ SKILLET ZUCCHINI

1½ pounds tiny zucchini, sliced in
   rounds
2 cups boiling water
1 pint cherry tomatoes
3 tablespoons butter

2 tablespoons lemon juice
¼ teaspoon salt
¼ teaspoon white pepper
¼ teaspoon honey
   Romano cheese, grated

In a skillet place the zucchini and cover with boiling water. Cook, covered, for 10 minutes.

Drain and return to the skillet with the tomatoes, butter, lemon juice, seasonings, and honey. Toss gently and simmer, uncovered, for 5 minutes more.

Serve sprinkled with Romano cheese.

Makes 4 servings.

◆ ONION PIE

A sweet onion pie and a salad will smooth the wrinkles out of any day.

1 cup Ritz cracker crumbs
¼ cup butter, melted
2 cups thinly sliced onions
2 tablespoons butter
2 eggs, beaten

¾ cup half-and-half
¾ teaspoon salt
   Dash white pepper
¼ cup grated smoked Cheddar or
   Gruyère cheese

In a small bowl combine the cracker crumbs and melted butter and press into an 8-inch pie pan.

In a skillet sauté the onions in the butter, covered, over low heat about 30 minutes until translucent. Place on the crust.

In a medium bowl combine the eggs, half-and-half, salt, and pepper and pour over the onions. Sprinkle cheese on top. Bake uncovered at 350° for 30 minutes.

Makes 4 servings.

◆ EASY APPLE PIE

Apple pie is a symbol of all we hold dear and you won't find an easier one than this. Serve it with vanilla ice cream or sharp Cheddar cheese.

3 cups peeled and sliced tart apples	1 9-inch prepared pastry shell, plus
1 cup sugar	dough for second crust
2 tablespoons cornstarch	2 tablespoons butter, cut in pieces
1 teaspoon ground cinnamon	

In a large bowl combine the apples, sugar, cornstarch, and cinnamon. Place in the pastry shell, dot with butter, and top with the second crust. Cut slits to allow for escaping steam. Bake at 350° for 50 minutes.

Makes 6 to 8 servings.

◆ BUTTER CAKE

Fix this for supper and you'll have coffee cake for morning.

1 18¼-ounce package Golden Butter cake mix	1 tablespoon butter flavoring
½ cup sugar	1 cup chopped pecans
⅔ cup vegetable oil	2 tablespoons firmly packed light brown sugar
4 eggs	2 teaspoons ground cinnamon
1 8-ounce carton sour cream	

Grease and flour a 10-inch stem or Bundt pan and set aside.

In a large bowl combine the cake mix and sugar. Add the oil, then the eggs one at a time, beating well after each addition. Add the sour cream, flavoring, and nuts.

In a separate bowl combine the brown sugar and cinnamon. Pour half the batter into the prepared pan and sprinkle with the sugar-cinnamon mixture. Pour in the remaining batter. Bake at 350° for 1 hour.

Cool in the pan for 15 minutes and turn out onto cake plate. Cake may be dusted with confectioners' sugar.

Makes 16 servings.

◆ FLOP CAKE

2	cups biscuit mix	1	cup sweetened flaked coconut
1	1-pound box light brown sugar	1	cup chopped pecans
4	eggs, beaten		

Grease and flour a 9 x 13 x 2-inch pan and set aside.

In a large bowl combine the biscuit mix and sugar. Add the eggs. The batter will be lumpy. Add the coconut and nuts. Pour into the prepared pan and bake at 350° for 30 minutes.

Cool in the pan and cut into squares. This cake will rise during baking and then flop.

Makes 15 servings.

◆ STRAWBERRY TEA

1	pint fresh strawberries, divided	½	cup lemon juice
4	cups strong English Breakfast tea, chilled	½	cup sugar

In a blender or food processor purée 1¼ cups strawberries. Strain the purée through a sieve into a pitcher and add the tea, lemon juice, and sugar. Garnish with the remaining strawberries. Serve over ice.

Makes 4 servings.

Flights of angels sing thee to thy rest.
William Shakespeare, 1600

◆ WHITE SANGRIA

3½	cups dry white wine	1	10-ounce bottle club soda
½	cup brandy	2	cups chopped fresh fruit
¼	cup sugar		

In a pitcher mix the wine, brandy, and sugar. Just before serving add the club soda and fruit.

Makes 10 servings.

DINNER FOR TWO

And we meet, with champagne and a chicken, at last.
Lady Mary Wortley Montagu, 1748

There are lots of ways to get to know each other. You can take in a movie together or a concert, check out the latest art exhibit, volunteer for a church singles songfest, spend Memorial Day weekend at a stock car race. Of course, none of these really work all that well. It takes a lot more than one movie to figure someone out. It's hard to shine at a public singing when you can't stay on key. And, frankly, the smell of burning rubber is not something you want in your hair.

Fortunately, there's another road to romance: quicker, cheaper, more reliable, infinitely more impressive. It's called "dinner for two" and it couldn't be easier. You don't have to be a good cook. Your silver doesn't have to match. It doesn't matter if you're a man or a woman. A stove would be nice, and a couple of saucepans, maybe a baking dish or two. Add one quick trip to the grocery and all glory can be yours: pork chops with apples and sour cream, angel biscuits, creamy spinach casserole, bacon-stuffed potatoes, a spicy shrimp tempura on a hot summer night.

Cooking for someone else says volumes about your character, taste, nature, intentions, all those things your mother told you to look for in "the other person." Honestly, now, who would you rather spend a fine, spring evening with: someone who drags you through discount malls looking for the best price on cocktail weenies, someone whose idea of romance involves seventy screaming teenagers and an electric guitar, or someone who calls you up one afternoon and says sweetly, "Drop by at eight. We'll start with cold lobster salad and stuffed mushrooms and then grill lamb chops on the porch. And by the way, there's cold buttered rum for dessert."? If you have to call your mother for the answer, you're in big trouble.

◆ WELSH RAREBIT

A lot of people think Welsh Rarebit has something to do with a rabbit. It doesn't. It's just an old and reliable combination of cheese, butter, and beer that will make your house smell great and your stomach feel loved. Even the swarthy vegetarian you met in the produce department early Sunday morning will go for this one.

1½ tablespoons butter	Dash white pepper
½ pound sharp Cheddar cheese, grated	¼ teaspoon dry mustard
	½ cup beer
¼ teaspoon salt	½ teaspoon Worcestershire sauce

In a saucepan melt the butter. Add the Cheddar cheese, salt, pepper, and mustard. Cook over very low heat, stirring constantly until the Cheddar cheese melts. Add the beer and Worcestershire sauce, mixing well. Serve on toast.
    Makes 2 servings.

◆ SALMON PÂTÉ

Salmon pâté conjures up images of ocean travel, violins, candlelight, heavy silver. A bowl of it, strategically placed, will classy up your den far better than that new wallpaper you haven't had time to hang.

1 14¾-ounce can salmon, drained and flaked	3 tablespoons sweet pickle relish
½ cup finely chopped onion	⅓ cup mayonnaise
⅓ cup finely chopped celery	1 pimiento, drained and finely chopped

In a large bowl combine all the ingredients and stir to mix. The pâté may be used to fill hors d'oeuvre cups or as a spread on crackers.
    Makes 2½ cups.

◆ BLEU CHEESE-DATE BALL

Bleu is French for "blue." The French are highly romantic. This recipe calls for sherry.... Now, you're on your own.

1 8-ounce package cream cheese, softened	½ cup pitted and chopped dates
	½ cup dry sherry
3 ounces bleu cheese, crumbled	1 cup chopped walnuts, divided

In a medium bowl combine the cheeses, dates, and sherry. Stir in a ½ cup walnuts. Form into a ball and roll in the remaining walnuts. Chill and serve with crackers or slices of fresh pears.
     Makes 2½ cups.

◆ EASY ONION DIP

1 1-ounce envelope onion soup mix	2 cups sour cream

In a medium bowl combine the soup mix and sour cream. Cover and chill 2 hours before serving.
     Serve with fresh vegetables for dipping.
     Makes 2 cups.

◆ BEER BREAD

Beer, honey, and bread are such a medieval combination you'll have to pin up your hair with this one and throw chunks of it to the dogs under the table. It also happens to be really good, and really good bread makes a lasting impression on anyone who eats it.

3 cups self-rising flour	1 tablespoon honey
1 12-ounce can beer	

Grease a 9 x 5-inch loaf pan and set aside.
     In a large bowl combine the ingredients, mixing well. Pour into the prepared loaf pan and bake at 350° for 30 minutes or until browned and a wooden pick inserted in center comes out clean. Turn out onto a wire rack to cool.
     Makes 12 slices.

◆ ANGEL BISCUITS

Angel biscuits are made with yeast, which makes the dough easy to handle and sure to rise. The beauty of this version is that you make it ahead, put it in the fridge, and take out and bake only what you need for each meal. That means you always have fresh biscuits. In some people's eyes, this constitutes a major miracle.

2	¼-ounce packages active dry yeast	1	teaspoon salt
2	tablespoons very warm water	1	teaspoon baking soda
5	cups self-rising flour	1	cup shortening
¾	teaspoon baking powder	2	cups buttermilk
¼	cup sugar		

In a small bowl dissolve the yeast in the water.

In a separate bowl combine the flour, baking powder, sugar, salt, and baking soda and cut in the shortening with a pastry blender until mixture resembles coarse meal. Add the yeast and buttermilk and knead for 30 seconds. Refrigerate until needed, up to five days.

When ready, roll out the dough on a floured surface to ½-inch thickness and cut with a biscuit cutter. You may fold the dough for Parker House rolls or stack two rounds for divided biscuits. Place the biscuits close together on an ungreased baking sheet and bake at 400° for 15 to 20 minutes.

Makes 60 biscuits.

Honey, we all deserve to wear white.
Susan Sarandon in Bull Durham, 1988

◆ PUFF BISCUITS

Puff biscuits are not really biscuits—they're more like shortbread fritters. No one you make them for will have had anything like them. You can even sprinkle them with ground cinnamon and serve them at breakfast.

	Shortening for frying	1	egg, beaten
2	cups all-purpose flour	½	to ¾ cup milk
1	tablespoon sugar	1	tablespoon butter, melted
2	rounded teaspoons baking powder		Confectioners' sugar
1	teaspoon salt		

In a heavy skillet heat 1½ inches of shortening to 375°.

In a large bowl combine the flour, sugar, baking powder, and salt and add the egg and enough milk to make a thick batter. Add the melted butter and drop by spoonfuls into the hot fat. Cook until brown and done in center. Serve hot sprinkled with confectioners' sugar.

Makes 6 servings.

◆ SHRIMP TEMPURA FOR TWO

There are men in this world who wouldn't marry a woman who couldn't fry. What makes them think they can't do it themselves is a mystery to us all.

12 large fresh shrimp, shelled and deveined but with tails left on	SAUCE:
2 cups all-purpose flour, divided	2 tablespoons soy sauce
2 eggs, beaten	2 tablespoons water
½ cup cold water	1 teaspoon sugar
Sesame or corn oil for frying	½ teaspoon seasoned salt
	1 teaspoon prepared horseradish

Place the shrimp in a bag with 1 cup flour and shake to coat.

In a medium bowl combine 1 cup flour, the eggs, and cold water, mixing until smooth. In a skillet heat 1½ inches of oil to 375°. Dip each flour-coated shrimp into the batter and fry in the hot oil for 1½ minutes. Remove and drain on paper towels.

Mix together the sauce ingredients and serve with the shrimp.

Makes 2 servings.

◆ BUTTERFLY SHRIMP

Butterfly shrimp is all glory and no effort. Simplicity is the key here. All you really need is a good butcher and a grill.

1 pound large fresh shrimp, shelled and deveined but with tails left on	¼ cup lemon juice
	1 tablespoon vegetable oil
	2 cloves garlic, minced

Split shrimp almost in half lengthwise, open like a book, and gently flatten. In a large bowl combine the lemon juice, oil, and garlic. Add the shrimp and toss to coat. Let stand for 15 minutes.

Thread four shrimp on each of six skewers or place in an oiled, hinged grill basket. Grill, turning occasionally, over moderately hot coals for 3 to 5 minutes or until shrimp are pink in color and lightly browned.

Makes 2 servings.

I'll be seeing you, in all the old, familiar places.
Irving Kahal, 1938

◆ GRILLED LAMB CHOPS

You can always go out to eat, but you can't always find good lamb chops. Grill them at home. They'll set you apart.

1 clove garlic, sliced	Freshly ground black pepper
2 tablespoons olive oil	3 lamb chops
1/3 cup fresh lime juice	

Slice garlic and marinate in oil for 2 to 4 hours.

Combine with lime juice and pepper. Marinate chops in dressing 8 hours or overnight.

Grill over moderately hot coals about 10 minutes on each side.

Makes 2 servings.

◆ LEMON SAUCE FOR GRILLED CHICKEN

1 clove garlic	2 teaspoons grated onion
1/2 teaspoon salt	1/2 teaspoon black pepper
1/4 cup vegetable oil	1/2 teaspoon dried thyme
1/2 cup lemon juice	

In a small bowl mash the garlic with the salt. Stir in the oil, lemon juice, onion, black pepper, and thyme. Chill for 24 hours.

Use to baste chicken on the grill.

Makes 3/4 cup.

◆ BAKED SALMON STEAKS

Okay, so maybe you don't have a grill. Cheer up. You can do amazing things with an oven, even a toaster oven.

2 fresh salmon steaks, 1 inch thick	1/2 cup sliced fresh mushrooms or 1
1 lemon, halved	4-ounce can mushrooms, drained
Seasoned salt to taste	2 tablespoons grated Parmesan
4 tablespoons mayonnaise	cheese
Grated nutmeg	

Grease a baking dish. In the dish place the steaks, not touching. Squeeze the juice of 1/2 lemon over each steak and sprinkle generously with seasoned salt. Spread 2 tablespoons mayonnaise over each steak and sprinkle lightly with nutmeg. Top with the mushrooms and 1 tablespoon Parmesan cheese each. Bake uncovered at 400° for 15 minutes.

Makes 2 servings.

◆ BAKED PORK CHOPS WITH APPLES

This recipe is amazingly easy and amazingly delicious. You might want to fix an extra chop—just in case someone wants seconds.

2 pork chops, 1½ inches thick	Sugar
Salt and pepper to taste	Sour cream
1 tart apple, unpeeled, halved and cored	

Sprinkle pork chops with salt and pepper and place in a baking pan. Place one apple half, cut-side down, on top of each chop and sprinkle with sugar. Bake uncovered at 350° for 40 to 50 minutes, basting often with the juices, until the meat is well browned.

Serve hot with juices thickened with the sour cream.

Makes 2 servings.

◆ BAKED CORNISH HENS

	Salt and pepper to taste	1	3-ounce can mushrooms, drained
3	Cornish hens	2	tablespoons chopped fresh parsley
½	cup butter	½	cup dry sherry
5	green onions, chopped	¼	cup water
2	stalks celery, chopped		

In a large casserole salt and pepper the hens liberally and brown in melted butter. Add the onions, celery, mushrooms, and parsley, cover, and bake at 300° for about 45 minutes. Watch closely and baste often with the pan juices, as Cornish hens finish cooking very quickly. Juices may be spooned over rice.

Makes 2 servings.

> This sort of thing may be tolerated by the French,
> but we are British—thank God.
> Lord Montgomery, 1965

◆ BROCCOLI AND RICE WITH CHEEZE WHIZ

½ 10¾-ounce can cream of chicken
    soup, undiluted
2 cups cooked white rice
1 10-ounce package frozen, chopped
    broccoli, cooked and drained

1 4-ounce can water chestnuts,
    drained and sliced
½ 8-ounce jar Cheeze Whiz
    Seasoned breadcrumbs

Grease a casserole dish and set aside. In a large bowl combine the soup, rice, broccoli, water chestnuts, and Cheeze Whiz, and pour into the prepared casserole dish. Top with the seasoned breadcrumbs and bake at 350° for 30 to 40 minutes.

Makes 2 servings.

◆ BAKED POTATOES

There are times in life when a baked potato is the only thing that will do.

Buy baking potatoes all approximately the same size and shape. Scrub well with a stiff brush and pat dry. Rub with shortening, bacon grease, butter, or olive oil. Sprinkle with garlic or onion salt. A potato rubbed with oil can go directly on the oven rack; shortening, bacon grease, and butter require a baking sheet or an iron skillet. Bake potatoes at 400° for 1 hour to 1 hour and 30 minutes until tender when pricked with fork. When done, slice lengthwise across tops and press in ends to fluff. Serve with butter, sour cream, yogurt, cheese sauce, chopped chives, and/or bacon bits.

◆ TWICE-BAKED POTATOES

Twice-baked potatoes are twice the trouble—there's no denying it. That's part of what makes them so special. The other part is the fact that they're absolutely wonderful. If you make someone twice-baked potatoes, they'll never forget it.

4 large baking potatoes
    Olive oil
2 tablespoons butter
½ cup sour cream
1 egg, beaten

½ teaspoon salt
    Dash white pepper
5 slices bacon, cooked and crumbled
    Parmesan cheese, grated

Scrub the potatoes, dry, and rub with olive oil. Bake on an oven rack at 400° for 1 hour to 1 hour and 30 minutes until fork tender.

Cut an oval slice off the top of each potato and scoop out the insides leaving a ¼-inch shell.

In a medium bowl mash the insides with a fork and add the butter, sour cream, egg, salt, and pepper. Beat well. Stir in the bacon. Stuff the potato shells with the mixture and sprinkle with Parmesan cheese. Bake at 400° until warmed through, about 20 minutes.

Makes 4 servings.

◆ BROCCOLI-CHEESE POTATOES

You can make a meal on broccoli-cheese potatoes, especially if you take up with the vegetarian. But, really, even the heartiest meat eater would be happy with these.

4	baking potatoes	2	tablespoons sour cream
	Olive oil	½	teaspoon Dijon mustard
1	10¾-ounce can Cheddar cheese soup, undiluted	1	cup broccoli florets, cooked

Scrub and dry the potatoes and rub them with olive oil. Bake on an oven rack at 400° for 1 hour to 1 hour and 30 minutes until fork tender. In a saucepan combine the soup, sour cream, and mustard. Add the broccoli and heat thoroughly. Split the potatoes and spoon the sauce over them.
Makes 4 servings.

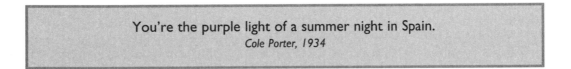

You're the purple light of a summer night in Spain.
Cole Porter, 1934

◆ EASY SPINACH CASSEROLE

This recipe is for two, but you might want to double it. If your evening goes well, you'll need extra helpings. If it doesn't, the leftovers will cheer you up the next day.

1	10-ounce package frozen, chopped spinach, thawed and wrung dry by hand	¼	cup butter, melted and divided
		½	cup seasoned breadcrumbs
			Paprika
1	3-ounce package cream cheese, softened		

Grease a small casserole dish and set aside. In a medium bowl combine the spinach, cream cheese, and 2 tablespoons melted butter. Spoon into the prepared casserole dish. Sprinkle with breadcrumbs and paprika and drizzle with the remaining 2 tablespoons of melted butter. Bake uncovered at 350° for 20 minutes.
Makes 2 servings.

◆ MARINATED GREEN BEAN SALAD

Marinated canned green beans may not sound great, but they are.

1 16-ounce can whole green beans,
   drained

MARINADE:
2 teaspoons olive oil
2 teaspoons tarragon vinegar
1 tablespoon finely chopped onion
1 tablespoon finely chopped fresh
   parsley
1/4 teaspoon salt
   Dash white pepper

DRESSING:
1/4 cup sour cream
1/4 cup mayonnaise
2 teaspoons lemon juice
2 teaspoons prepared horseradish
1 teaspoon finely chopped onion
1/2 teaspoon dry mustard

Place the green beans in a large bowl.
    In a medium bowl mix together all the ingredients for the marinade and pour over the green beans. Cover and chill overnight. Before serving combine in a small bowl all the ingredients for the dressing. Drain the beans and add the dressing.
    Makes 2 to 4 servings.

◆ CUCUMBER-AVOCADO MOLD

1 3-ounce package lemon-flavored
   gelatin
1/2 cup hot water
1 cup sour cream
3/4 teaspoon salt

2 tablespoons lemon juice
1/2 cup minced cucumber
1 cup diced avocado
2 tablespoons minced onion

Grease a 3-cup mold and set aside. In a medium bowl dissolve the gelatin in the hot water. Add the sour cream, beating until smooth. Add the salt, lemon juice, cucumber, avocado, and minced onion and stir. Pour into the prepared mold and chill until set.
    Makes 4 servings.

◆ FRESH SPINACH SALAD

1 pound fresh spinach
2 2.8-ounce cans French-fried onions

1 8-ounce bottle garlic salad dressing

Wash and dry the spinach, remove the stems, and tear the leaves into manageable pieces. Place the leaves in a salad bowl and toss with the onions. Just before serving, pour the dressing over the spinach.
    Makes 4 servings.

◆ CHOCOLATE LOVER'S MOUSSE

Some of the most romantic of desserts are made with that pedestrian household staple—unflavored gelatin. If you've never used it, you must learn now. Practice by yourself the first time. This mousse is a good one to learn on because you beat the gelatin into the whipped cream rather than folding the whipped cream into the gelatin. And really, after two or three tries you'll have no trouble at all.

1 teaspoon unflavored gelatin	¼ cup cocoa
1 tablespoon cold water	1 cup whipping cream
2 tablespoons boiling water	1 teaspoon vanilla extract
½ cup sugar	Shaved chocolate

In a small bowl sprinkle the gelatin over the cold water and let stand 1 minute. Add the boiling water and stir until gelatin is dissolved. In a separate bowl stir together the sugar, cocoa, whipping cream, and vanilla. Beat on medium speed of an electric mixer, scraping the bottom of the bowl occasionally, until mixture is stiff. Add the gelatin mixture and beat until well blended. Spoon into dessert dishes or champagne glasses. Sprinkle with shaved chocolate. Chill 1 hour before serving.

    Makes 4 servings.

> You know the nice thing about buying food for a man is that
> you don't have to laugh at his jokes.
> *Veronica Lake in* Sullivan's Travels, *1941*

◆ PECAN SQUARES

2 cups crushed graham crackers	1 cup semisweet chocolate morsels
1 14-ounce can sweetened condensed milk	½ cup chopped pecans
	1 teaspoon almond extract

Grease and flour an 8-inch square baking pan and set aside. In a medium bowl mix all the ingredients. Pour into the prepared pan and bake at 325° for 25 to 30 minutes.

    Let cool in the pan before cutting into squares.

    Makes 16 squares.

◆ CHOCOLATE-ALMOND PIE

You'd better be sure you really like someone before you fix them a chocolate pie. You might end up with more than you bargained for.

9.3 ounces milk chocolate
2 tablespoons butter
1 teaspoon instant coffee granules
1 tablespoon amaretto liqueur
1 8-ounce carton whipped topping, thawed

1 9-inch prepared Chocolate Wafer Pastry Shell (recipe follows)
¼ cup chopped almonds

In the top of a double boiler melt the chocolate and butter over hot water. Remove from the heat and add the coffee granules and amaretto. Cool.

In a large bowl pour mixture into the whipped topping and blend well. Pour into the prepared pastry shell and chill.

Sprinkle with chopped nuts.

Makes 8 servings.

◆ CHOCOLATE WAFER SHELL

1 9-ounce box Famous Chocolate Wafers, crushed

⅓ cup butter, melted

In a medium bowl mix the ingredients and press into a 9-inch pie plate. Chill.

◆ FRUIT CRISP

There's something immensely soothing about hot fruit crisp with vanilla ice cream melting on it. It goes well with conversation, movies, news, companionable silence. It's the perfect late-night dessert.

1 1-pound 5-ounce can peach or apple pie filling
1 cup all-natural granola

¼ teaspoon ground cinnamon
3 tablespoons butter, melted
Ice cream

In an 8-inch pie plate spread the pie filling. In a small bowl toss together the granola, cinnamon, and melted butter and spoon over the filling. Bake at 375° for 20 minutes or until bubbly and browned.

Serve warm with ice cream.

Makes 4 servings.

◆ COLD BUTTERED RUM DESSERT

Nothing could be easier—or more romantic—than this.

1 pint butter-pecan ice cream, soft-
   ened
	2 ounces dark rum
	   Shaved chocolate

In a blender or food processor blend together the ice cream and rum until smooth. Pour into small glasses and chill.

Sprinkle with shaved chocolate before serving.

Makes 2 servings.

We deserve each other.
George Sanders in All About Eve, *1950*

◆ CHOCOLATE-BRANDY CREAM

1 6-ounce package semisweet choco- late morsels	¼ teaspoon salt ¾ cup hot milk
1 tablespoon brandy	Whipped topping, thawed
1 tablespoon sugar	

In a blender mix the chocolate, brandy, sugar, and salt until smooth. Add the hot milk gradually. Chill for 3 to 4 hours.

Serve topped with whipped cream.

Makes 4 servings.

◆ CHABLIS COOLER

Superfine sugar	*½ teaspoon vanilla extract*
1 ounce grenadine	*2 ounces vodka*
2 tablespoons lemon juice	*Pink Chablis, chilled*

With superfine sugar, sugar-frost two tall, 14-ounce glasses and add three ice cubes to each.

In a container mix the grenadine, lemon juice, vanilla, and vodka and pour half into each glass. Fill the glasses to the rim with Chablis. Stir.

Makes 2 servings.

SUMMER

It's too darn hot.
Cole Porter, 1949

Sometimes it's just too hot to eat. A hundred degrees in the shade, not a cloud in the sky, the drought of the decade well into its eighth week. Your thighs are sticking together. Every molecule in your body is crying out for ice. Life is nothing but one long, slow, breathless effort, not a pleasant experience nor one you bargained for and, no thanks, it's not that you don't appreciate the effort that went into that truly attractive aspic, but, really, you don't have much appetite today.

No appetite? On the contrary. There's a world of food waiting for just such an emergency: cold curried asparagus soup, batterfried shrimp, fresh tomatoes stuffed with pesto and angel hair, wilted lettuce, boiled shrimp, ratatouille tourte, peach shortcake, summer citrus tea. Hot weather food is pure delight. It cools you down and startles your taste buds, all at the same time. There's no limit to what you can do once the temperature hits ninety, given the right ingredients. A handful of vine-ripened tomatoes, one sweet onion, and a green bell pepper in a food processor with a little oil and vinegar and some fresh dill and sour cream, and you've got a cold gazpacho that will revolutionize your thinking.

Hot weather is a chance to eat fried green tomatoes with hot pepper sauce, fresh sole in tarragon and cream, mesquite-grilled steak, lemon pie. It's not something you'd want to miss. There are some things August was simply made for.

◆ BISCUIT BREAD

You probably wouldn't want to make this in July in a kitchen without air condition-ing, but if you can stand the extra heat, you'll be glad to have it. It cooks on the same principle as corn bread, tastes like a light biscuit, and you don't have to roll out the dough. Serve it in wedges with butter and honey.

2   cups self-rising flour   ½   cup vegetable oil
1   cup milk

Liberally grease an 8-inch cast-iron skillet and place in oven to heat. In a medium bowl combine all the ingredients and mix well. Pour the batter into the hot skillet and bake at 400° for 18 to 20 minutes or until golden brown.
    Makes 8 servings.

◆ SUMMER CORNPONE

Cornpone is unleavened corn bread, a traditional dish of Native Americans cooked originally on a hot rock. This version is practically a meal in itself. You can't cook this on a rock, but you can trade out vegetables for variety—okra instead of corn, hot pepper instead of green chilies, summer squash. And, since it cooks on top of the stove, it won't heat up your kitchen.

1   8¾-ounce can cream-style corn   2   eggs, beaten
1   large tomato, peeled and diced   ½   teaspoon salt
1   medium onion, chopped   ½   teaspoon black pepper
1   clove garlic, minced   ½   cup half-and-half
1   teaspoon chopped green chilies,   1   cup white cornmeal
    drained   Vegetable oil for frying

In a large bowl combine the corn, tomato, onion, garlic, and chilies.
    In a separate bowl combine the eggs, salt, pepper, and half-and-half and pour over the corn mixture, stirring gently. Gradually add the cornmeal, stirring until even-ly mixed and all the cornmeal is absorbed. The batter will be very sticky. On the stove top heat a lightly greased 10-inch skillet to 375°. Spoon the batter evenly into the skil-let and reduce the heat to medium-low. Cover and cook 10 to 15 minutes until the underside is golden brown.
    Remove the lid and flip to the other side. Cook uncovered 5 to 8 minutes more.
    Makes 6 servings.

◆ COLD GAZPACHO

2 medium tomatoes, peeled and
   chopped
1 small cucumber, scored and
   chopped
1 small onion, chopped
½ green bell pepper, chopped
1 clove garlic, minced

1 tablespoon olive oil
1 tablespoon wine vinegar
   Dash Tabasco sauce
1 24-ounce can vegetable juice cocktail
   Sour cream
   Fresh dill weed

In a food processor pulse the vegetables until coarse. Add the olive oil, vinegar, Tabasco sauce, and vegetable juice and process until the soup is the desired consistency. Cover and refrigerate overnight.

Serve chilled with sour cream and fresh dill.

Makes 6 servings.

◆ NOODLES IN CREAM

In a snootier context, this would be made with linguine or capellini and called "Alfredo," and you would have to sit up straight at a table and make polite conversation while you ate it. On a hot night at home, you can make it with wide noodles in your bare feet. It's still full of butter and cream—and it's still wonderful.

1 8-ounce box wide egg noodles,
   cooked and drained
¼ cup butter
¼ cup whipping cream

1 clove garlic, pressed
   White pepper to taste
1 teaspoon seasoned salt
   Fresh parsley, chopped

In a large saucepan combine the hot noodles with the butter, cream, garlic, and seasonings. Return to the stove and cook over low heat until the noodles have absorbed most of the cream. Place in a warm serving dish and sprinkle with fresh parsley.

Makes 4 servings.

> They sowed the duller vegetables first, and a pleasant feeling of righteous
> fatigue stole over them as they addressed themselves to the peas.
> E. M. Forster, 1920

◆ BAKED SUMMER VEGETABLES

Summer is the season of farmers' markets in church parking lots on alternate Tuesday afternoons so breathless and bright that you begin to wonder if beating that old lady with the cane out of the last of the fresh dill was such a good idea after all. This lovely summer dish, a combination of vegetables, cheeses, and cream, happens to use the canned and frozen varieties. It's only mildly cheating—you can still buy an onion from a farmer—and it's far the more charitable approach.

2 10-ounce packages frozen chopped
    broccoli, thawed
1½ cups cottage cheese
½ cup sour cream
3 eggs, lightly beaten
2 tablespoons minced onion

1 16-ounce can whole kernel corn,
    drained
1 tablespoon all-purpose flour
    Salt and pepper to taste
½ cup grated Parmesan cheese

In a greased 2-quart casserole place the broccoli. In a large bowl combine the cottage cheese, sour cream, eggs, onion, corn, and flour. Season to taste with salt and pepper. Pour over the broccoli. Sprinkle with Parmesan cheese. Bake covered at 325° for 20 minutes.

    Uncover and bake for 30 to 45 minutes more or until the mixture is set and top is lightly browned.

    Makes 8 servings.

◆ RATATOUILLE

Ratatouille as a side dish or over rice sets the standard for summer vegetables. You can also make it into a tourte straight out of a French brasserie. Make the ratatouille as usual and mix it with two beaten eggs, ¾ cup of crumbled feta cheese, and maybe a little light cream. Pour it into a prepared 9-inch pastry shell, sprinkle with grated Romano, and bake at 350° for 30 to 40 minutes. Serve it topped with sour cream or yogurt cheese. Like everything made with eggplant, it's even better the second day.

3 baby or 1 small eggplant, diced
2 small yellow squash, diced
1 small zucchini, diced
1 medium onion, thinly sliced
3 cloves garlic, thinly sliced
2 tablespoons extra-virgin olive oil
1 small green bell pepper, thinly
    sliced

1 medium tomato, peeled and diced
    Salt to taste
    Freshly ground white pepper
½ teaspoon crushed coriander seeds
1 cup loosely packed fresh cilantro

Salt the diced eggplant and squashes and place in a colander in the sink under a heavily weighted plate for 2 to 3 hours until the bitter juices drain out. In a skillet sauté the onion and garlic in olive oil, covered, over medium-low heat about 20 minutes until just translucent. Add the bell pepper, squashes, eggplant, tomato, salt, white pepper, and coriander. Simmer uncovered over low heat 20 minutes more, stirring occasionally. Add the cilantro and cook 5 minutes more. Salt to taste.

    Makes 4 servings.

◆ BAKED ZUCCHINI

6 *very small zucchini, thinly sliced*
2 *medium tomatoes, peeled and*
    sliced
2 *medium sweet onions, thinly sliced*
    Salt to taste

Freshly ground white pepper
2 *teaspoons dried dill weed*
½ *cup grated Parmesan cheese*
½ *cup seasoned breadcrumbs*

Grease a 1½-quart casserole dish. In the order given, layer one third each of the zucchini, tomatoes, onions, salt, pepper, dill weed, and Parmesan cheese in the prepared casserole dish, repeating layers until the casserole is full. Top with the breadcrumbs. Cover with foil and bake at 400° for 45 minutes. Remove the foil for the last 10 minutes to let the casserole brown.
  Makes 4 servings.

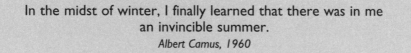

In the midst of winter, I finally learned that there was in me
an invincible summer.
Albert Camus, 1960

◆ SUMMER SQUASH CASSEROLE

If you were blindfolded on a desert island, and someone gave you a bite of squash casserole, you would say, "Summer." And you would be right.

2 *pounds yellow squash, sliced*
1 *medium onion, chopped*
½ *teaspoon salt*
1 *10¾-ounce can cream of chicken*
    soup, undiluted

1 *8-ounce carton sour cream*
1 *8-ounce can water chestnuts, sliced*
½ *cup butter, melted*
1 *8-ounce package herb-seasoned*
    stuffing mix

Grease a 9 x 13-inch baking dish and set aside. In a pot cook the squash and onion in a small amount of salted water until just tender. Drain. Add the soup, sour cream, and water chestnuts. In a large bowl combine the melted butter and stuffing mix. Pour half the stuffing mixture into the prepared baking dish. Add the squash mixture. Cover with the remaining stuffing. Bake uncovered at 350° for 30 minutes.
  Makes 9 servings.

◆ ANGEL HAIR PESTO IN PLUM TOMATOES

You can fix angel hair pesto any season of the year, but only when the temperature passes ninety can you stuff it into vine-ripened plum tomatoes. It takes a hot summer sun to ripen a tomato properly. Any Britisher who brags to you about the "super" tomatoes he grows on his moss-covered patio is delusional.

½ pound angel hair pasta, cooked and drained	8 plum tomatoes, hollowed out
3 tablespoons extra-virgin olive oil	Romano cheese, grated
1 7-ounce container pesto sauce	Pine nuts, chopped
	Fresh parsley, chopped

In a large bowl toss the angel hair with the olive oil and pesto. Stuff into the hollowed-out tomatoes and sprinkle with the Romano cheese, pine nuts, and fresh parsley. Chill before serving.

Makes 6 to 8 servings as an appetizer, 2 to 3 for supper.

◆ BELL PEPPER STEAK

Another stove-top skillet meal. Try to find a green bell pepper that has started to turn orange-red. The color means the flavor is intensifying. If you can keep one on your windowsill until it turns bright-colored and leathery, the flavor will be exquisite. Sometimes, though, they just rot. It's impossible to tell ahead of time which will turn properly and which won't.

1 pound boneless beef sirloin or top round, ¾-inch thick and sliced across the grain into thin strips	2 cloves garlic, minced, or ¼ teaspoon garlic powder
2 tablespoons olive oil, divided	¼ teaspoon black pepper
2 cups thinly sliced sweet bell pepper, green, red, and/or orange	1 10¾-ounce can Italian tomato soup, undiluted
1 medium onion, sliced and separated into rings	½ cup hot water
1 teaspoon dried oregano	4 cups cooked fusilli or spaghetti
	Sour cream

In a 10-inch skillet over medium-high heat brown the beef one half at a time in 1 tablespoon olive oil, stirring often. Remove the meat and set aside. Reduce the heat to medium, add the second tablespoon of olive oil and cook the bell peppers, onion, oregano, garlic, and black pepper until tender, stirring often. Stir in the soup and water and heat to boiling. Reduce the heat and return the beef to the skillet to heat thoroughly. Serve over pasta or rice with sour cream.

Makes 4 servings.

◆ BAKED FILLET OF FISH

There exists in certain families the occasional aunt or nephew happily content to spend the summer lying in a hammock waiting for the fish to bite. Such people are to be cherished. There is little else on a hot summer night like a fresh fillet of fish.

2 or 3 pounds fish fillets, any kind
  Salt and pepper
½ cup butter
  Juice of 1 lemon

1 tablespoon dry white wine
  Parmesan cheese, grated
  Paprika to taste

Season the fillets with salt and pepper. Place the butter in a shallow baking dish and brown at 450°. Place the fillets flesh-side down in the sizzling butter and return to the oven for 10 to 15 minutes. Turn carefully, baste with the juices, and sprinkle with the lemon juice, white wine, Parmesan cheese, and paprika. Return to the oven about 5 minutes more until done. The fish will flake with a fork when done. Serve with pan juices.

Makes 4 servings.

◆ CHEESE SAUCE FOR EGGS OR FISH

2½ tablespoons butter
2 tablespoons all-purpose flour
1 cup half-and-half
  Salt to taste
  Freshly ground white pepper

¼ teaspoon ground nutmeg
2 tablespoons grated Swiss cheese
2 tablespoons grated Parmesan
  cheese

In a saucepan melt butter over medium heat and stir in the flour with a wire whisk until it begins to brown. Gradually pour in the half-and-half, stirring constantly. Season with the salt, white pepper, and nutmeg. Remove from the heat and stir in the cheeses until melted.

Makes 1½ cups.

◆ SOLE IN SHRIMP SAUCE

3 pounds sole fillets
1 tablespoon butter
   Salt to taste
⅔ cup dry white wine, divided
1 tablespoon all-purpose flour
2 cups heavy cream

1 pound cooked shrimp, finely
   chopped
1 4-ounce can mushrooms, drained
   and finely chopped
   Fresh parsley, chopped

Butter and heat a baking dish. Place the fillets in the prepared dish, sprinkle with salt and pour in ⅓ cup wine. Bake at 400° for 20 minutes, basting often. Remove the fillets to a platter. In the dish thicken the fish stock with the flour and add the cream, shrimp, and mushrooms. Add the remaining wine. Pour over the fillets and garnish with parsley.

Makes 6 servings.

◆ BOILED SHRIMP

You can meet the boats by the wharf at sunset and fight stray cats for a peck of fresh shrimp, or you can buy a block flash-frozen from the grocer. Either way, you're going to have yourself a shrimp boil. Cover your table with newspapers, set out saucers of shrimp sauce among the boiled corn and sliced tomatoes and cucumbers, and tell everybody to sit down and peel their own.

4 quarts water
½ onion, sliced
1 clove garlic
1 bay leaf
2 stalks celery with leaves, broken in
   thirds

3 tablespoons salt
¼ teaspoon cayenne pepper
1 lemon, sliced
2 tablespoons shrimp seasoning
4 pounds fresh shrimp

In a large pot simmer all the ingredients except the shrimp for 30 minutes. Add the shrimp. Cook 5 to 8 minutes until the shrimp is pink in color. Drain and serve on newspapers with cocktail sauce.

Makes 8 servings.

◆ BATTER-FRIED SHRIMP

2 eggs, lightly beaten
2 tablespoons milk
1 pound fresh shrimp, peeled and
      deveined but with tails intact

Cracker meal
Salt and pepper to taste
Vegetable oil for frying

In a shallow bowl mix the eggs and milk. Dip each shrimp into the egg mixture and roll in the cracker meal to which salt and pepper have been added. In a skillet heat 1 ½ inches of oil to 375° and fry the shrimp until a deep, golden brown. Drain on paper towels and serve hot with cocktail sauce.

Makes 4 servings as an appetizer, 2 for supper.

◆ COLD CURRIED ASPARAGUS SOUP

You can add half-and-half to practically any undiluted canned soup and with a little curry powder or cumin or dill have yourself an elegant cold bisque.

1 10¾-ounce can cream of asparagus
      soup, undiluted
1½ cups half-and-half

½ teaspoon curry powder
Fresh or dried chives, chopped
Additional cream

In a serving dish mix together the soup, half-and-half, and curry powder and chill. Serve cold sprinkled with chopped chives and drizzled with cream.

Makes 4 servings.

> A land without mercy, without shade. If you sit under an olive tree you
> are not shaded; the leaves are like little flickering tongues of fire.
> *Iris Origo, 1944*

◆ MESQUITE-GRILLED STEAKS

8 1½-inch thick T-bone steaks
2 teaspoons seasoned salt
1 12-ounce can or bottle beer
8 large cloves garlic, minced

Freshly ground black pepper

Mesquite wood chips, soaked in
   water overnight

Trim the fat around the steaks to desired thickness. Sprinkle both sides of each steak evenly with the salt, beer, and garlic. Pierce steaks with a fork on each side, cover, and let stand at room temperature for 1 hour. Heat coals in a grill. Place the soaked mesquite chips directly on the hot coals. Grill the steaks 8 to 10 minutes per side. Sprinkle with pepper.

Makes 8 servings.

> Ho! 'Tis the time of salads.
> *Laurence Sterne, 1765*

◆ COOL CUCUMBER SALAD

1 3-ounce package lime gelatin
1 cup boiling water
1 3-ounce package cream cheese,
   softened

1 cup mayonnaise
1 tablespoon tarragon vinegar
1 tablespoon grated onion
1 cup grated cucumber

Grease a 4-cup mold and set aside. In a large bowl dissolve the gelatin in the boiling water. In a separate bowl combine the cream cheese, mayonnaise, and vinegar, mixing well. Stir the cream cheese mixture into the gelatin and add the onion and cucumber. Pour into the prepared mold and chill until set.

Makes 6 servings.

◆ WILTED LETTUCE SALAD

People used to call this "killed lettuce" and you got it in the summer in cafeterias with floor-to-ceiling mirrors and Art Deco lamps and organists who played "The Yellow Rose of Texas" while white-coated waiters named Slim carried your tray to a table on the edge of the balcony. It's the hot bacon grease that does it. If you're not going to use bacon, don't bother to make it.

1	large bunch Bibb or red-leaf lettuce	1	teaspoon sugar
1	small sweet onion, finely chopped	2	tablespoons cider vinegar
	Freshly ground black pepper	½	teaspoon salt
6	slices bacon, fried crisp and crumbled, with drippings reserved		

Wash the lettuce and tear into pieces in a salad bowl. Add the onions and pepper. To the hot bacon drippings add the sugar, vinegar, and salt and pour immediately over the lettuce. Toss lightly. Add the bacon and toss again.

Makes 4 servings.

◆ THREE-PEA SALAD

1	19-ounce can chickpeas, drained and rinsed	½	cup thinly sliced onion
1	16-ounce can black-eyed peas, drained and rinsed	1	medium green bell pepper, chopped
1	17-ounce can English peas, drained	½	cup sugar
1	8-ounce jar cocktail onions, undrained	½	cup vegetable oil
		½	teaspoon salt
		¼	teaspoon pepper

In a large bowl combine all the ingredients and toss well. Cover and chill overnight. The salad will keep in the refrigerator for several days.

Makes 10 servings.

◆ TOMATO ASPIC WITH CLOVES

1	pint tomato juice	1	3-ounce package lemon-flavored gelatin
2	stalks celery, chopped in thirds		
5	whole cloves	1	tablespoon cider vinegar
1	small onion		

Grease a 9-inch square pan and set aside. In a saucepan simmer the tomato juice, celery, cloves, and onion for 15 minutes. Strain and in a large bowl pour the hot mixture over the gelatin. Add the vinegar. Pour into the prepared pan and chill until firm. Cut in 3-inch squares to serve.

Makes 9 servings.

◆ VANILLA-WAFER CAKE

2 cups sugar	½ cup milk
1 cup butter	1 cup chopped pecans
6 eggs	1 7-ounce bag flaked coconut
1 12-ounce box vanilla wafers, crushed fine	

Grease and flour a 10-inch stem pan and set aside. In a large bowl cream the sugar and butter. Add the eggs one at a time, beating well after each addition. Add the vanilla wafers and mix well. Add the milk. Add the nuts and coconut. Bake at 325° in the prepared pan for 1 hour and 30 minutes to 1 hour and 45 minutes.

Makes 16 servings.

◆ EASY LEMON PIE

You put the whole lemon, rind and all, into this pie. It may spoil you forever for the pale shadows of the "lemon-flavored."

3 eggs	2 tablespoons lemon juice
1 lemon, unpeeled, quartered, and seeded	¼ cup butter, melted
1¼ cups sugar	1 9-inch prepared pastry shell, unbaked

In a blender or food processor combine the eggs, lemon, sugar, and lemon juice and process until smooth. Add the butter and process a few seconds longer. Pour the mixture into the pastry shell. Bake at 350° for 30 to 35 minutes. Serve with French vanilla ice cream.

Makes 8 servings.

◆ FRUIT PIE SQUARES

1 18¼-ounce package yellow cake mix, reserving 1 cup	2 16-ounce cans pie filling, any kind
¾ cup butter, melted and divided	¼ cup sugar
1 egg, beaten	1 teaspoon ground cinnamon

Grease the bottom only of a 9 x 13 x 2-inch cake pan. In the pan stir together the cake mix (less 1 cup reserved), ½ cup melted butter, and the egg. Spread the pie filling on top of the batter. Combine the reserved cake mix with the reserved melted butter, the sugar, and the cinnamon and sprinkle over the pie filling. Bake at 350° for 45 minutes. Serve with vanilla ice cream.

Makes 12 servings.

◆ PEACH SHORTCAKE

You can make strawberry shortcake the year around—frozen berries work just fine. Peach shortcake, on the other hand, is a different proposition. Frozen peaches are not the same and if you forget to make this while the peaches are fresh, come December you will be filled with regret.

1	18¼-ounce package yellow cake mix	2	tablespoons cornstarch
3½	cups peeled and sliced fresh peaches	⅛	teaspoon ground nutmeg
		2	tablespoons butter
½	cup cold water	½	cup whipping cream, whipped, or 1 cup whipped topping, thawed
½	cup sugar		

In a 9 x 13 x 2-inch pan prepare and bake the cake mix according to the directions on the package. Cool completely and set aside. In a large saucepan combine the peaches, water, sugar, and cornstarch. Cook over medium heat until thickened, stirring constantly. Remove from the heat and stir in the nutmeg and butter. Spoon the whipped cream over the cooled cake and pour the peach mixture over the whipped cream. Serve immediately.

Makes 12 servings.

◆ BANANA-RUM POUND CAKE

Desperate for something to do with those spotted bananas the children, quite sensibly, refuse to touch? Got some rum left from your last luau? Two bites of this cake and you'll be transported to the tropics. The children can fend for themselves.

3	tablespoons sliced almonds	½	cup sour cream
1	large ripe banana, mashed	⅛	teaspoon ground nutmeg
2	eggs, beaten	1	8-ounce carton whipped topping, thawed
¼	cup dark rum		
1	1-pound package pound cake mix	1	tablespoon dark rum

Grease a 9 x 5-inch loaf pan, sprinkle it with almonds, and set aside. In a large bowl combine the banana, eggs, and rum and beat in the cake mix until smooth. Beat in the sour cream and nutmeg. Pour the batter into the prepared pan and bake at 325° for 1 hour and 10 minutes to 1 hour and 15 minutes. Cool in the pan 10 minutes. Turn out and cool completely on a wire rack before cutting. Serve with rum-flavored whipped topping.

Makes 8 servings.

◆ SUMMER MARGARITAS

In hot weather, liquid intake is just as critical as food. The great majority of people you see wandering around with plastic water bottles in their hot, sweaty hands would much prefer a glass of something cold from your fridge. You'd better keep your supply up.

Lime wedges
Salt
2 cups fresh lime juice
1½ cups tequila

½ cup Triple Sec or other orange-flavored liqueur
Cracked ice

Rub the rims of 8 cocktail glasses with lime wedges. Place the salt in a saucer. Spin the rim of each glass in the salt. Set the prepared glasses aside. In a mixer combine the remaining ingredients, shaking well. Pour into the prepared glasses.
    Makes 8 servings.

Water, water, every where,
Nor any drop to drink.
Samuel Taylor Coleridge, 1798

◆ SUMMER CITRUS PUNCH

3 cups fresh orange juice, chilled
2 cups fresh grapefruit juice, chilled
1 cup fresh lemon juice, chilled
1 cup fresh lime juice, chilled

¾ cup sugar
1 cup sparkling mineral water, chilled
Fresh strawberries
Canned pineapple chunks, drained

In a large container combine the fruit juices and the sugar, stirring until the sugar dissolves. Add the mineral water. Serve over ice and garnish with strawberries and pineapple chunks.
    Makes 8 servings.

◆ LEMONADE WITH SPICED TEA CUBES

¾ cup fresh lemon juice
½ cup sugar
2 cups cold water

Frozen spiced tea cubes
Lemon slices

In a large container combine the lemon juice, sugar, and water, stirring until the sugar dissolves. Pour over spiced tea cubes (recipe follows) and garnish with lemon slices.
   Makes 3 cups.

◆ SPICED TEA CUBES

1½ cups water
10 whole cloves
2 2-inch sticks cinnamon

4 regular tea bags
1½ cups cold water

In a saucepan combine 1½ cups water, cloves, and cinnamon sticks and bring to a boil. Reduce the heat and simmer 5 minutes. Remove from the heat and pour over the tea bags. Cover and let steep 10 minutes. Strain and discard the tea bags and spices. Add 1½ cups cold water to the tea mixture. Pour the tea into ice cube trays and freeze.
   Makes 2 dozen cubes.

◆ SUMMER TEA I

You can dazzle sweaty people with fruit punch for a while, but sooner or later they come back for iced tea.

3 tablespoons loose tea
6 fresh mint leaves
2 quarts boiling water

1 cup sugar
1 cup fresh orange juice
1 cup fresh lemon juice

In large container combine the tea and mint. Add the boiling water, cover, and let steep 7 minutes. Strain and add the remaining ingredients, stirring well. Serve over ice.
   Makes 2½ quarts.

◆ SUMMER TEA 2

1	quart boiling water	½	cup lemon juice
6	regular tea bags	½	cup white grape juice
1	cup sugar	1	quart cold water

In a large container pour the boiling water over the tea bags, cover, and let steep 5 minutes. Discard the tea bags. Add the remaining ingredients, stirring until the sugar dissolves. Serve over ice.

Makes 10 servings.

10

WINTER

...rest had seemed the sweetest thing under a roof.
Edward Thomas, 1915

There's something about cold weather that calls for shepherd's pie. Maybe it's the mashed potatoes; maybe it's the beef and mushrooms or the peas. Maybe it's the invigorating hint of Worcestershire. Whatever it is, when the thermometer hits thirty, you've got to have it—that and some black bean soup with chopped chives and Parmesan, green bean casserole, French-fried onion rings, cheese biscuits, peach cobbler, pudding cake. If you've ever considered braised pork chops in white wine and mustard, this is the time.

Cold weather cooking is a pleasure all around. One pot of beef-and-beer stew can transform a house. You can barbecue spareribs, mix up a hot fruit compote, bake a cheese-noodle casserole so rich in sour cream you'll think you've died and gone to heaven.

People need good food in winter. Darkness comes early. Tempers are short. The wind outside cuts right through your clothes. Inside is cozy warmth, cottage cheese-dill bread hot from the oven, sweet butter, orange tea. There's spinach soufflé on the warming tray, Cheddar cheese soup with jalapeño peppers, meat loaf crusty with catsup and brown sugar. Supper is in front of the fire and after the news we're having hot chocolate with whipped cream. It makes a person glad to be home.

◆ COTTAGE CHEESE-DILL BREAD

This is a yeast bread with all of the benefits and none of the bother. Bake it on a cold fall afternoon in the middle of college football season and serve it hot at halftime with sweet butter in front of a fire.

½ teaspoon sugar	1 teaspoon salt
¼ cup very warm water	1 cup small-curd cottage cheese
1 ¼-ounce envelope active dry yeast	¼ teaspoon baking powder
1 egg	2½ cups all-purpose flour
1 tablespoon instant minced onion	Melted butter
1 tablespoon butter, softened	Coarse salt
2 teaspoons dried dill seed	Additional dill seed

Grease a 1-quart round baking dish and set aside. In a small bowl dissolve the sugar in very warm water and sprinkle the yeast on top. Let stand about 5 minutes until foamy.

In a large bowl beat the egg slightly. Add the onion, butter, dill seed, salt, cottage cheese, and baking powder. Stir until well blended. Add the yeast mixture and just enough flour to make a soft dough that is still easy to stir. Place the dough in the prepared baking dish and cover with plastic wrap. Let rise in a warm place about 1 hour until doubled in bulk.

Bake the bread at 350° for 1 hour.

Turn out on a wire rack, brush the top with melted butter, and sprinkle with coarse salt and additional dill seed.

Makes 8 to 10 servings.

◆ HOT PEPPER-CHEESE CRACKERS

You can make these ahead of time and serve them with sliced apples and pears and a glass of old port.

½ cup butter, softened	½ teaspoon salt
2 cups shredded sharp Cheddar cheese	¼ teaspoon cayenne pepper
1½ cups all-purpose flour	1 tablespoon chopped fresh or dried chives

In a large bowl cream the butter and Cheddar cheese until smooth. In a separate bowl combine the flour, salt, cayenne, and chives, and add to the cheese mixture, blending well. Shape the dough into 1-inch balls. Place 2 inches apart on ungreased baking sheets. Flatten each ball to ⅛-inch thickness with the bottom of a glass dipped in flour. Prick the top with a fork. Bake at 350° for 12 to 15 minutes. Let cool on a wire rack. Store in an airtight container.

Makes 48 crackers.

◆ MINIATURE CHEESE MUFFINS

2 cups biscuit mix	1 8-ounce carton sour cream
½ cup butter, melted	½ cup shredded yellow cheese

Grease miniature muffin tins and set aside. In a large bowl combine all the ingredients, mixing well. Spoon into the prepared tins, filling each half full. Bake at 450° for 10 to 12 minutes.

Makes 48 muffins.

> Never again will I spend a winter in this accursed
> bucket shop of a refrigerator called England.
> *Rudyard Kipling, 1928*

◆ BLACK BEAN SOUP

Listen carefully. This is an emergency. At the first hint of winter, make yourself a pot of black bean soup. Then snow, ice, subzero temperatures, or gale-force winds, let winter do its worst—you won't care. If the power goes out, you can heat it over the fire.

3 10¾-ounce cans black bean soup, undiluted	2 teaspoons instant minced onion
2 10½-ounce cans beef consommé	1 cup Burgundy wine
¼ cup lemon juice	Sour cream
3 cups water	Chopped chives

In a large saucepan combine the soups and mix until smooth. Add the lemon juice, water, and onion. Bring to a boil, stirring frequently, and immediately reduce heat. Simmer covered for 15 minutes. Add the Burgundy. Serve with sour cream and chopped chives.

Makes 2½ quarts or 10 servings.

◆ FRENCH ONION SOUP

It's a long weekend in a dark month. There's ice on the windowpanes, basketball on television, a stack of magazines on the floor by your chair, lazy conversation. The only thing that would make this better is a nice bowl of hot soup. It's a good thing you made some.

2	large onions, thinly sliced	½	cup dry sherry
¼	cup butter, melted	2	cups toasted bread cubes
3	cups beef broth	7	teaspoons grated Parmesan cheese
2	cups chicken broth	7	4-inch square slices mozzarella
2	cups water		cheese
¼	teaspoon white pepper		

Separate the onions into rings and sauté covered in the butter over low heat about 30 minutes until translucent, not brown. Add the broths, water, and pepper and bring to a boil. Immediately reduce the heat and simmer uncovered for 30 minutes. Remove from the heat and stir in the sherry. Place seven oven-proof soup bowls on a baking sheet. Ladle the soup into each. Top with bread cubes, 1 teaspoon Parmesan cheese, and one slice mozzarella cheese. Broil 6 inches from heat until the cheese melts.

Makes 7 servings.

> Still falls the rain—
> *Edith Sitwell, 1940*

◆ CLAM CHOWDER

4	bacon slices, diced	2	cups water
1	medium onion, diced	1	8-ounce can minced clams with
2	potatoes, diced		juice
1	stalk celery, diced	2	tablespoons diced parsley
2	carrots, sliced in thin rounds		
1	14½-ounce can stewed tomatoes, mashed with juice		

In a pot boil the bacon, onion, potatoes, celery, carrots, and tomatoes in water until tender. Add the minced clams and parsley. Heat thoroughly.

Makes 4 servings.

◆ CREAM OF CORN SOUP

You might be able to buy cream of corn soup in a can, but it won't be this good.

1 *medium onion, chopped*	¼ *teaspoon black pepper*
1 *tablespoon vegetable oil*	3 *cups half-and-half*
3 *tablespoons all-purpose flour*	1 *17-ounce can whole kernel corn,*
1 *teaspoon salt*	*drained and coarsely chopped*

In a saucepan sauté the onion in oil until transparent, not browned. Add the flour, stirring constantly with a wire whisk until brown and bubbly. Add the salt and pepper. Gradually add the half-and-half, stirring constantly until thick and bubbly. Add the corn and heat thoroughly.

Makes 4 servings.

◆ MEAT LOAF

Even children who bolt at the sight of a green vegetable will take seconds on this meat loaf.

1½ *pounds ground round beef*	1½ *teaspoons salt*
¼ *pound pork sausage*	¼ *teaspoon black pepper*
¼ *cup finely chopped onion*	¼ *cup finely chopped green bell pep-*
¼ *cup finely chopped celery*	*per*
½ *cup catsup, plus additional for top*	¼ *cup firmly packed dark brown*
1 *egg, beaten until fluffy*	*sugar*

Grease a 9 x 5-inch loaf pan and set aside.

In a large bowl mix all the ingredients and place in the prepared pan. Top with catsup and brown sugar. Bake uncovered at 350° for 1 hour and 30 minutes.

Makes 4 to 6 servings.

◆ STOVE-TOP CRAB

2	tablespoons butter		Salt and cayenne pepper to taste
4	large mushrooms, thinly sliced	1¼	cups heavy cream
2	teaspoons grated onion	2	teaspoons finely minced parsley
2	fresh tomatoes, peeled and chopped	1	teaspoon chopped fresh chives
		1	jigger brandy
2	7-ounce cans crab meat, drained, or 1 pound imitation crab meat	2	cups cooked white rice

In a 2-quart casserole melt the butter. Add the sliced mushrooms and cook 5 minutes. Add the onion and tomatoes and cook another 5 minutes. Add the crab meat in large lumps. Season and heat. Add the cream, stirring gently. Let boil 1 minute, no longer, and add the parsley, chives, and brandy. Serve at once in shallow soup plates over cooked rice.

Makes 4 servings.

◆ PORK CHOPS IN WHITE WINE

6	pork chops, thickly cut		Brown sugar
2	teaspoons prepared mustard	6	thin lemon slices
	Salt and pepper to taste	1	cup dry white wine
¼	teaspoon dried dill weed		Sour cream

In a lightly greased skillet over medium heat brown the chops on either side. Drain the excess fat. Spread one side of each chop with mustard and sprinkle with the seasonings and brown sugar. Place one lemon slice on each chop. Add the wine, cover, and simmer on low heat about 50 to 60 minutes until tender.

Remove the chops from the skillet and keep warm. Remove the excess fat from the skillet, thicken drippings with sour cream, and spoon over the meat.

Makes 6 servings.

◆ BEEF-AND-BEER STEW

You can make this stew on a Friday evening in the teeth of the worst winter hurricane on record and eat it all weekend. If you're lucky, you'll still be snowed in on Monday.

2 pounds stew beef or chuck, cut in 1-inch cubes	1 10½-ounce can beef consommé
¼ cup shortening or bacon grease	1 12-ounce can or bottle beer
1 teaspoon salt	4 carrots, chopped in 1-inch pieces
½ teaspoon black pepper	4 potatoes, quartered
½ teaspoon dried marjoram	6 onions, quartered
¼ teaspoon dried tarragon	Salt to taste
½ teaspoon dried basil	¼ cup all-purpose flour
2 bay leaves	¼ cup water

In a skillet brown the meat in the hot shortening. Add the seasonings, consommé, and beer. Cover and simmer 1 hour and 30 minutes.

Add the vegetables and continue cooking about 45 minutes until tender. Salt to taste.

In a small bowl mix the flour and water and stir into the stew until thickened.

Makes 6 servings.

◆ BARBECUED SPARERIBS

5 tablespoons sugar	1 teaspoon salt
3 tablespoons honey	1 cup hot chicken broth
3 tablespoons soy sauce	4 pounds spareribs
2 tablespoons catsup	

In a medium bowl mix all the ingredients except the ribs, pour over the ribs, and marinate for 2 hours.

Bake at 300° for 2 to 3 hours, basting every 30 minutes.

Makes 6 servings.

> I remember the leg of Welsh mutton and the turnips on the table that day had the finest flavor imaginable.
> *William Hazlitt, 1823*

◆ SHEPHERD'S PIE

2 to 3 cups cubed cooked lamb or
    beef
1 10-ounce package frozen peas
1 10¾-ounce can cream of mushroom
    soup, undiluted
½ teaspoon salt
⅛ teaspoon black pepper
1 small onion, chopped
1 teaspoon Worcestershire sauce

2 cups prepared mashed potatoes
    (one 4-serving recipe of instant
    mashed potatoes, or 2 medium
    potatoes cooked and mashed
    with ¼ cup milk and 2 table-
    spoons butter)
½ cup grated Parmesan cheese
    Paprika

Grease a 2-quart casserole dish. In the dish layer the meat and peas evenly.

In a medium bowl mix the soup, salt, pepper, onion, and Worcestershire sauce and spread over the peas. Spread the mashed potatoes over the top. Sprinkle with Parmesan cheese and paprika. Bake at 375° for 45 to 60 minutes until light golden brown and bubbly.

Makes 4 servings.

◆ QUICK VEGETABLE DRESSING

1 cup mayonnaise

2 tablespoons prepared spicy mustard

Mix and pour over vegetables, hot or cold.

◆ GREEN BEAN-CELERY SOUP CASSEROLE

One of the all-time greats: No home should ever be without the possibility of it.

2 14½-ounce cans green beans,
    drained
2 2.8-ounce cans French-fried onion
    rings

1 10¾-ounce can cream of celery
    soup, undiluted

In a casserole place the green beans and mix in one can of onion rings. Pour the soup over the top. Bake at 350° for 30 minutes.

Pour the second can of onions over the top and bake for 5 minutes more.

Makes 6 to 8 servings.

◆ CHEESE-NOODLE CASSEROLE

4 ounces egg noodles, uncooked	⅛ teaspoon garlic powder
1 cup sour cream	Salt and pepper to taste
1 cup cottage cheese	Parmesan cheese, grated
1 egg, lightly beaten	Chopped chives
1 small onion, finely chopped	Extra sour cream
1 teaspoon Worcestershire sauce	

Grease a 1½-quart baking dish or ring mold and set aside.

In a pot cook and drain the noodles according to the directions on the package.

In a large bowl combine the noodles, sour cream, cottage cheese, egg, onion, Worcestershire sauce, and seasonings. Pour into the prepared dish or ring mold. Sprinkle with Parmesan cheese and bake at 325° for 1 hour.

Sprinkle with chives and additional Parmesan cheese before serving and top with extra sour cream.

Makes 6 servings.

◆ BARLEY CASSEROLE

You may never have to hike to freedom over snow-covered mountains in the moonlight. But if you do, this barley casserole will see you through.

¼ cup butter	3 pimientos, coarsely chopped and drained
1½ cups pearl barley, uncooked	2 cups chicken broth
2 medium onions, chopped	1 teaspoon salt
¾ pound mushrooms, trimmed and thinly sliced	⅛ teaspoon white pepper

Grease a 2-quart casserole dish and set aside.

In a saucepan melt the butter. Add the barley, stir, and cook until the barley begins to brown. Add the onions and mushrooms and sauté over low heat until the vegetables are tender. Transfer the mixture to the prepared casserole dish. Add the pimientos, broth, salt, and pepper. Cover and bake at 350° for 50 to 60 minutes or until the barley is tender and all liquid is absorbed.

Makes 6 servings.

◆ CHEDDAR-LENTIL LOAF

Lentils play a powerful role in human history. When Esau sold his birthright to his brother Jacob, it was for a porridge of red ones. This lentil loaf is especially easy because you throw everything in a food processor. For lunch the next day, you can eat the leftovers on toast with mustard and ripe olives.

½ pound sharp Cheddar cheese, cubed
2 cups lentils, cooked or canned and drained
½ small onion
½ teaspoon salt

Freshly ground black pepper
¼ teaspoon dried thyme
1 cup soft breadcrumbs, firmly packed
1 egg, slightly beaten
1 tablespoon butter, softened

Grease a 9 x 5-inch loaf pan and set aside.

In a food processor combine the Cheddar cheese, lentils, and onion and process until coarsely ground. Add the salt, pepper, and thyme and process 5 seconds. Add the breadcrumbs, egg, and butter and process 10 seconds more. Press into the prepared pan and bake at 350° for 45 minutes.

Serve with tomato or mustard sauce.

Makes 5 servings.

◆ HOT FRUIT COMPOTE

Maybe this is fruit; maybe it's dessert. Whatever it is, it's one of the original comfort foods. Fix it on a really cold night. You'll make someone very, very happy.

1 1-pound can peaches, drained
1 1-pound can apricots, drained
1 1-pound or 16-ounce can black cherries with juice
1 cup firmly packed brown sugar
Juice and grated rind of 1 lemon
Juice and grated rind of 1 orange

TOPPINGS:
1 8-ounce carton sour cream mixed with 2 tablespoons firmly packed brown sugar or 1 cup whipped topping, thawed, mixed with 1 tablespoon Cointreau liqueur

In a 2-quart casserole dish combine the peaches, apricots, cherries, brown sugar, lemon juice and rind, and orange juice and rind, and mix well. Bake uncovered at 350° for 45 minutes.

Serve topped with sour cream flavored with brown sugar or whipped cream flavored with Cointreau.

Makes 8 servings.

◆ BAKED APRICOTS

2   15-ounce cans apricot halves,
      drained
1   8-ounce box Ritz crackers, crushed

½   cup firmly packed brown sugar
½   cup butter, cut in bits

Fill a large buttered baking dish with alternate layers of apricots, cracker crumbs, brown sugar, and butter. Bake covered at 350° for 30 minutes.
   Uncover and bake for 30 minutes more.
   Makes 10 servings.

◆ PINEAPPLE SALAD

1   17- or 20-ounce can crushed pineap-
      ple with juice
2   3-ounce packages orange-flavored
      gelatin

2   cups buttermilk
1   8-ounce carton whipped topping,
      thawed

In a saucepan heat the pineapple and juice. Dissolve the gelatin in the hot liquid. Cool 30 minutes and add the buttermilk. Mix well. Fold in the whipped topping. Chill overnight in a glass bowl.
   Makes 8 to 10 servings.

◆ PINEAPPLE-LEMON MOLD

1   3-ounce package lemon-flavored
      gelatin
1   cup boiling water
¾   cup pineapple juice
1   tablespoon lemon juice

¼   cup crushed pineapple, drained
1   cup shredded sharp Cheddar
      cheese
1½   cups whipped topping, thawed

Grease a 1½-quart mold and set aside.
   In a large bowl dissolve the gelatin in the boiling water. Add the pineapple and lemon juice and chill until the mixture is the consistency of uncooked egg whites.
   Fold the in pineapple, Cheddar cheese, and whipped topping. Pour into the prepared mold. Chill until firm.
   Makes 6 to 8 servings.

◆ APPLE-PECAN COBBLER

Snowed in again? Tired of bought cookies? Bake a cobbler—canned fruit, nuts, sugar, a flour crust. Since most of the ingredients can sit in your cupboard indefinitely, you're never more than minutes away from one.

1	21-ounce can apple pie filling	1	tablespoon sugar
¼	cup chopped pecans	¼	teaspoon ground cinnamon
½	cup biscuit mix		Dash grated nutmeg
1	tablespoon firmly packed brown sugar		Vanilla ice cream or whipped topping, thawed
3	tablespoons buttermilk		

Grease a 1½-quart casserole dish. In the dish combine the pie filling and pecans.

In a large bowl combine the biscuit mix and brown sugar. Stir in the buttermilk, mixing well. Drop biscuit dough in 6 spoonfuls onto the pie filling. In a small bowl combine the sugar, cinnamon, and nutmeg and sprinkle over the cobbler. Bake at 400° for 30 minutes.

Serve with vanilla ice cream or whipped topping.

Makes 4 servings.

◆ THREE-MINUTE COBBLER

½	cup butter	¾	cup milk
1	cup all-purpose flour	¼	teaspoon salt
1	cup sugar	1	16-ounce can fruit pie filling, any kind
2	teaspoons baking powder		

In a small casserole melt the butter. Stir in the flour, sugar, baking powder, milk, and salt until smooth. Pour the fruit on top but don't stir. Bake at 350° for 1 hour.

Makes 6 to 8 servings.

◆ PEACH COBBLER

1 29-ounce can peaches in heavy syrup	1 cup biscuit mix
¼ teaspoon ground nutmeg	1 tablespoon butter
¼ teaspoon ground cinnamon	Whipped topping, thawed

Grease a 10 x 6 x 2-inch pan and set aside. Drain ¼ cup syrup from peaches and reserve. Empty peaches with the remaining syrup into the prepared pan. Sprinkle with the nutmeg and cinnamon.

In a medium bowl combine the biscuit mix, reserved syrup, and butter, stirring with a fork until blended. Drop by spoonfuls over the peaches in 6 equal portions. Bake at 425° 20 to 25 minutes. Serve with whipped topping.

Makes 6 servings.

◆ PUDDING CAKE

Pudding cake speaks to the eternal mystery of transfiguration. No one will know how you do it. No one will stop eating long enough to ask.

1 cup all-purpose flour	2 tablespoons vegetable oil
¾ cup sugar	1 cup finely chopped walnuts or pecans
¼ cup plus 2 tablespoons cocoa, divided	1 cup firmly packed brown sugar
2 teaspoons baking powder	1¾ cups hot water
¼ teaspoon salt	Whipped topping, thawed
½ cup milk	

Grease and flour an 8-inch square cake pan and set aside.

In a large bowl combine the flour, sugar, 2 tablespoons cocoa, baking powder, salt, milk, oil, and nuts. Beat vigorously until well blended. Pour into the prepared cake pan.

In the same bowl mix the brown sugar, ¼ cup cocoa, and hot water. Pour slowly over the batter in the pan. Bake at 350° for 45 minutes. The pudding will become thick and rich and sink to the bottom of the pan.

Cool in pan on a wire rack. Serve with whipped topping.

Makes 6 to 8 servings.

◆ APPLE PIE

On those occasions when you really need to cheer someone up—especially when it's you—apple pie is the way to go. It's far more than fruit and crust. It's a promise from days gone by of better days to come.

¾ cup sugar
1 tablespoon all-purpose flour
1 teaspoon ground cinnamon
¼ teaspoon ground nutmeg
1 quart peeled and sliced tart apples

1 9-inch prepared pastry shell, plus 1 extra pie crust
1 tablespoon butter
   Additional sugar

In a large bowl combine the sugar, flour, cinnamon, and nutmeg until well blended. Stir in the apples. Pour the mixture into the prepared pie crust. Dot with butter. Cover with the extra pie crust, cutting slits in a star pattern to allow for escaping steam. Sprinkle the top with sugar. Bake at 350° for 40 minutes.

Cool on a wire rack.

Makes 6 to 8 servings.

◆ HOT CHOCOLATE

A cold wind outside, a warm heart—hot chocolate. It's a cardinal rule of winter.

2 1-ounce squares unsweetened chocolate
¼ cup sugar

   Dash salt
1 cup water
4 cups milk

In a saucepan combine the chocolate, sugar, salt, and water. Stir over low heat until chocolate melts. Gradually stir in the milk and heat slowly just to boiling. Beat with a rotary beater until frothy.

Makes 5 servings.

◆ MEXICAN CHOCOLATE

4 cups milk
5 1-ounce squares semisweet chocolate

2 2-inch sticks cinnamon
1 teaspoon vanilla extract

In a saucepan combine the milk, chocolate, and cinnamon. Cook over low heat, stirring, just until chocolate melts. Remove from the heat. Discard the cinnamon sticks and stir in the vanilla. Beat with a rotary beater until frothy.
   Makes 4 servings.

◆ HOT BUTTERED RUM

Say you're on a ski weekend in a mountain lodge with nine old friends who won't stop talking and let you go to sleep. Get up and fix them some hot buttered rum. You'll all sleep like babies.

1 quart water
3 Constant Comment tea bags
2 cups apple cider or apple juice

¾ cup firmly packed light brown sugar
1½ cups golden rum
5 teaspoons butter

In a large saucepan bring the water to a boil. Add the tea bags, cover, and let steep 5 minutes. Remove the tea bags and stir in the apple cider, sugar, and rum. Heat to steaming. Ladle into mugs and drop ½ teaspoon butter on top of each.
   Makes 10 servings.

◆ HOT APPLE CIDER

1 quart apple cider
1 teaspoon whole cloves

2 sticks cinnamon

In a pot combine all the ingredients. Heat well, cover, and let steep 30 minutes. Do not boil. Serve hot.
   Makes 4 servings.

HOLIDAYS

I drink to the general joy of the whole table.
William Shakespeare, 1610

You might as well not celebrate the holidays if you're going to mess with the food. Every family has its ghosts of holidays past: the fateful Thanksgiving Uncle Colonel put vodka in the pumpkin soup; the dismal Christmas Eve your children converted to vegetarianism; Easter without lamb; Fourth of July without hot dogs. The horror, the horror. The simple truth is holidays are food and people should get what they want.

Half the fun of getting together with friends and relatives two or three times a year is the anticipation. The other half is the eating: roast turkey with corn bread stuffing, scalloped oysters, candied sweet potatoes with marshmallow crème, cranberry relish, mandarin orange salad, pumpkin pie, coconut cake It's simple. It's steady. It works.

Tradition is all a matter of cheating time. The maple mousse your mother made is now your own, and someone else will remember your hands folding in the egg whites. Sour cream potatoes, herbed onion bread, chicken in rum-raisin sauce, oyster stew, whiskey cake, eggnog, hot mulled wine—they're all more than something to eat. What they do is link us together through space, through time. For one day at least, one holiday, everything old really is new again.

◆ VEGETABLE DIP

When your life is one big house party of family and friends and you need some way to get them out from under your feet so you can get the meals on the table, try dips. Chop up a big plate of vegetables. Boil up a big pile of shrimp. Set out a couple of jig-saw puzzles on the card tables. And leave them to it.

1½ cups mayonnaise	1 teaspoon prepared mustard
2 hard-cooked eggs, finely grated	Dash garlic salt
1 small onion, finely chopped	Tabasco sauce to taste
1 teaspoon Worcestershire sauce	½ cup sour cream

In a medium bowl combine all the ingredients and chill for 2 to 3 hours.
    Serve with fresh vegetables.
    Makes 2½ cups.

> Happy families are all alike; every unhappy family
> is unhappy in its own way.
> Leo Tolstoi, 1875

◆ CHILI SAUCE DIP

1 cup mayonnaise	1 teaspoon dry mustard
⅓ cup minced onion	1 teaspoon white pepper
¼ cup catsup	Dash paprika
¼ cup chili sauce	Dash Tabasco sauce
2 cloves garlic, minced	

In a medium bowl combine all the ingredients and chill for 2 to 3 hours.
    Serve with boiled shrimp or fresh vegetables.
    Makes 2 cups.

◆ TOASTED ONION-HERB BREAD

Pass a plate of this out to the vegetable-shrimp-dip crowd and you'll have the kitchen all to yourself.

1   clove garlic, minced
½   cup butter
1   14-ounce loaf French bread,
        unsliced

¼   teaspoon celery seed
½   teaspoon dried Italian seasoning
½   teaspoon instant minced onion

In a skillet sauté the garlic in the butter until translucent, not brown.

Cut the bread into 1-inch slices and place on a baking sheet. Brush the slices with the butter-garlic mixture and sprinkle with the celery seed, Italian seasoning, and onion. Cover with foil and bake at 400° for 10 to 15 minutes.

Makes 6 servings.

> One of those no-neck monsters hit me with a hot buttered biscuit!
> *Tennessee Williams, 1955*

◆ CREAM BISCUITS

Cream biscuits are like angel biscuits but softer. The dough is easy to handle and you can leave it in the fridge until you need it. Use a sharp-edged biscuit or cookie cutter so as not to mash the edges.

1   ¼-ounce package active dry yeast
2   tablespoons very warm water
4   cups all-purpose flour

1½   teaspoons salt
1   tablespoon baking powder
1   pint whipping cream

In a small bowl dissolve the yeast in the warm water.

In a large bowl sift the flour, salt, and baking powder.

In a mixing bowl combine the cream and yeast. Add the dry ingredients and mix well. Cover and store in the refrigerator until needed. Roll out the dough on a floured surface, kneading in more flour if necessary. Cut into biscuits and place on an ungreased baking sheet. Brush the tops with butter and let stand 1 hour.

Bake the biscuits at 450° for 12 to 15 minutes.

Makes 60 biscuits.

◆ EGGNOG BREAD

This sweet bread is so full of fruit you can serve it for breakfast.

2	eggs, beaten	1	teaspoon salt
¾	cup sugar	1	cup commercial eggnog
¼	cup butter, melted	½	cup candied cherries
2¼	cups all-purpose flour	½	cup golden raisins
2	teaspoons baking powder	½	cup chopped pecans

Grease and flour a 9 x 5-inch loaf pan and set aside.

In a large bowl combine the eggs, sugar, and butter. In a separate bowl combine the flour, baking powder, and salt. Add the flour mixture alternately with the eggnog, beginning and ending with the flour. Stir in the cherries, raisins, and pecans. Pour the batter into the prepared loaf pan. Bake at 350° for 1 hour and 10 minutes or until a wooden pick inserted in the center comes out clean.

Cool in the pan for 10 minutes. Remove to a wire rack and cool completely before slicing.

Makes 1 loaf or serves 10.

◆ OYSTER STEW

Holidays begin in some homes with oyster stew. Serve this as a prechurch snack if you're going to early services or as a light supper after midnight.

1	cup milk	½	teaspoon salt
1	cup heavy cream	⅛	teaspoon white pepper
1	pint oysters with juice		Dash Tabasco sauce
¼	cup butter		

In a small saucepan scald the milk and cream.

In a separate saucepan heat the oysters in own juice until edges curl. Add the butter, salt, pepper, and Tabasco sauce. Add the milk and cream and cook 1 minute. Serve at once.

Makes 4 servings.

◆ PLUM SOUP

You could serve plum soup at Christmas for the color alone.

3½ cups ripe plums, peeled, pitted, and
      diced
1¾ cups apple juice
1   cup water

1   3-inch stick cinnamon
½   teaspoon vanilla extract
¼   teaspoon ground allspice
     Heavy cream

In a medium saucepan combine the plums, apple juice, water, and cinnamon. Bring to a boil, reduce heat, and simmer covered for 30 minutes.

Remove from the heat and stir in the vanilla and allspice. Discard the cinnamon stick.

Into a blender or food processor pour half the mixture and process until smooth. Repeat with the remainder. Chill and serve cold with a drizzle of heavy cream in the center.

Makes 4½ cups or serves 6.

But angry people are not always wise; and in seeing him at last look somewhat nettled, she had all the success she expected.

Jane Austen, 1813

◆ ROQUEFORT VICHYSSOISE

2   cups finely chopped onion
¼   cup butter
4   cups chicken broth
2   cups peeled and diced potatoes
¼   teaspoon salt
⅛   teaspoon white pepper

6   ounces Roquefort cheese, crumbled
      and divided
½   cup dry white wine
2   cups buttermilk
2   tablespoons minced fresh parsley

In a large Dutch oven sauté the onion in the butter until translucent, not brown. Stir in the broth, potatoes, salt, and pepper and bring to a boil. Reduce the heat and simmer uncovered 15 minutes or until the potatoes are tender.

Into a blender or food processor spoon half the potato mixture and process until smooth. Repeat with the remainder. Return to the Dutch oven. Add 4 ounces of Roquefort cheese and the wine and cook over low heat, stirring constantly until the Roquefort cheese melts, about 5 minutes. Cool. Cover and refrigerate for 4 hours.

Stir in the buttermilk. Serve with the remaining Roquefort cheese and parsley on top.

Makes 8 to 10 servings.

◆ CRANBERRY RELISH

2 medium cooking apples, chopped	4 cups fresh or frozen cranberries
½ cup dark raisins	¼ cup firmly packed light brown sugar
1 6-ounce can frozen apple juice con-centrate, thawed	

In a heavy saucepan combine all the ingredients and bring to a boil over medium heat. Reduce the heat and simmer covered 15 minutes, stirring occasionally. Chill before serving.

Makes 4 cups.

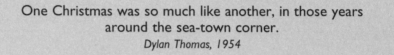

One Christmas was so much like another, in those years
around the sea-town corner.
Dylan Thomas, 1954

◆ ROAST STUFFED TURKEY

You can get out of roasting the turkey for years, but sooner or later it's going to catch up with you. Be gracious, take courage, and follow these simple directions. After about the second hour, your house will smell like heaven. A word of warning: Turkey meat left on the bone overnight will breed salmonella. Strip the carcass immediately after dinner, freeze the bones for soup stock, and store the leftover meat in a separate container.

Wash the thawed turkey and rub outside with vegetable oil. Fill the cavity three-fourths full of stuffing. Ten cups of stuffing will fill a ten-pound turkey. Place the stuffed turkey on a rack in a roasting pan. Do not cover. Place in an oven which has been preheated to 450° and immediately reduce the heat to 350° and roast for 20 to 25 minutes per pound for a small bird. For a larger bird—18 to 25 pounds—allow 13 to 15 minutes per pound.

If you do not wish to stuff the bird, place a quartered onion and several pieces of cut celery in the cavity during roasting. Baste the turkey frequently with the juices after the first 30 minutes of cooking. Allow 1 pound of turkey per serving.

One never knows when the blow may fall.
Graham Greene, 1949

◆ BASIC BREADCRUMB DRESSING FOR TURKEY

You can stuff a turkey with just about anything—oysters, sausage, mushrooms, chestnuts, corn bread, celery, onion. Allow 1 cup of dressing for every pound of bird. Sprinkle the body cavity with salt and stuff lightly. Dressing baked in the bird's cavity soaks up fats and juices during cooking—great news for taste but a singularly dangerous invitation to salmonella. Never leave the dressing inside a bird overnight. Remove it from the cavity immediately after dinner and store in a separate container.

You may prefer to bake the dressing separately in a greased 9 x 13 x 2-inch pan uncovered at 400° for 20 minutes. Or you can form it into patties and bake it on a greased baking sheet.

FOR A TEN-POUND TURKEY:

2 small onions, chopped	1 teaspoon salt
2 stalks celery with leaves, chopped	Freshly ground black pepper
1 cup butter	1/4 cup chopped fresh parsley
1 tablespoon poultry seasoning or ground sage	10 cups stale bread cubes or crumbs
	Turkey broth to moisten

In a skillet sauté the onion and celery in the butter until tender, not brown. In a large bowl combine the seasonings and bread and toss together with the onion mixture. Add additional turkey broth to barely moisten.

Variations: *Mushroom Dressing.* In a skillet sauté 1 pound of mushrooms, brushed and thinly sliced, with the onion and celery.

Corn Bread Dressing. Substitute corn bread crumbs for all or part of the bread-crumbs. Ham or bacon drippings may be used for part of the butter.

Sausage Dressing. In a skillet brown 8 to 12 ounces of bulk sausage. Remove the sausage and sauté the onion and celery in the drippings. Add to the crumbs and proceed with the recipe.

◆ OYSTER-MUSHROOM DRESSING

2 cups breadcrumbs	2 teaspoons salt
3/4 cup chopped celery leaves	1/8 teaspoon paprika
3 tablespoons diced bacon	1 tablespoon Worcestershire sauce
1 quart oysters, coarsely chopped	Turkey broth to moisten
1/4 pound mushroom caps, halved and sautéed in butter	

In a large bowl mix the ingredients by tossing lightly with a fork. Pack loosely in the cavity of the bird and truss the legs. Or, the dressing may be baked separately in a greased 9 x 13 x 2-inch pan uncovered at 400° for 20 minutes.

◆ TURKEY-ALMOND CASSEROLE

After the holiday dinner, after the days and nights of cold turkey sandwiches, you're still going to have some meat left. This is one of the special pleasures of holiday cooking: turkey casserole, turkey hash, turkey salad. There are many people counting the days until the end of the year who much prefer leftover turkey to the first cut.

½ cup slivered almonds	2 cups cooked rice
2 tablespoons butter	1 cup half-and-half
2 cups chopped cooked turkey	½ teaspoon salt
1 10¾-ounce can cream of mushroom soup, undiluted	¼ cup dry white wine
	1 cup buttered breadcrumbs

Grease a 1½-quart casserole dish and set aside. In a skillet brown the almonds in butter. Combine the turkey, soup, rice, half-and-half, salt, and wine and place in the prepared casserole dish. Top with the crumbs and bake at 350° for 45 minutes.

Makes 4 servings.

◆ CHICKEN IN RUM-RAISIN SAUCE

3 tablespoons dark raisins	½ cup heavy cream
3 tablespoons dark rum	1 tablespoon sliced almonds, toasted
3 pounds chicken pieces	Fresh parsley, chopped
Salt and pepper to taste	

In a small bowl soak the raisins in the rum for 30 minutes.

Arrange the chicken skin-side up in a 9 x 13 x 2-inch baking pan. Season with salt and pepper to taste. Bake uncovered at 450° for 20 minutes or until the chicken begins to turn brown.

Add the heavy cream. Continue baking, basting with sauce, about 20 minutes more until the chicken is tender and juices run clear.

Stir in the rum-raisin mixture. Arrange the chicken on a warm platter. Spoon the sauce over chicken and sprinkle with toasted almonds and fresh parsley.

Makes 4 servings.

◆ APRICOT CHICKEN

3 or 4 pounds chicken pieces,
    skinned
1 8-ounce bottle French dressing

1 1-ounce package onion soup mix
1 10-ounce jar apricot preserves
¼ cup dry sherry

Grease a baking dish and place the chicken in it. In a large bowl combine the dressing, soup, preserves, and sherry, pour over chicken, and marinate 2 hours in the refrigerator.

Bake at 350° for 1 hour.

Serve over rice or noodles.

Makes 4 to 6 servings.

> I like to be particular in dates,
> Not only of the age, and year, but moon;
> They are a sort of post house, where the Fates
> Change horses.
> George Gordon, Lord Byron, 1819

◆ BAKED HAM

In some families turkey on the table means Thanksgiving; ham means Christmas. You can glaze it, slice it, stuff it, then make sandwiches, salads, and pâtés. Always buy more than you think you'll need to begin with.

Choose a fully cooked whole or half ham or a canned ham. Score the ham, inserting whole cloves in the corners. Bake uncovered. Glaze during the final 15 to 20 minutes.

TIMETABLE FOR BAKED HAM:
Fully Cooked Whole Ham
10 to 14 pounds
325°
10 to 15 minutes per pound

Fully Cooked Half Ham
5 to 7 pounds
325°
18 to 24 minutes per pound

Picnic Shoulder
5 to 8 pounds
325°
25 to 30 minutes per pound

Canned Ham
4 to 5 pounds
325°
18 to 24 minutes per pound

Glazes: *Brown Sugar.* Combine 1 cup firmly packed dark brown sugar with 2 tablespoons all-purpose flour, ½ teaspoon dry mustard, ⅛ teaspoon ground cinnamon, and 3 tablespoons dry sherry. Mix well and spread on the ham.

Jelly. Melt 1 cup currant or apple jelly and spread on the ham.

Orange Marmalade. Melt 1 cup orange marmalade and spread on the ham.

Pineapple. Combine 1 cup firmly packed dark brown sugar with ¼ teaspoon ground cloves and ¾ cup crushed pineapple, drained. Spread on the ham.

◆ SCALLOPED OYSTERS

⅔ cup firmly packed soft breadcrumbs
1   cup Ritz cracker crumbs
½ cup butter, melted
1½ pints oysters, drained with liquor
     reserved

¾ teaspoon salt
    Freshly ground black pepper
2   tablespoons chopped fresh parsley
½ teaspoon Worcestershire sauce
3   tablespoons heavy cream

Grease a 1-quart casserole dish and set aside.

In a large bowl mix the breadcrumbs, cracker crumbs, and butter. Place half the crumb mixture in the prepared casserole dish. Add half the oysters and sprinkle with half the salt, pepper, and parsley. Add the remaining oysters and sprinkle with the remaining salt, pepper, and parsley. Mix ⅓ cup of oyster liquor with the Worcestershire sauce and cream and pour over the oysters. Top with the remaining crumb mixture. Bake at 350° for 45 minutes or until puffy and brown.

Makes 4 servings.

◆ SWEET POTATO-CRANBERRY CASSEROLE

1   16- or 20-ounce can sweet potatoes,
     drained
½ cup firmly packed dark brown
     sugar
2   tablespoons butter
1   cup fresh cranberries
½ cup orange juice

WALNUT TOPPING:
½ cup chopped walnuts
2   tablespoons butter, melted
1   tablespoon firmly packed brown
     sugar
½ teaspoon ground cinnamon

Grease a 1½-quart casserole dish. Arrange half the potatoes in the dish. Sprinkle with ¼ cup brown sugar. Dot with butter. Sprinkle with ½ cup cranberries. Repeat the layers. Pour the orange juice over all. Cover and bake at 350° for 45 minutes.

Uncover, spread with the walnut topping. Bake 10 minutes more.

Makes 6 to 8 servings.

◆ CANDIED SWEET POTATOES

¾ cup firmly packed dark brown
    sugar
1 teaspoon salt
1 1-pound 13-ounce can sweet pota-
    toes, drained and sliced

¼ cup butter
½ cup miniature marshmallows or
    marshmallow crème

Grease a 1½-quart casserole dish and set aside. In a medium bowl mix the sugar and salt. Place one layer of potatoes in the bottom of the prepared casserole dish. Sprinkle with half the sugar mixture and dot with butter. Repeat the layers. Bake uncovered at 375° for 30 minutes or until glazed.

Top with the marshmallows for last 5 minutes.

Makes 6 servings.

◆ SOUR CREAM POTATOES

Baked potatoes are not generally considered holiday fare. Potatoes scalloped with sour cream, however, are.

6 medium waxy potatoes
1 cup breadcrumbs
1¼ cups milk, divided
1 8-ounce carton sour cream

3 eggs, hard-cooked and sliced
Salt and pepper to taste
Butter

Boil the potatoes in their jackets until tender. Slice. Grease a 1 ½-quart casserole and cover the bottom with the breadcrumbs.

In a medium bowl mix ¼ cup milk with the sour cream. Layer half the potatoes and eggs in the prepared casserole dish and season with salt and pepper. Cover with half the sour cream mixture. Repeat the layers. Top with breadcrumbs and dot with butter. Pour 1 cup milk around the sides of the casserole dish. Bake at 350° for 1 hour.

Makes 6 servings.

◆ STUFFED PEARS

3 ripe pears, peeled, cored, and
    halved
2 teaspoons lemon juice
1 3-ounce package cream cheese,
    softened
3 tablespoons heavy cream

¼ teaspoon dried tarragon
½ cup sliced celery
½ cup pitted and chopped dates
    Lettuce leaves
½ cup chopped walnuts

Sprinkle the pear halves with the lemon juice.

In a medium bowl combine the cream cheese, heavy cream, and tarragon. Stir in the celery and dates. Spoon one sixth of the mixture on each pear half. Arrange on lettuce leaf and sprinkle with nuts. Cover and chill 1 to 2 hours.

Makes 6 servings.

◆ CAN OPENER AMBROSIA

1 16-ounce can fruit cocktail, drained
1 11-ounce can mandarin oranges,
    drained
1 16-ounce can pear halves, drained
    and chopped

1 10-ounce jar maraschino cherries,
    drained and chopped
1 3½-ounce can flaked coconut
1 8-ounce carton whipped topping,
    thawed

In a large bowl combine the fruit and coconut and toss well. Fold in the whipped topping. Cover and chill for 2 to 3 hours.

Makes 8 servings.

◆ PUMPKIN CHEESECAKE

You can start making pumpkin cheesecake at Halloween. No one will complain.

1 10-inch prepared graham cracker crust (recipe follows)	1 tablespoon pumpkin pie spice Sour cream topping (recipe follows)
4 8-ounce packages cream cheese, softened	
1½ cups sugar	**SOUR CREAM TOPPING:**
3 eggs	2 8-ounce cartons sour cream
1 cup whipping cream	½ cup sugar
2 15-ounce cans pumpkin, drained	2 teaspoons vanilla extract
2 teaspoons vanilla extract	

Line a springform pan with graham cracker crust and set aside.

In a large bowl with an electric mixer blend the cream cheese with the sugar until smooth. Add the eggs one at a time, beating well after each addition. Add the whipping cream, pumpkin, vanilla, and spice, blending thoroughly. Pour into the prepared springform pan. Bake at 300° for 1 hour and 30 minutes or until set. Remove and let stand 10 minutes.

Smooth sour cream topping over top. Cool thoroughly before removing sides of springform pan. Chill.

Makes 16 servings.

◆ GRAHAM CRACKER CRUST

1 teaspoon butter, softened	¼ cup sugar
1¼ cups graham cracker crumbs	¼ cup butter, melted
1 teaspoon ground cinnamon	

Brush a 10-inch springform pan with soft butter. In a medium bowl mix the graham crumbs, cinnamon, sugar, and melted butter. Press onto the bottom of the pan.

◆ EASY PUMPKIN PIE

1	3¾-ounce package instant vanilla pudding mix
½	cup milk
1	15-ounce can pumpkin, drained

¾	teaspoon pumpkin pie spice
1	9-inch prepared pastry shell, baked
	Whipped topping, thawed

In a large bowl combine the pudding mix, milk, pumpkin, and spice and beat well. Pour into a cooked pastry shell and chill for 2 to 3 hours. Top with the whipped topping.

Makes 6 to 8 servings.

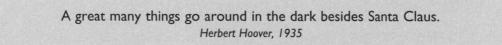

A great many things go around in the dark besides Santa Claus.
Herbert Hoover, 1935

◆ PUMPKIN CAKE

You can also make cakes out of pumpkin—really good cakes—but cooking the jack-o'-lantern on All Saints' Day doesn't work all that well. Ornamental pumpkins tend to be stringy, and field pumpkins are so big you'd have to hire a hoist to get one in your kitchen. Buy canned pumpkin, instead, and drain off the liquid. It's much easier and you'll never know the difference.

3	cups sugar
3	cups all-purpose flour
1	tablespoon baking powder
1	tablespoon baking soda
1	tablespoon ground cinnamon
¾	teaspoon salt
1½	cups vegetable oil
3¼	cups canned pumpkin, drained
4	eggs, lightly beaten

CREAM CHEESE ICING:

1	1-pound box confectioners' sugar
1	8-ounce package cream cheese, softened
½	cup butter, softened
2	teaspoons vanilla extract
½	cup chopped dark raisins

Grease and flour three 9-inch cake pans and set aside.

In the large bowl of an electric mixer combine the sugar, flour, baking powder, soda, cinnamon, and salt. Add the oil and beat until moistened. Add the pumpkin and beat until well blended. Add the eggs and beat 1 minute more. Do not overbeat. Pour the batter into the prepared cake pans, smoothing the tops with a spatula. Bake at 325° for 40 minutes. Cool thoroughly in pans on wire racks.

For the icing, in a large bowl combine the sugar, cream cheese, butter, and vanilla. Mix until smooth. Add the raisins. Turn the cakes out, fill, and ice as a 3-layer cake.

Makes 16 servings.

◆ COCONUT CAKE

1   18¼-ounce box yellow or white
    cake mix
2   tablespoons vegetable oil

COCONUT ICING:
3   6-ounce packages frozen coconut
1   8-ounce carton sour cream
1½ cups confectioners' sugar

In a large bowl prepare the cake following the directions on the box, adding 2 table-spoons oil. When the cake is done and cooled, mix all the ingredients for the icing and spread. Store in refrigerator.

Makes 16 servings.

◆ BOURBON CAKE

Before legalized liquor, everyone had a bootlegger who brought the whiskey into town for the Christmas cakes. You could hear him coming blocks away in a souped-up wreck of a car with enormously powerful springs on the back axle designed to normalize the weight of the liquor in the trunk. By the time he'd finished his deliveries, his car was jacked up in back like a fighting grasshopper. The state troopers knew who he was, of course, but they all had cakes of their own to soak, and besides, it was Christmas. Now, you just go down to the liquor store and hand over your credit card—not nearly as colorful, but the cakes taste the same.

2   cups whole red candied cherries
1½   cups dark raisins
2   cups bourbon
1½   cups butter
2⅓   cups sugar
2⅓   cups firmly packed light brown
       sugar

6   eggs, separated
5   cups all-purpose flour, divided
2   teaspoons ground nutmeg
1   teaspoon baking powder
4   cups chopped pecans

In a large bowl combine the cherries, raisins, and bourbon. Cover and let stand overnight at room temperature.

Drain the fruits and reserve the bourbon. Grease and flour a 10-inch stem pan and set aside.

In a large bowl cream the butter and sugars together, add the egg yolks, and beat well.

In a separate bowl combine ½ cup flour, the nutmeg, baking powder and the pecans and set aside. Add the remaining flour and bourbon alternately to the butter mixture, beating well.

In a separate bowl beat the egg whites until stiff and fold into the batter. Fold the fruits and pecan-flour mixture into the batter. Pour into the prepared stem pan and bake at 275° for 3 hours and 30 minutes.

Cool and remove from the pan. Fill the center hole with cheesecloth soaked in the bourbon. Wrap in heavy foil and store at room temperature in a tightly covered container for at least one week before serving.

Makes 16 servings.

◆ SOUR CREAM POUND CAKE

This is the only pound cake recipe you'll ever need.

1¼ cups butter, softened
3 cups sugar
6 eggs
3 cups all-purpose flour

¼ teaspoon baking soda
1 8-ounce carton sour cream
1 teaspoon vanilla extract
1 teaspoon almond extract (optional)

Grease and flour a 10-inch stem or Bundt pan and and set aside.

In a large bowl cream the butter and sugar until light and fluffy. Add the eggs one at a time, beating well after each addition. In a separate bowl combine the flour and soda and add alternately with the sour cream. Add the vanilla. Pour into the prepared pan and bake at 325° for 1 hour and 30 minutes.

Let cool in the pan 10 minutes before removing.

Makes 15 servings.

◆ RUM CAKE

1 cup chopped pecans
1 18¼-ounce package yellow cake
    mix
1 3¾-ounce package instant vanilla
    pudding mix
½ cup water
½ cup vegetable oil
½ cup white rum
4 eggs

GLAZE:
1 cup sugar
¼ cup water
½ cup butter
3 ounces white rum

Grease and flour a 10-inch stem pan, sprinkle nuts over the bottom, and set aside.

In a large bowl mix well all the cake ingredients except the eggs. Add the eggs one at a time, beating well after each addition. Pour the batter over the nuts in the prepared pan. Bake at 325° for 1 hour.

Ten minutes before the cake is done, in a saucepan combine the sugar, ¼ cup water, and butter, and heat to boiling. Boil 1 minute, remove from heat, and stir in the rum. Pour the glaze over the cake as soon as it comes out of the oven. Allow the cake to absorb the glaze and repeat until all the glaze is absorbed. Remove the cake from the pan while still warm.

Makes 16 servings.

◆ MAPLE MOUSSE

2 ¼-ounce envelopes unflavored
   gelatin
½ cup cold water
1 cup pure maple syrup
4 eggs, separated
½ cup firmly packed dark brown
   sugar

2 cups whipping cream, whipped, or
   1 8-ounce carton whipped topping, thawed
Chopped pecans

Grease a large soufflé dish and set aside.

In a saucepan soften the gelatin in the cold water and heat over low heat until dissolved. Add the syrup.

In a small bowl beat the egg yolks and add to the syrup mixture. Cook over moderate heat, stirring constantly, until the custard thickens slightly and coats the spoon. Add the brown sugar and stir to dissolve. Cool to room temperature.

In a medium bowl beat the egg whites until stiff. In a separate bowl whip the cream. Fold the whipped cream into the custard, then fold in the egg whites. Turn into the prepared soufflé dish and chill until firm.

Sprinkle with pecans.

Makes 8 servings.

◆ VIENNESE ORANGE COFFEE

6 to 8 tablespoons ground coffee
2 teaspoons grated orange rind
¼ teaspoon ground cinnamon

1 tablespoon brandy
6 cups water

Place the coffee in the basket of an automatic drip coffeepot. Sprinkle with the orange rind, cinnamon, and brandy. Brew as directed.

Serve with cream and sugar.

Makes 8 cups.

◆ CHOCOLATE-ALMOND COFFEE

6	to 8 tablespoons ground coffee	¼	cup chopped almonds, toasted
1	tablespoon cocoa	¼	teaspoon almond extract
¼	teaspoon ground nutmeg	6	cups water

Place the coffee in the basket of an automatic drip coffeemaker. Sprinkle the remaining ingredients over the grounds. Brew as directed.

Serve with cream and sugar.

Makes 8 cups.

◆ CHRISTMAS FRUIT TEA

2	quarts cranberry juice	1	cup orange juice
1	45-ounce can pineapple juice	4	3-inch sticks cinnamon
1	6-ounce can frozen lemonade con-centrate, thawed	3	whole nutmegs
2	cups apple juice	1½	teaspoons ground ginger

Pour the juices into a thirty-cup electric percolator. Place cinnamon, nutmegs, and ginger in the percolator basket. Perk through a complete cycle. Let stand 1 hour.

Serve hot.

Makes 1 gallon or 32 servings.

◆ HOT MULLED WINE

Hot mulled wine is for low, late-night conversations on cold, starry nights when children you haven't seen for a long, long time are sleeping quietly upstairs in their old beds.

2	quarts Burgundy or other dry red wine	3	3-inch sticks cinnamon
2	quarts apple juice	1½	teaspoons whole cloves
		1	teaspoon whole allspice

In a large container combine the wine and apple juice. Tie the spices in a cheesecloth and add to the wine mixture. Cover and chill overnight.

Into a large Dutch oven pour the mixture and bring to a boil. Reduce the heat and simmer 3 to 5 minutes. Remove the spice bag. Serve hot.

Makes 1 gallon or 32 servings.

12

COOKOUT & BARBECUE

I only work with the previously dead.
Big Arthur, 1987

You're sitting out back on a hot summer evening. The sun has finally set below the rim of trees. An evening star shines dimly through opalescent clouds. Cicadas are gearing up for the nighttime din. Suddenly, in a flash, it comes to you: All's right with the world. "This," you say to yourself, "is breaking news." You look around for the TV cameras, the microphones, the on-the-spot reporters trampling through the aspidistra. But everything looks pretty much the same: tag ends of sunset in a western sky, shadows deepening in the hedge, fireflies rising from the dewy grass. Then you have it—the smell. Meat juices sizzling down the hot night air, a hint of lighter fluid on charcoal briquettes, roasting corn, hot dog buns, wilted lettuce. You don't have to know where it is. You don't even have to be invited. It's a cookout, and you were right—all is right with the world.

Cooking out-of-doors changes everything. People who can't otherwise boil water start suddenly slathering orange-mustard sauce on grilled chicken. Barbecued beans are never spicier, coleslaw creamier, summer squash fresher, watermelon sweeter than on a cookout. Black cherry salad, lemonade pie, crusty baked pineapple and vanilla ice cream—every bite is the best thing you've ever put in your mouth.

Troubles disappear on a cookout. People talk to each other. Children play tag in the dark. It won't last forever, but for one short space there is nothing in this world more important than friends and food.

That is breaking news.

◆ BISCUIT STICKS

2¼ cups biscuit mix
⅔   cup milk

2 tablespoons butter, melted

In a large bowl stir the biscuit mix and milk until blended. On a floured surface roll the dough with hands into a ½-inch diameter stick. Cut into 3-inch pieces. Brush with melted butter. Bake at 450° for 10 minutes.
    Makes about 10.

◆ ONION-PARMESAN BREAD

1 14-ounce loaf French bread,
      unsliced
½ cup mayonnaise

½ cup grated Parmesan cheese
¼ cup finely chopped onion

Slice the bread in half lengthwise. Place each half cut-side up on a baking sheet.
    In a medium bowl combine the mayonnaise, Parmesan cheese, and onion, and spread on the cut sides of the bread halves. Bake at 375° for 15 minutes or until golden brown.
    Cut crosswise into half-moon slices.
    Makes 12 servings.

◆ BEER BISCUITS

Always let beer batter sit for a while at room temperature. The chemical reaction of the flour and the beer makes these biscuits light and gives them the texture of good yeast bread. This is an exceptionally easy version.

1 20-ounce package biscuit mix
1 12-ounce can or bottle beer, room
      temperature

2 tablespoons sugar

Grease 2½-inch muffin tins and set aside. In a large bowl mix all the ingredients and let stand at least 30 minutes.
    Spoon into the prepared muffin tins, filling each half full, and bake at 375° for 20 minutes.
    Makes 12 biscuits.

BARBECUE SAUCE FOR CHICKEN

Nothing sets the mood for a cookout better than the smell of barbecue sauce simmering away all afternoon in the kitchen.

2 cups butter
1 12-ounce bottle Worcestershire
 sauce
2 tablespoons A-1 sauce

Juice of 1 lemon
Tabasco sauce to taste
8 cloves garlic, pressed

In a large saucepan mix all the ingredients and simmer for 2 to 3 hours.
 Makes 3 cups.

> Full many a flower is born to blush unseen,
> And waste its sweetness on the desert air.
> *Thomas Gray, 1750*

HONEY-LIME BARBECUE SAUCE

3 cloves garlic, finely chopped
¼ cup extra-virgin olive oil
1 teaspoon salt
1 teaspoon white pepper
¼ teaspoon dried oregano
1 tablespoon finely chopped fresh
 basil

1½ cups tomato purée
¼ cup honey
 Juice of 2 limes
½ cup red wine
¼ cup finely chopped fresh parsley

In a skillet sauté the garlic in the oil over medium heat until tender.
 Add the salt, pepper, oregano, basil, tomato purée, and honey and simmer for 15 minutes.
 Add the lime juice and wine and simmer for 10 minutes more. Just before removing from the stove, add the parsley. Use to baste beef, chicken, or pork.
 Makes 2½ cups.

◆ ORANGE MUSTARD SAUCE

1 cup tomato juice
½ cup orange marmalade

1 tablespoon Dijon mustard

In a 1½-quart saucepan over medium-high heat combine all the ingredients. Heat to boiling, stirring constantly. Reduce the heat to low and cook 10 minutes or until the sauce thickens, stirring often.

Use the sauce to baste grilled chicken, pork chops, or flank steak.

Makes 1 cup.

◆ ONION-MARINATED FLANK STEAK

You can grab a cut of beef from the butcher, scoot home and throw it on the grill, and eat perfectly well. Or you can marinate it in the fridge for a couple of days in sour cream and onion and spices. It's definitely a step up and one you won't regret.

1 medium onion, coarsely chopped
¼ cup vegetable oil
¼ cup sour cream
2 teaspoons salt

2 teaspoons ground ginger
1½ teaspoons ground cumin
½ teaspoon black pepper
1 2½-pound flank steak

In a food processor or blender combine the onion and vegetable oil and process until finely chopped. Add the sour cream, salt, ginger, cumin, and pepper and process until blended. Place the steak in a deep, glass baking dish and pour the marinade over it. Cover and refrigerate, turning once, for 24 to 48 hours.

Grill the steak 6 inches from the coals, turning once and basting with the marinade, 15 to 20 minutes for medium-rare.

Transfer to a carving board and let stand 5 minutes before slicing diagonally against the grain.

Makes 8 servings.

All shall be well and all shall be well and all manner of thing shall be well.
Dame Julian of Norwich, 14th century

◆ VELVEETA BURGERS

You can buy your fine cuts of meat, and you can marinate and baste and slice. But the truth is nothing beats a well-grilled hamburger and a slice of Velveeta.

1 pound ground chuck	2 teaspoons prepared mustard
2 tablespoons chopped green bell pepper	½ teaspoon chili powder
2 teaspoons chopped banana pepper	¼ teaspoon salt
1 tablespoon dried onion flakes	⅛ teaspoon black pepper
1 tablespoon prepared horseradish	4 hamburger buns
2 teaspoons Worcestershire sauce	Lettuce leaves
	4 ⅔-ounce slices Velveeta cheese

In a large bowl combine the ground chuck, peppers, onion flakes, horseradish, Worcestershire sauce, and seasonings and mix well. Shape into 4 patties and place on a grill over medium coals. Grill 4 to 5 minutes on each side.

Place hot patties in the buns with the lettuce and Velveeta cheese.

Makes 4 servings.

◆ PINEAPPLE PORK CHOPS

An ocean breeze, a rustling palm, a mouthwatering whiff of pineapple, pork, and charcoal. *The Twilight Zone* was canceled years ago. This must really be the South Pacific.

6 1-inch-thick pork chops	⅓ cup vegetable oil
1 20-ounce can pineapple slices, drained, with syrup reserved	¼ cup minced onion
¼ cup pineapple syrup	1 clove garlic, minced
½ cup soy sauce	1 tablespoon firmly packed dark brown sugar

Place chops in a large shallow dish.

In a large bowl combine the syrup, soy sauce, oil, onion, garlic, and sugar, mixing well, and pour over the chops. Cover and marinate in refrigerator for 2 to 3 hours.

Remove chops, reserving the marinade. Grill the chops over medium coals 40 to 50 minutes, turning frequently and basting with the marinade.

Place a pineapple ring on top of each chop during the final minutes of cooking.

Makes 6 servings.

◆ WESTERN BARBECUE BEANS

You can't have a barbecue without beans. And you can't make barbecued beans without a lot of ingredients. So stop whining and make your list. You can bake them while you simmer the barbecue sauce. Your neighbors will line up for blocks.

1½ pounds ground beef
1½ teaspoons salt
¼ teaspoon black pepper
1 clove garlic, minced
3 tablespoons vegetable oil
¼ cup finely chopped onion
½ cup tomato juice
⅓ cup chili sauce

¼ cup diced sweet pickles
   Tabasco sauce to taste
½ teaspoon Worcestershire sauce
2 15-ounce cans pork and beans
½ cup catsup
2 tablespoons firmly packed dark
      brown sugar
1 large onion, cut into rings

In a large skillet combine the beef, salt, pepper, and garlic. Sauté in vegetable oil over medium heat until lightly browned. Add the onion and sauté until tender. Remove from the heat and add the tomato juice, chili sauce, pickles, Tabasco sauce, Worcestershire sauce, and beans. Pour into a bean pot and cover the top with the catsup, brown sugar, and onion rings. Bake uncovered at 325° for 1 hour.

Makes 8 servings.

◆ FIVE-BEAN BEER POT

1 cup minced onion
1 clove garlic, minced
1 tablespoon dry mustard
¼ cup firmly packed dark brown
      sugar
2 cups beer
   Salt and pepper to taste
1 15-ounce can butter beans, drained

1 15½-ounce can red kidney beans,
      drained
1 15-ounce can pinto beans, drained
1 1-pound 1-ounce can green lima
      beans, drained
1 15-ounce can great Northern beans,
      drained

In a bowl combine the onion, garlic, dry mustard, brown sugar, and beer. Mix well and season to taste with salt and pepper.

In a large casserole or bean pot layer the beans one kind at a time, adding some of the beer mixture between each layer. Pour the remaining beer mixture over the top. Cover and bake at 325° for 1 hour or place over low heat on stove top and simmer for 40 minutes.

Makes 6 servings.

◆ CHEDDAR-SQUASH CASSEROLE

5 cups warm, cooked yellow squash, slightly drained	1 cup breadcrumbs
¼ cup butter	3 eggs, slightly beaten
½ cup minced onion	**TOPPING:**
1 cup grated Cheddar cheese	¼ cup breadcrumbs
1 teaspoon salt	1 tablespoon butter, melted
½ teaspoon white pepper	

Grease a 2-quart casserole dish and set aside.

In a large bowl mix all the ingredients in the order given and pour into the prepared casserole dish. Bake at 350° for 40 minutes.

Top with buttered breadcrumbs and bake 20 minutes more or until the center is firm.

Makes 12 servings.

Pigeons on the grass alas.
Gertrude Stein, 1927

◆ PENNY CARROTS

When the children sneak these out of the dish with their grubby little hands you must promise to look the other way. It was you, after all, who told them to eat their vegetables. You just neglected to tell them vegetables could be so good.

2 pounds carrots, sliced crosswise ¼-inch thick	⅔ cup sugar
1 onion, sliced in rings	1 10 ¾-ounce can condensed tomato soup, undiluted
1 green bell pepper, chopped	2 teaspoons Worcestershire sauce
1 cup cider vinegar	1 tablespoon dry mustard
⅔ cup vegetable oil	Salt and pepper to taste

In a pot cook the sliced carrots in salted water until just tender. Drain. Mix with the remaining ingredients and chill overnight.

Makes 12 servings.

◆ MEXICAN GREEN BEANS

4   14½-ounce cans whole green
      beans, drained, with liquid
      reserved
1   tablespoon minced onion

6   tablespoons vegetable oil
½   cup chili sauce
3   tablespoons sugar
    Tabasco sauce to taste

Into a skillet pour one third the bean liquid with the beans and cook over high heat for 15 minutes.

Reduce the heat to medium, add the remaining ingredients, and cook for 15 minutes more.

Makes 12 servings.

◆ CARROT-CABBAGE COLESLAW

Mayonnaise-based coleslaw needs time for the flavors to blend. Don't mix this up and serve it directly—people will think they're back in the school cafeteria and start running for the exits. Make it, instead, the day before, let it marinate, and serve it very cold.

2   cups shredded cabbage
1   carrot, shredded
⅓   cup mayonnaise

1   teaspoon cider vinegar
1   teaspoon sugar

In a bowl combine the cabbage and carrot. In a separate bowl mix the mayonnaise, vinegar, and sugar and add to the cabbage mixture. Chill overnight.

Makes 4 servings.

◆ BLACK CHERRY SALAD MOLD

Black cherry gelatin is the color of the sky on a July night in the dark of the moon when a thunderstorm is moving up the coast. The sherry is in honor of your great-aunt who never once made Jell-O without wine.

1   3-ounce package cherry-flavored
      gelatin
1   16-ounce can small, black cherries,
      pitted, with juice reserved

1   cup dry sherry

Grease a mold and set aside. In a large bowl dissolve the gelatin in ½ cup boiling cherry juice. Add the sherry and cherries. Pour in the prepared mold and chill until set.

Makes 6 servings.

◆ TOSSED MANDARIN SALAD

Whoever was the first to put together bleu cheese, mandarin oranges, and avocado deserves, at the very least, an entire generation of namesakes.

2 11-ounce cans mandarin oranges,
    drained
1 large avocado, sliced
1 8-ounce bottle bleu cheese dressing

2 medium onions, thinly sliced
½ head iceberg lettuce
½ head Bibb or Boston lettuce

In a large bowl marinate the oranges, avocado, and onions in the bleu cheese dressing in the refrigerator overnight. Tear the lettuce into bite-sized pieces. Toss all the ingredients and serve.
    Makes 8 servings.

◆ LEMONADE PIE

Bands are playing. Bunting flutters in the breeze. Festive crowds throng the marketplace. It's a cookout. You're eating lemonade pie, and you're very, very happy.

1 8-ounce carton whipped topping,
    thawed
1 14-ounce can sweetened condensed
    milk

1 6-ounce can frozen lemonade con-
    centrate, thawed
2 9-inch prepared graham cracker
    pastry shells

Mix together the whipped topping, condensed milk, and concentrate and blend thoroughly. Pour into the graham cracker crusts and refrigerate at least 2 hours before serving.
    Makes 2 pies or 16 servings.

◆ GRAHAM CRACKER PASTRY SHELL

1½ cups graham cracker crumbs
    (approximately 15 crackers)
½ cup butter, melted

3 tablespoons sugar
   Dash ground cinnamon

In a medium bowl mix all the ingredients and press into a 9-inch pie plate.

◆ LEMON CHESS PIE

This may well be the best pie you'll ever put in your mouth.

4   eggs
1   cup sugar
1   cup light corn syrup
1/3   cup lemon juice

Grated rind of 1 lemon
1   heaping tablespoon all-purpose
    flour
1   9-inch prepared pastry shell

In a large bowl beat the eggs with an electric mixer at slow speed. Gradually add the sugar, corn syrup, lemon juice, grated rind, and flour until well blended. Pour into the prepared pastry shell and bake at 325° about 40 minutes until the filling is set.
    Makes 6 to 8 servings.

◆ CINNAMON BARS

You can share a piece of pie with an old friend on a glider under the stars, but a bar cookie travels. Wrap it in a paper napkin, stick it in your pocket, and eat it at midnight in bed while you watch summer lightning from an upstairs window.

1   cup butter, softened
1   cup sugar
1   egg, separated
2   cups all-purpose flour

1   tablespoon, plus 1 teaspoon ground
    cinnamon
1   cup chopped pecans

Cream butter and sugar until light and fluffy. Add egg yolk, flour, and cinnamon and blend well. Press mixture into an ungreased 15 x 10 x 1-inch jelly roll pan. Brush egg white over surface and cover with chopped pecans pressed lightly into dough. Bake at 325° for 25 to 30 minutes. Cool in pan before cutting into bars.
    Makes 4 dozen.

◆ CHOCOLATE-PECAN SQUARES

2 1/2   cups all-purpose flour
1 1/2   teaspoons baking powder
1/2   teaspoon salt
2/3   cup butter
2 1/4   cups firmly packed light brown
    sugar

3   eggs
2   teaspoons lemon juice
1   cup chopped pecans
1   6-ounce package semisweet
    chocolate morsels

Grease and flour a 9 x 13 x 2-inch baking pan and set aside.

In a large mixing bowl combine the flour, baking powder, and salt. In a large saucepan melt the butter. Add the sugar. Add the eggs one at a time, beating well after each addition. Add the lemon juice, flour mixture, pecans, and chocolate. Stir well. Pour into the prepared pan and bake at 350° for 25 minutes.

Cut into 1½-inch squares while warm and cool completely in pan.

Makes 36 squares.

◆ STRAWBERRY SHORTCAKE

It's the middle of May. The days are longer, the nights brighter. School's not out yet, but neither are the mosquitoes. You still need a sweater after dark, and the markets are full of strawberries. The shortcake part is easy.

2⅓ cups biscuit mix
½ cup milk
3 tablespoons sugar
3 tablespoons butter, melted
1 quart fresh strawberries or 2 1-
pound packages frozen
strawberries

1 8-ounce carton whipped topping,
thawed

In a large bowl stir together the biscuit mix, milk, sugar, and butter to form a soft dough. Spread in an ungreased 8-inch square pan. Bake at 425° for 15 to 20 minutes or until golden brown.

Cool slightly in the pan before slicing into squares. Place on serving plates topped with strawberries and whipped topping.

Makes 8 servings.

◆ BAKED PINEAPPLE DESSERT

If you're very, very lucky, someone will make homemade vanilla ice cream and you can spoon it on top of your baked pineapple. If not, you can just eat the pineapple.

8 slices canned pineapple, drained,
with juice reserved
½ cup firmly packed light brown sugar
2 tablespoons butter

1 teaspoon ground cinnamon
½ cup graham cracker crumbs
½ cup pineapple juice

In a shallow pan place the pineapple slices.

In a medium bowl cream the sugar, butter, and cinnamon, mix with the crumbs, and spoon on top. Pour the juice over and around the pineapple. Bake at 350° for 25 minutes.

Let cool and serve 1 pineapple slice topped with a large spoonful of ice cream.

Makes 8 servings.

◆ PINEAPPLE DAIQUIRI SALAD

1 15½-ounce can crushed pineapple, drained, with juice reserved
Water
2 ¼-ounce envelopes unflavored gelatin

½ cup light rum
1 6-ounce can frozen limeade concentrate, thawed
8 to 10 ice cubes

Grease a 4-cup mold and set aside.

In a measuring cup measure the pineapple juice and add enough water to make 1 cup. In a blender combine ½ cup of the juice mixture and the gelatin and process 15 seconds. Let stand 1 minute.

In a saucepan bring the remaining ½ cup of reserved liquid to a boil and add to the gelatin mixture. Process until the gelatin dissolves. Add the rum and limeade and process briefly. Add the ice cubes one at a time, processing until smooth. Stir in the pineapple and pour into the prepared mold. Chill until firm.

Makes 8 servings.

The answer lies out there in the swamps.
Tom Stoppard, 1968

◆ COFFEE SODA

5 cups black coffee
1¼ cups sugar
2½ cups club soda
2½ cups cream soda

5 tablespoons vanilla extract
7 tablespoons whipped topping, thawed

While coffee is hot mix with the sugar to dissolve. Let cool and add the remaining ingredients. Serve with ice cream on top.

Makes 10 servings.

13

PICNIC

"Take my camel, dear," said my Aunt Dot, as she climbed down
from this animal on her return from High Mass.
Rose Macaulay, 1956

The picnic is the modern equivalent of the saintly pilgrimage. You
have some place to go. It's largely symbolic. You leave behind you
all of ordinary life with its burden of care and woe. You concentrate
on the immediate. On both pilgrimage and picnic you carry with
you everything you need for the duration of the journey. On a picnic that means food.

There are two things about picnics that set them apart from
everyday life: First, the cooking is almost always done before you
set out, and second, most things end up between two slices of
bread. Sure, you've got your mock fried chicken, your deviled eggs,
your stove-top beans, your summer macaroni, your picnic corn.
Nothing tastes better at sunset on a windy beach than a syrupy
mixture of canned pork and beans and diced Spam heated over a
driftwood fire and topped off with a slice of chocolate chip-date
cake, maybe an oatmeal pie or a sack of blond brownies. The rest,
happily, is mainly sandwiches and a person could live forever on
sandwiches: cream cheese and green onion, deviled ham, frankfurters on whole wheat, bologna and hard-cooked eggs, fish sticks
on onion rolls with mayonnaise and sweet pepper relish.

On picnics as on pilgrimages food tastes better, the air is fresher, the land is always new, people are transformed. The sound of
waves crashing on the rocky beach is a song you're hearing for the
first time—or the thousandth. The truth is you've made this trip
before and you've seen the light. And like any true pilgrim you'll be
back.

◆ SPICY MUSTARD

With a little lemon juice and horseradish, you could dress up the moon.

1½ cups mayonnaise	1 tablespoon prepared horseradish
½ cup prepared Creole mustard	2 tablespoons lemon juice

In a medium bowl combine all the ingredients and blend well. Cover and chill at least 3 hours.
　　Makes 2½ cups.

◆ COOKED MAYONNAISE

There is nothing quite as classy as homemade mayonnaise. Traditional mayonnaise, however, is made with uncooked eggs, and one sad fact of the end of this millennium is the salmonella rampant in the U.S. egg supply. Uncooked eggs are an invitation to disaster. This cooked mayonnaise is not as delicate as the recipes we used to make, but it's better than anything commercial.

¼ cup sugar	¼ cup water
2 teaspoons all-purpose flour	¼ cup cider vinegar
1 teaspoon dry mustard	2 eggs, beaten
½ teaspoon salt	1 tablespoon butter

In a saucepan combine the sugar, flour, mustard, and salt. Gradually stir in the water and vinegar. Add the eggs, beating well with a wire whisk. Add the butter. Cook over medium heat until the mixture comes to a boil, beating constantly. Cover and chill.
　　Makes 1¼ cups.

A Jug of Wine, a Loaf of Bread—and Thou
Beside me singing in the Wilderness—
Edward Fitzgerald, 1859

◆ STACKED SANDWICHES

Only the true sandwich lover will understand that sometimes, no matter what goes inside it, you have to put butter on the bread.

1 3-ounce package cream cheese, softened	12 slices rye bread
	Lettuce leaves
2 tablespoons chopped green onion	2 3-ounce packages roast beef, thinly sliced
1 tablespoon soy sauce	
1 tablespoon dry sherry	4 3-ounce packages ham, thinly sliced
3 tablespoons butter, softened	

In a medium bowl combine the cream cheese, onion, soy sauce, and sherry. Spread the butter on one side of each slice of bread. Spread the cream cheese mixture over the butter. On six bread slices on top of the cream cheese mixture arrange the lettuce, roast beef, and ham. Top with the remaining bread. Cut the sandwiches in half before serving.

Makes 6 sandwiches.

◆ FISH-STICK ROLLS

At last, a respectable use for that old childhood staple: fish sticks.

3 tablespoons mayonnaise	1 10.1-ounce package frozen fish sticks
2 tablespoons sweet pickle relish, drained	
	4 French rolls, split lengthwise
2 teaspoons prepared mustard	1 large tomato, peeled and sliced
1/4 teaspoon dried dill weed	2 cups shredded iceberg lettuce

In a small bowl combine the mayonnaise, relish, mustard, and dill. Mix well and set aside.

Cook the fish sticks according to the directions on the package. Spread the mayonnaise mixture on the bottom half of the French rolls. Place four fish sticks on the mayonnaise. Top with the tomato, lettuce, and 1 heaping tablespoon of mayonnaise mixture. Cover with the roll top.

Makes 4 sandwiches.

◆ BOLOGNA-EGG SANDWICHES

Call it "baloney" if you will—it still makes a great sandwich. You might have to go off by yourself to eat it, but on a picnic nobody's going to complain.

4 slices bologna, chopped	¼ cup mayonnaise
4 hard-cooked eggs, chopped	1 teaspoon instant minced onion
1 stalk celery, chopped	Leaf lettuce
¼ cup sweet pickle relish, drained	4 onion rolls, split lengthwise

In a medium bowl combine the bologna, eggs, celery, relish, mayonnaise, and onion, stir well, and chill. Arrange the lettuce leaves on the bottom half of each onion roll. Top with the filling and cover with the roll top.
    Makes 4 sandwiches.

◆ DEVILED HAM SANDWICHES

1 4-ounce can deviled ham	1 teaspoon instant minced onion
2 hard-cooked eggs, finely chopped	1 teaspoon prepared mustard
3 tablespoons finely chopped dill pickle	Mayonnaise
	Sandwich bread

In a medium bowl combine the ham, eggs, pickle, onion, and mustard, stirring well. Chill.
    Spread the mayonnaise on the sandwich bread and top with the deviled ham mixture.
    Makes 1 cup or 2 sandwiches.

◆ FRANKFURTERS ON WHOLE WHEAT

Don't change even one of these ingredients and make sure you have plenty for seconds.

8 frankfurters	Creole-style mustard
8 slices whole grain bread	8 dill pickles, sliced lengthwise
Mayonnaise	4 slices American cheese

Broil or grill the frankfurters according to the directions on the package. Let cool slightly and cut lengthwise into two long pieces. Spread the bread slices for the bottom of the sandwiches with mayonnaise, the top slices with mustard. On four bread slices place two pickle slices, four frankfurter slices, and one slice of American cheese. Top with the remaining bread.
    Makes 4 sandwiches.

◆ MOCK FRIED CHICKEN

3 pounds chicken pieces	1 teaspoon garlic salt
1 cup milk	1 teaspoon paprika
2 cups corn flakes crumbs	½ teaspoon grated nutmeg
1 teaspoon celery salt	

Grease a broiler pan and set aside.

Soak the chicken in milk for 1 hour.

In a shallow bowl combine the corn flake crumbs, salts, paprika, and nutmeg, mixing well. Remove the chicken from the milk and roll in the crumb mixture, coating well. Place the chicken on the prepared pan, and bake uncovered at 400° for 45 minutes or until juices run clear.

Makes 4 to 6 servings.

◆ CLASSIC POTATO SALAD

If you take someone on a picnic without potato salad, they'll make you go back home and get it.

1 cup mayonnaise	1 cup sliced celery
2 tablespoons cider vinegar	½ cup chopped onion
½ teaspoon salt	¼ cup chopped pimiento-stuffed green
¼ teaspoon black pepper	olives
4 cups peeled and cubed cooked	2 hard-cooked eggs, chopped
potatoes	Paprika

In a large bowl combine the mayonnaise, vinegar, salt, and pepper until smooth. Add the potatoes, celery, onion, olives, and eggs and toss well to coat. Sprinkle with paprika, cover, and chill.

Makes 5 cups or 8 servings.

> Spring again, and the long white road unrolling itself southward from Paris. How could one resist the call?
> *Edith Wharton, 1908*

◆ SALMON-POTATO SALAD

Good cooks have a habit of doctoring recipes, for which we are all grateful. This hearty picnic salad probably started out as just another potato salad. You could make it with tuna, and instead of celery substitute chopped cucumber, and maybe a little dry sherry for the lemon juice, and a teaspoon of dill weed. Rice—how about rice instead of potato?

1	7½-ounce can salmon, drained	2	tablespoons sweet pickle relish, drained
1	medium potato, peeled, cooked, and cubed	1	tablespoon lemon juice
1	hard-cooked egg, chopped	3	tablespoons mayonnaise
½	cup chopped celery		Salt and pepper to taste
3	green onions, finely chopped		

In a large bowl combine all the ingredients, tossing well. Chill before serving.
Makes 4 servings.

◆ PICNIC CORN

Corn-on-the-cob is best eaten out-of-doors. It's messy; it sticks in your teeth; it gets all over your hands. And it's absolutely delicious—especially this one boiled in butter and milk. You'll never get it off your shirtfront and you just won't care. It would be most thoughtful, too, if you were to stop by a farm on your way home and offer the cobs to a pig.

2	quarts water	1	cup butter
2	quarts milk	12	very fresh ears white corn, shucked and cleaned
	Salt and pepper to taste		

In a large pot bring the water and milk to a slow boil. Add the salt, pepper, butter, and corn and boil about 10 minutes until done. Remove the pot from the heat and leave the corn in it for up to an hour before serving.
Makes 8 to 10 servings.

I don't much care if I never see a mountain in my life.
Charles Lamb, 1801

◆ SUMMER MACARONI SHELLS

This is a baked macaroni, so if you're taking it on a picnic you'll have to use one of those lovely woven baskets with the nested serving dishes and the checkered napkins color-coordinated with the flatware handles. Or you could sling it over your shoulder in a plastic grocery sack.

1 cup small shell pasta, uncooked	Dash cayenne pepper
1 pimiento, chopped	3 eggs, beaten
1 green bell pepper, chopped	2 slices white bread, trimmed of
1 tablespoon chopped fresh parsley	crusts and cubed
1 tablespoon chopped onion	1½ cups grated sharp Cheddar cheese,
½ teaspoon salt	divided
½ cup butter	1½ cups half-and-half

Grease a 2-quart casserole dish and set aside.

In a pot cook and drain the pasta according to the directions on the package.

In a large bowl combine the cooked pasta, pimiento, bell pepper, parsley, onion, salt, butter, and cayenne. In a separate bowl combine the eggs, bread cubes, and 1 ¼ cups of Cheddar cheese. Add the pasta mixture. Pour into the prepared casserole dish. Pour the cream over the top and sprinkle with the remaining ¼ cup Cheddar cheese. Bake at 350° for 50 minutes.

Makes 6 servings.

◆ DEVILED EGGS

Twenty-four deviled eggs should serve ten to twelve people. They should, but they won't. There's hardly a person alive who won't eat three or four and then start looking around for more. Perhaps you should double this recipe.

12 hard-cooked eggs, halved with	3 tablespoons mayonnaise
yolks removed	3 tablespoons sour cream
1 teaspoon dry mustard	1 tablespoon cider vinegar
¼ teaspoon salt	1 teaspoon Worcestershire sauce
Dash cayenne pepper	Paprika

In a medium bowl mash the egg yolks with a fork and add the mustard, salt, cayenne pepper, mayonnaise, sour cream, vinegar, and Worcestershire sauce. Mix until fluffy. Fill the egg halves with the yolk mixture and sprinkle with paprika.

Makes 24 deviled eggs.

◆ STOVE-TOP BEANS

1	15-ounce can pork and beans, undrained	¼	cup finely chopped onion
1	15½-ounce can red kidney beans, drained and rinsed	1	clove garlic, pressed
		1	teaspoon prepared mustard
½	cup prepared salsa	1	tablespoon molasses

In a saucepan combine all the ingredients over medium heat and heat to boiling. Reduce the heat and simmer for 30 minutes, stirring occasionally.

Makes 4 to 6 servings.

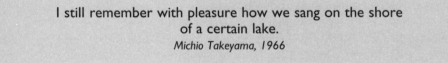

I still remember with pleasure how we sang on the shore of a certain lake.
Michio Takeyama, 1966

◆ LAKE MIXTURE

This is the true story of Lake Mixture. On a lake trip in the 1950s, these very ingredients were all that was salvaged from a canoe capsizing. Picture yourself on a muddy beach. You're wet. You're cold. You've lost your paddle. The sun is going down. The wind is rising. You manage finally to start a fire between two rocks. You do, by some miracle, still have a can opener and a pot. You dump everything into the pot and heat it over the fire. And for the next forty years you take Lake Mixture to every picnic, every outing, every dinner on the grounds. There's a similar story about the origin of mayonnaise, but it doesn't involve a canoe. It's enough to make a person believe in fate.

3	15-ounce cans pork and beans	¼	cup molasses
2	12-ounce cans Spam, cubed		Juice of ½ lemon
2	tablespoons tomato paste		Grated rind of ½ lemon

In a Dutch oven combine all the ingredients. Simmer on a stove or over a campfire for 1 hour. Good hot or cold.

Makes 10 servings.

◆ CREAM CHEESE POUND CAKE

3 cups sugar	6 eggs
¾ cup butter	2 teaspoons vanilla extract
1 8-ounce package cream cheese, softened	3 cups all-purpose flour

Grease and flour a 10-inch stem pan and set aside.

In a large bowl cream the sugar and butter. Cut the cream cheese into three parts and add alternately with the eggs one at a time, beating well after each addition. Add the vanilla. Add the flour 1 cup at a time. Pour into the prepared stem pan and bake at 300° for 1 hour and 45 minutes. Cool in the pan 10 minutes.

Makes 16 servings.

◆ OATMEAL PIE

Even if you have to delegate one person to walk ahead carrying this pie out in front like a totem, you have to take it on your picnic.

3 eggs, beaten	1 cup, plus 2 tablespoons rolled oats, raw
¾ cup sugar	Pinch salt
¾ cup firmly packed light brown sugar	1½ teaspoons vanilla extract
1⅛ cups light corn syrup	1 10-inch prepared deep-dish pastry shell, unbaked
¾ cup whipping cream	
6 tablespoons butter, melted	
1½ cups flaked coconut	

In a large bowl combine all the ingredients except the pastry shell, mixing well. Pour into the prepared pastry shell. Bake at 350° for 45 to 55 minutes or until browned and set.

Makes 15 servings.

◆ BLOND BROWNIES 2

Blond brownies tend to be denser than chocolate. In a hip pocket, denseness can be a virtue.

2 cups all-purpose flour	2 eggs, beaten
2 teaspoons baking powder	1 teaspoon vanilla extract
¼ teaspoon salt	1 cup pecan pieces
½ cup butter	
2 cups firmly packed light brown sugar	

Grease and flour a 9 x 13 x 2-inch baking pan and set aside.

In a large bowl combine the flour, baking powder, and salt. In a saucepan melt the butter and remove from the heat, stirring in the sugar while still hot. Add the eggs and vanilla. Add the dry ingredients and nuts. Spread in the prepared pan. Bake at 350° for 20 to 25 minutes. Do not overbake.

Cut into bars while still warm.

Makes 48 bars.

◆ APPLESAUCE SKILLET CAKE

2 cups all-purpose flour	1 cup sugar
1 teaspoon ground cinnamon	1 tablespoon cocoa
1 teaspoon baking powder	1 cup sweetened applesauce
½ teaspoon grated nutmeg	½ cup vegetable oil
½ teaspoon ground cloves	

Lightly grease a 9-inch iron skillet and place in oven to heat.

In a large bowl mix together the flour, cinnamon, baking powder, nutmeg, cloves, sugar, and cocoa. Add the applesauce and oil. Pour into the prepared skillet and bake at 350° for 35 minutes.

Cool in the pan on a wire rack.

Makes 8 servings.

◆ STIRRED DATE CAKE

Date cakes are wise choices for picnics in rugged terrain because if—heaven forbid—you should lose your bearings, you can always sit down where you are and eat cake until the search team arrives. At which point you can offer some to your rescuers. One good date cake could sustain the lot of you for days.

1½ cups boiling water	½ teaspoon salt
1 heaping cup pitted and chopped dates	1 teaspoon ground cinnamon
	1 teaspoon vanilla extract
1 teaspoon baking soda	½ cup firmly packed light brown sugar
¾ cup shortening	½ cup pecan or walnut pieces
1 cup sugar	½ cup semisweet chocolate morsels
2 eggs	
1½ cups, plus 2 tablespoons all-purpose flour	

Grease and flour a 9 x 13 x 2-inch pan and set aside.

In a large bowl pour the boiling water over the dates and let stand until cool. Stir in the baking soda.

In a separate bowl cream the shortening and sugar. Add the eggs and beat until fluffy. Add to the date mixture.

In a separate bowl combine the flour, salt, and cinnamon and add to the date mixture. Add the vanilla. Pour into the prepared pan.

In a separate bowl combine the brown sugar, nuts, and chocolate and sprinkle over the batter. Bake at 350° for 40 minutes.

Cool in the pan before cutting into squares.

Makes 15 servings.

> Going up that river was like traveling back to the
> earliest beginnings of the world.
> *Joseph Conrad, 1902*

◆ TANGY PUNCH

1 cup orange-flavored instant breakfast drink powder
3 cups water
3 cups pineapple juice, chilled

2 tablespoons frozen lemonade concentrate, thawed
1 33.8-ounce bottle ginger ale, chilled

In a gallon container mix the instant drink powder, water, pineapple juice, and lemonade concentrate and chill. Add the ginger ale and seal in individual canteens or ther-
moses.
    Makes ½ gallon.

◆ TOMATO ZINGER

2 cups tomato juice
1 quart clam and tomato juice cocktail
2 teaspoons Worcestershire sauce

¾ teaspoon crushed celery seed
¾ teaspoon white pepper
1½ teaspoons lemon juice
¼ teaspoon Tabasco sauce

In a container combine all the ingredients, mixing well. Chill thoroughly.
    Seal in individual canteens or thermoses.
    Makes 6 cups.

◆ SPANISH SANGRIA

1 25.4-ounce bottle Burgundy wine
¼ cup brandy
2 tablespoons Cointreau liqueur

3 cups red Hawaiian Punch
3 oranges, thinly sliced
2 lemons, thinly sliced

In a 3-quart pitcher combine the liquids. Mix well. Add the fruit, stirring gently. Cover
and chill at least 4 hours.
    Seal in a wide-mouthed thermos.
    Makes 3 quarts.

14

BUFFET

He looked about as inconspicuous as a tarantula on angel food.
Raymond Chandler, 1940

They come at the end of particularly tedious operas when the soprano has been dying since intermission, and three arias and a spirited duet into Act Five you begin to wonder if a bass flute qualifies as a blunt instrument. They come during mind-numbing cocktail parties just about the time you admit to yourself that alcohol isn't really going to help. They come with office seminars, political strategy sessions, international peace talks, community relations weekends at seedy mountain resorts so far from civilization you wouldn't have a prayer if you walked out. They're buffets, and they make the world a better place. Anything you want to eat in any quantity, spread out for easy access on long, crowded tables: rare roast beef with horseradish and sour cream, salmon mousse, hot Italian sausage and bell pepper roasted in olive oil and red wine, rice pilaf, sherried mushrooms, red velvet cake.

The beauty of a buffet is that you're on your own. You have a plate. You have a fork. You have a large, squarish napkin. Who's to say you're the one pigging out on deep-fried rice-and-cheese balls? How much, after all, is too much ratatouille? Who's keeping track of the coconut cream pie?

Buffets are your reward for a life well lived. You're a good citizen. You work hard. You respect your elders. You almost always vote in national elections. Community relations are dear to your heart. So, too, are crab balls in remoulade sauce, honey-glazed ham, applesauce-bran muffins, and chocolate-raspberry cheesecake. You get one—you get the other. It's another of life's simple harmonies.

◆ DEEP-FRIED RICE-AND-CHEESE BALLS

Don't try to make this for a hundred people—you'll be in the kitchen all night. Rather, put them out at an intimate buffet. They'll get everybody's attention.

2 eggs, lightly beaten
2 cups cooked white rice, cold
4 ounces mozzarella cheese, cut into ½-inch cubes

¾ cup seasoned Italian-style bread-crumbs
Vegetable oil for deep frying

In a large bowl gently stir the eggs and rice together. On top of 1 tablespoon of rice mixture place a cube of mozzarella cheese and top with 1 additional tablespoon of rice. Shape into a ball, roll in the breadcrumbs, place on waxed paper, and refrigerate for 30 minutes.

Line a large baking dish with paper towels and place in a 250° oven. Heat 1½ inches of oil in a skillet or deep-fat fryer to 375°. Fry the balls 4 or 5 at a time for about 5 minutes or until golden brown. Transfer to the baking dish in the oven to drain. The balls may be kept warm in oven for up to 10 minutes.

Makes 6 servings.

> As with tragic opera, things got worse after the interval.
> Tom Stoppard, 1977

◆ CRAB BALLS

2 7-ounce cans crab meat, drained, or 1 pound imitation crab meat
2 tablespoons milk
2 tablespoons mayonnaise
¾ teaspoon salt
¼ teaspoon cayenne pepper
¼ teaspoon black pepper
1 teaspoon dried parsley flakes

1 tablespoon finely diced green bell pepper
1 teaspoon celery seed
1 teaspoon dry mustard
2 teaspoons Worcestershire sauce
1 egg, beaten
6 soda crackers, crushed
Vegetable oil for frying

In a large bowl combine all the ingredients except the cracker crumbs and oil and refrigerate for at least 1 hour.

Shape into balls the size of a large marble. Roll in the crushed cracker crumbs. Heat 1 inch of oil in a skillet to 375° and fry the balls 5 or 6 at a time. Brown on all sides, turning once. Drain on paper towels and serve at once with Remoulade Sauce (recipe follows).

Makes 40 balls.

◆ REMOULADE SAUCE

Remoulade gets its name from celery and it's made for seafood.

2 cups mayonnaise	½ cup horseradish mustard
2 hard-cooked eggs, finely chopped	1 teaspoon Worcestershire sauce
1 cup finely chopped celery hearts	1 teaspoon sugar
3 cloves garlic, pressed	½ teaspoon white pepper
3 tablespoons dry mustard	1 teaspoon salt
2 tablespoons red wine vinegar	

In a large bowl combine all the ingredients and mix thoroughly. Store in the refrigerator in a tightly covered jar. Keeps indefinitely.

Makes 1 quart.

I have the heart and stomach of a king.
Elizabeth I of England, 1588

◆ BATTER-FRIED SHRIMP

2 pounds fresh jumbo shrimp	1 teaspoon salt
1 3-ounce bag shrimp boil	½ teaspoon cayenne pepper
1 cup cracker meal	Vegetable oil for frying
1 5-ounce can evaporated milk	

In a pot cook the shrimp in boiling water seasoned with shrimp boil until barely pink. Dip in cold water, shell, and devein. In a shallow bowl make a batter of cracker meal, milk, salt, and pepper.

In a skillet heat 1 inch of oil to 375°. Dip the shrimp in the batter and fry in hot oil for 4 to 5 minutes.

Serve with Remoulade Sauce.

Makes 6 servings.

◆ DROP BISCUITS

You may think you can't make biscuits, but that's just because you haven't made drop biscuits.

2	cups all-purpose flour		2	tablespoons shortening
4	teaspoons baking powder		¾	cup milk, plus 2 tablespoons
½	teaspoon salt			

In a large bowl combine the flour, baking powder, and salt and with a pastry blender cut in the shortening until the mixture resembles coarse meal. Make a well in the center, pour in the milk, and stir with a fork until just moistened. Do not overstir. Drop by spoonfuls onto an ungreased baking sheet. Bake at 400° for 10 to 12 minutes.
    Makes 24 biscuits.

◆ CHEESE BISCUITS

2	cups all-purpose flour		¾	cup grated yellow cheese
4	teaspoons baking powder		⅓	cup milk
½	teaspoon salt		⅓	cup water
2	tablespoons shortening			

In a large bowl combine the flour, baking powder, and salt and with a pastry blender cut in the shortening until the mixture resembles coarse meal. Add the yellow cheese. Make a well in the center, pour in the milk and water, and stir with a fork until just moistened. Do not overstir. Roll out on a floured surface to ½-inch thickness and cut with biscuit or cookie cutters. Transfer to an ungreased baking sheet. Bake at 400° for 10 to 12 minutes.
    Makes 24 biscuits.

◆ APPLESAUCE-BRAN MUFFINS

1½ cups 100-percent bran cereal	1 teaspoon ground cinnamon
1½ cups applesauce	½ teaspoon ground ginger
1 egg, beaten	½ cup dark raisins
¼ cup butter, melted	
½ cup firmly packed light brown sugar	**GLAZE:**
1½ cups all-purpose flour	½ cup confectioners' sugar
1 tablespoon baking powder	1 tablespoon applesauce

Grease 12 2½-inch muffin cups and set aside. In a large bowl mix the bran, applesauce, egg, butter, and brown sugar. Let stand 5 minutes.

In a separate bowl combine the flour, baking powder, cinnamon, and ginger. Stir in the bran mixture until just blended. The batter will be lumpy. Stir in the raisins. Spoon the batter into the prepared muffin cups. Bake at 400° for 15 to 18 minutes.

Remove from the pan, cool slightly, and drizzle with a glaze of confectioners' sugar and applesauce. Serve warm.

Makes 12 muffins.

Note: For miniature muffins, bake at 400° for 10 to 12 minutes.

Makes 36 miniature muffins.

◆ SPOON ROLLS

¼ cup sugar	¾ cup butter, melted
2 cups very warm water	1 egg, beaten
1 ¼-ounce envelope dry yeast	4 cups self-rising flour

Grease 2½-inch muffin tins and set aside.

In a large bowl dissolve the sugar in the warm water and sprinkle the yeast on the surface about 5 minutes to proof. When the yeast is foamy, add the butter, egg, and flour. Mix thoroughly. Keep in the refrigerator until ready to use.

Drop the batter by spoonfuls into the prepared muffin tins and bake at 350° for 20 minutes.

Makes 24 rolls.

◆ SALMON MOUSSE

A good salmon mousse counters a multitude of sins. "Well, yes, of course she is tiresome and hard to get along with. And there is that unfortunate 'habit' she can't seem to break. But...you have to admit the woman makes a fine salmon mousse." See how it works?

2	¼-ounce envelopes unflavored gelatin	1	tablespoon vinegar
1	14¾-ounce can salmon, drained, with juice reserved	1	medium onion, quartered
	Water	1	cup mayonnaise
3	tablespoons lemon juice	2	cups roughly chopped celery or cucumber
1	tablespoon Worcestershire sauce	2	teaspoons dried dill weed
		1	cup whipping cream, whipped

Grease a 6-cup mold or serving dish and set aside.

In a measuring cup measure the salmon juice and add enough water to equal 1½ cups. In a saucepan over low heat dissolve the gelatin in the juice mixture, stir, and set aside.

In a food processor place the salmon, lemon juice, Worcestershire sauce, vinegar, onion, mayonnaise, celery or cucumber, and dill weed. Add the gelatin. Process until smooth. Fold in the whipped cream and pour into the prepared mold or serving dish. Refrigerate overnight.

Makes 12 servings.

◆ HONEY HAM

If you try to put on a buffet without glazed ham people will stand around with pained looks on their faces waiting for you to go out and buy some.

1	7-pound smoked pork picnic shoulder	1	6-ounce can frozen orange juice concentrate, thawed and undiluted
	Water		
2	cups sugar	1	teaspoon whole cloves
1	cup honey		

Make diagonal slits, ½ inch apart, halfway through the ham until the knife touches the bone. Place the ham in a deep bowl and cover with water. Stir in the sugar and soak for 2 days in the refrigerator.

Drain. Set the ham in a roasting dish lined with enough heavy-duty foil to completely wrap it. Cover with the honey and orange juice concentrate. Insert the cloves randomly over the top. Wrap the ham tightly in the foil. Bake at 200° for 6 to 7 hours, unwrapping and basting occasionally with the honey glaze.

When the ham is cooked, unwrap and bake at 450° for 15 minutes for slightly crispy skin.

Makes 10 to 12 servings.

◆ RARE ROAST BEEF

A lot of people credit their attendance at buffets solely to the rare roast beef.

2 to 4 beef ribs (4½ to 12 pounds)
½ cup all-purpose flour

1 teaspoon salt
½ teaspoon pepper

Cooking chart:

Ribs	Pounds	Minutes
2	4½ to 5	25 to 30
3	8 to 9	40 to 50
4	11 to 12	55 to 60

Warm the roast to room temperature. In a shallow, dry pan place the roast fat-side up and rub with a mixture of flour, salt, and pepper. Add no water to the pan. Place the pan in the oven and bake uncovered at 500° according to time chart above. When the cooking time is finished, turn the heat off and leave the roast in oven for 2 to 3 hours without opening the oven door. Slice very thin and serve with Horseradish Cream Sauce (recipe follows).

Makes 6 to 12 servings.

◆ HORSERADISH CREAM SAUCE

If you're not a meat eater, you'll have to find something else on the buffet table to dip into this horseradish sauce. If no one's looking, you could eat it with a spoon.

¼ cup prepared horseradish, drained
¼ teaspoon salt
¼ teaspoon pepper

1 tablespoon cider vinegar
½ cup whipping cream, whipped, or 1
   cup whipped topping, thawed

In a medium bowl mix the horseradish, salt, pepper, and vinegar. Fold in the whipped cream.

Makes 1 cup.

◆ BUFFET CHICKEN

8   boned chicken breast halves
8   slices bacon
4   ounces chipped beef
1   10¾-ounce can cream of mushroom
      soup, undiluted

1   8-ounce carton sour cream
    Slivered almonds

Grease an 8 x 12-inch baking dish and set aside. Wrap each chicken breast half in one slice of bacon. Cover the bottom of the prepared baking dish with chipped beef. Place the chicken on top.

In a medium bowl blend the soup and sour cream and pour over the chicken. Sprinkle with slivered almonds. Bake uncovered at 275° for 3 hours.

Spoon the gravy over rice.

Makes 6 to 8 servings.

◆ ASPARAGUS-CRAB CASSEROLE

Asparagus casseroles are hard to come by, a phenomenon difficult to understand when you consider how truly good they are. You could make this one with turkey or chicken instead of crab, mozzarella instead of Cheddar.

2   15-ounce cans green asparagus
      spears, drained
½   pound Cheddar cheese, grated
2   pounds imitation crab meat, shred-
      ded
3   7-ounce cans sliced mushrooms,
      drained

2   10¾-ounce cans cream of mush-
      room soup, undiluted
½   cup breadcrumbs
½   cup chopped almonds
    Paprika

Grease a 9 x 13 x 2-inch casserole dish. Line the dish with asparagus spears sprinkled with a third of the Cheddar cheese. Add the crab. Add another third of the Cheddar cheese. Cover with the mushrooms and mushroom soup. Top with the crumbs and almonds. Add the remaining Cheddar cheese and dust with paprika. Bake at 350° for 40 minutes.

Makes 10 to 12 servings.

 SAUSAGE AND PEPPERS

3 green bell peppers	1 pound hot Italian sausage
3 tablespoons olive oil	¾ cup red wine
Salt and pepper to taste	

Remove the stems and seeds from the peppers and cut into large chunks.

In an oven-proof baking dish sauté the peppers in the olive oil until they begin to soften. Sprinkle with salt and pepper, lift out of the dish, and set aside.

Brown the sausages in the same dish and add the wine. Cover and bake at 350° or 40 minutes or until the sausage is no longer pink.

Uncover and add the sautéed peppers. Bake for 30 minutes more.

Makes 2 to 4 servings.

◆ RICE PILAF

½ cup finely chopped onion	½ teaspoon saffron
1 clove garlic, minced	¼ teaspoon dried thyme
⅓ cup butter	⅛ teaspoon black pepper
2 cups white rice, uncooked	1 bay leaf
1 tablespoon chopped fresh parsley	2 13¾-ounce cans chicken broth
2 teaspoons salt	1½ cups water

In a 2-quart casserole over medium heat sauté the onion and garlic in butter until translucent, not brown.

Stir in the rice and sauté until the rice turns a milky color. Add the parsley, salt, saffron, thyme, pepper, and bay leaf.

In a saucepan combine the chicken broth and water and bring to a boil. Pour over the rice. Cover and bake at 350° about 25 minutes until the liquid is absorbed.

Makes 8 servings.

> It is bad manners...to eat greedily, as I do. I often bite my tongue and sometimes my fingers, in my haste.
> *Michel de Montaigne, 1558*

◆ SHERRIED SPINACH WITH MUSHROOMS

3   10-ounce packages frozen, chopped
    spinach
¼   cup butter
1   teaspoon Worcestershire sauce
1   teaspoon lemon juice
1   cup sour cream

1   4-ounce can sliced mushrooms,
    drained
Salt to taste
Freshly ground black pepper
¼   cup dry sherry

In a pot cook the spinach according to the directions on the package. Drain, wring dry by hand, and heat in a saucepan with the butter until the butter is melted. Add the Worcestershire sauce, lemon juice, sour cream, mushrooms, salt, and pepper. Add the sherry. Mix well and simmer 2 to 3 minutes over medium heat.

    Makes 8 to 10 servings.

◆ MUSHROOM-HAM CASSEROLE

¼   cup butter
¼   cup all-purpose flour
3   4-ounce cans chopped mushrooms,
    drained, with liquid reserved
Water
½   cup heavy cream

4   hard-cooked eggs, chopped
1   cup chopped cooked ham
Onion salt to taste
2   tablespoons dry sherry
Breadcrumbs

Grease a 1½-quart casserole dish and set aside.

    In a heavy saucepan over medium heat melt the butter and add the flour, stirring with a wire whisk until browned. In a measuring cup measure the mushroom liquid and add enough water to equal ½ cup. Add the mushroom liquid and cream, stirring until smooth. Add the mushrooms, eggs, ham, onion salt, and sherry. Pour into the prepared casserole dish and top with breadcrumbs. Bake at 350° for 30 minutes.

    Makes 6 servings.

◆ RASPBERRY-ORANGE SALAD

2　cups cranberry juice cocktail
2　3-ounce packages raspberry-fla-
　　vored gelatin
2　11-ounce cans mandarin oranges,
　　drained, with juice reserved

2　8-ounce cartons sour cream
½　cup chopped pecans

Grease a 9-inch square pan and set aside.

In a saucepan heat the cranberry juice to boiling. Stir in the gelatin and 1 cup juice from the oranges. Chill in the refrigerator to the consistency of uncooked egg whites.

Fold in the oranges, sour cream, and nuts. Pour into the prepared pan and refrigerate until set.

Makes 12 servings.

◆ CARROT-APPLE-RAISIN MOLD

2　¼-ounce envelopes unflavored
　　gelatin
2　tablespoons sugar
1¾　cups boiling water
1⅓　cups mayonnaise

¼　cup lemon juice
3　cups shredded carrots
1　medium apple, finely chopped
1　cup dark raisins

Grease an 8-inch square pan and set aside.

In a large bowl mix the gelatin and sugar. Add the boiling water and stir until the gelatin is completely dissolved. With a whisk blend in the mayonnaise and lemon juice. Fold in the carrots, apple, and raisins. Turn into the prepared pan. Chill until set.

Makes 10 servings.

◆ TOMATO ASPIC

There was a time when a tomato aspic was the making of a cook. Legends grew up around individual recipes; widows raised children on the proceeds. It's still hard to imagine a proper buffet without one.

2   16-ounce cans stewed tomatoes, drained with juice reserved
    Water
3   tablespoons cider vinegar

2   3-ounce packages lemon-flavored gelatin
2   tablespoons finely chopped onion
    Dash salt

Grease a 6 x 8-inch dish and set aside.

In a measuring cup measure the tomato juice and add enough water to equal 2 cups. In a saucepan bring the tomato juice mixture and the vinegar to a boil. Add the gelatin and stir until dissolved. Add the tomatoes, onion, and salt and pour into the prepared dish. Chill until set.

Makes 6 servings.

◆ PICKLE-PECAN SALAD

Yes—pickles. It also calls for ginger ale. Try it. You'll be amazed.

2   cups ginger ale, divided
1   3-ounce package lime-flavored gelatin
1   cup thinly sliced sweet gherkins (slice crosswise)

1   cup chopped pecans
    Mayonnaise
    Additional chopped pecans

Grease a 9-inch square pan and set aside.

In a saucepan bring 1 cup of ginger ale to a boil. In a large bowl dissolve the gelatin in the boiling ginger ale. Add the second cup of ginger ale and chill until the mixture is the consistency of uncooked egg whites. Add the pickles and nuts, stirring until well mixed. Pour into the prepared pan and chill until set.

Serve with mayonnaise and additional chopped pecans.

Makes 8 servings.

◆ 7-UP CAKE

1½ cups butter	2 tablespoons lemon extract
3 cups sugar	¾ cup 7-Up
5 eggs	3 cups all-purpose flour

Grease and flour a 10-inch stem pan and set aside.

In a large bowl cream the butter and sugar until light and fluffy. Add the eggs one at a time, beating well after each addition.

In a medium bowl combine the lemon extract and 7-Up and beat into the creamed mixture alternately with the flour. Pour the batter into the prepared pan and bake at 350° for 1 hour to 1 hour and 15 minutes. Cool in the pan for 10 minutes.

Makes 16 servings.

◆ EASY COCONUT PIE

1 13-ounce can evaporated milk	3 tablespoons all-purpose flour
3 eggs	3 tablespoons vegetable oil
1 cup sugar	½ teaspoon vanilla extract
1 cup flaked coconut	

Grease and flour a 9-inch pie plate and set aside.

In a food processor combine all the ingredients and process until well blended. Pour into the prepared pie plate. Bake at 325° for 40 minutes or until set. Let pie cool before serving.

Makes 8 servings.

◆ CHOCOLATE-RASPBERRY CHEESECAKE

12 ounces cream cheese, softened
½ cup sugar
½ teaspoon vanilla extract
2 eggs
½ cup frozen raspberries, thawed and
    well drained
1 9-inch prepared chocolate wafer
    pastry shell

GLAZE:
1 teaspoon butter
1 1-ounce square unsweetened bak-
    ing chocolate
¼ cup confectioners' sugar
1 teaspoon dark corn syrup
2 teaspoons boiling water
½ teaspoon vanilla extract

In the bowl of an electric mixer beat the cream cheese until fluffy. Gradually add the sugar and vanilla. Add the eggs one at a time, beating well after each addition. Fold in the raspberries, reserving a few for garnish.

Place the prepared crust on a baking sheet and fill with the raspberry mixture. Bake at 325° for 35 minutes. Cool completely on a wire rack and chill.

For the glaze, in a saucepan stir together the butter, unsweetened chocolate, confectioners' sugar, corn syrup, and boiling water over low heat until chocolate is melted. Remove from the heat and stir in the vanilla. Pour over the chilled cheesecake and chill for 3 hours more. Garnish with the reserved raspberries.

Makes 8 servings.

◆ GLAZED FRUIT TART

This tart looks like something you brought back from a weekend in Paris.

2 ¼-ounce envelopes unflavored
    gelatin
1 cup half-and-half, cold
1 cup half-and-half, boiling
2 3-ounce packages cream cheese,
    softened
⅓ cup sugar
¼ cup apricot brandy or Cognac
1 teaspoon vanilla extract
1 cup ice cubes (6 to 8)
4 cups sliced fresh fruit, any combina-
    tion of bananas, oranges, peach-
    es, strawberries, blueberries, or
    cherries

CRUST:
3 cups graham cracker crumbs
    (approximately 30 crackers)
1 cup melted butter
⅓ cup sugar
¼ teaspoon ground cinnamon

GLAZE:
½ cup apricot preserves
2 tablespoons apricot brandy or
    Cognac

In a blender sprinkle the unflavored gelatin over the cold half-and-half and let stand 3 minutes. Add the hot half-and-half and blend about 2 minutes until the gelatin is completely dissolved. Add the cream cheese, sugar, brandy, and vanilla. Blend at high speed until smooth. Add the ice cubes one at a time, blending at high speed until the ice is melted. Let stand about 10 minutes until the mixture is slightly thickened.

For the crust, in a large bowl mix all the ingredients and press into a 15 x 10 x 1-inch jelly roll pan. Evenly spread the mixture onto the prepared crust and top with the fruit.

For the glaze, in a small saucepan heat the preserves with the brandy, stirring until blended. Carefully brush over the fruit. Chill until firm.

Makes 16 servings.

◆ RED VELVET CAKE

When a crowd of people are standing around a buffet table and it comes time for dessert, half of them will start looking for the red velvet cake. It's a little extra trouble, but you might as well buckle down and make one.

½ cup shortening (not butter)
1½ cups sugar
2 eggs
¼ cup cocoa
1 ounce red food coloring, or up to ¼ cup for a deep-red cake
1 teaspoon salt
1 teaspoon vanilla extract
1 cup buttermilk
2½ cups all-purpose flour

1 tablespoon cider vinegar
1 teaspoon baking soda

ICING:
2 3-ounce packages cream cheese
3 cups confectioners' sugar
1 teaspoon butter, softened
1 tablespoon bourbon
½ cup chopped pecans or walnuts
½ cup chopped dark raisins

Grease and flour two 9-inch cake pans and set aside.

In the large bowl of an electric mixer cream the shortening and sugar until fluffy. Add the eggs one at a time, beating well after each addition. Beat the mixture 1 minute on medium speed.

In a separate bowl blend the cocoa and red food coloring to make a paste and add it and the salt to the creamed mixture.

In a separate bowl combine the vanilla and buttermilk and add alternately with the flour to creamed mixture, beating constantly.

In a separate bowl blend the vinegar and baking soda and beat in. Pour the batter into the prepared pans and bake at 350° for 25 to 30 minutes.

Let cool in pans on a wire rack before removing.

For the icing, in a large bowl combine the cream cheese, sugar, butter, and bourbon. Add the nuts and raisins. Spread the icing between the cake layers and over the top and sides.

Makes 12 to 15 servings.

◆ HOT TEA FOR TWENTY-FIVE

½   cup tea leaves or 20 small bags   *4½   quarts cold water*

Preheat a 6-quart serving pot by filling with boiling water. Heat cold water to just boiling. Empty the serving pot, add the tea leaves and cover with freshly boiled water. Let steep 3 to 5 minutes. Remove the tea leaves. Keep the tea warm on low heat.
    Makes 25 servings.

◆ ICED TEA FOR TWENTY-FIVE

½   cup tea leaves or 20 small bags   *4½   quarts cold water*

Preheat a 6-quart serving pot by filling with boiling water. Heat cold water to just boiling. Empty the serving pot, add the tea leaves and cover with freshly boiled water. Let steep 5 minutes.
    Remove the tea leaves. Pour over ice cubes.
    Makes 25 servings.

15

PARTY

The only emperor is the emperor of ice cream.
Wallace Stevens, 1923

So you're invited to this party. And you don't really want to go, but you're short on excuses and you figure you can just slip in, say hello, grab a quick drink, and be on your way with no one the wiser. So you get there. And right in the middle of the front hall is the one person you've been avoiding for months. And your heart sinks. It can't, you're thinking to yourself, get any worse than this. And then you see another one and another. It's a bleak moment—there's no denying it. So you're sidling toward the nearest exit hoping no one notices, and someone hands you a cup of raspberry sparkle and a chicken wing, and there on the sideboard next to the sausage-cheese balls you see some hot Velveeta dip and a plate of bacon twists. And the next thing you know you're in for the duration. Why, after all, turn down strawberries with chocolate cream?

People go to parties for the food. They may tell you it's the conversation, but they're lying. Generally speaking, the same people go to the same parties season after season, year after year. They all know the same stories; they tell them over and over; they do not—like popular romance—improve in the telling. The only thing that varies at parties is the food and that makes all the difference. On the strength of a good wine punch or a cup of orange blossoms, you can for a short while get along with Attila the Hun. You might even decide you like him. Guacamole, hot crab dip, sesame seed twists, Scottish shortbread, marshmallow-devil's food squares: all in all, it's not a bad system.

◆ NUTS AND BOLTS

In the 1950s, you couldn't throw a party without Nuts and Bolts, and the truth is people still gravitate to it in a crowd. It's just so tasty—all that Worcestershire and salt, not to mention the full cup of butter. It's got to be the inspiration for those high-energy health snacks hikers and cyclists carry around now in their fanny packs.

1	cup butter	1	10-ounce bag pretzel sticks
2	tablespoons Worcestershire sauce	1	10-ounce box Cheerios
	Garlic salt	2	8-ounce cans dry-roasted peanuts
	Celery salt	¼	cup pecan halves
1	12-ounce box Rice Chex		

In a saucepan melt the butter and add the Worcestershire sauce, garlic, and celery salts. In a large bowl mix the sauce thoroughly with the cereals, pretzels, and nuts. Spread in a 9 x 13 x 2-inch pan and bake at 200° for 1 hour, stirring every 20 minutes.
    Makes 6 quarts.

◆ PIZZA CRACKER APPETIZER

You can make tiny pizzas on just about anything, including flour tortillas and English muffins. It's all just an excuse, anyway, to get to the pepperoni and cheese.

1	10-ounce box round whole wheat crackers	8	ounces mozzarella cheese, grated
1	14-ounce jar pizza sauce	1	8-ounce package sliced pepperoni

On each cracker place 1 tablespoon pizza sauce, 1 tablespoon grated mozzarella cheese, and one slice pepperoni. Run under the broiler immediately for 2 or 3 minutes until the cheese is melted and bubbly. Serve immediately.
    Makes 50 appetizers.

> Let them eat cake!
> *Marie Antoinette, 1770*

◆ CHEESE COCKTAIL BISCUITS

There are many versions of these relatives of the cheese straw, including some with confectioners' sugar and cayenne—a volatile combination and quite addictive. This one is especially good with pecan halves on top.

½	cup butter, room temperature	1	teaspoon salt
1	5-ounce jar sharp Old English cheese, room temperature	⅛	teaspoon cayenne pepper Pecan halves
1½	cups all-purpose flour		

In a large bowl cream the butter until light and fluffy. Gradually beat in the Old English cheese. Slowly add the flour, salt, and cayenne. The dough will be very soft. Cover and chill until firm.

Form into 2 quarter-sized rolls, wrap in waxed paper, and chill again. The dough will last in refrigerator 1 month.

To serve, slice the rolled dough into ¼-inch pieces. Decorate with pecans, place on an ungreased baking sheet, and bake at 350° for 12 to 15 minutes or until lightly browned.

Remove immediately to a wire rack to cool.

Makes 60 to 72 biscuits.

> Egbert came into the large, dimly lit drawing-room with the air of a man who is not certain whether he is entering a dovecote or a bomb factory, and is prepared for either eventuality.
>
> *H. H. Munro, 1930*

◆ STUFFED MUSHROOMS

1	pound large mushrooms	⅓	cup olive oil, divided
⅓	cup grated Parmesan cheese	⅓	cup butter, melted
1	8-ounce package herb-seasoned stuffing mix		

Brush the mushrooms. Remove and chop the stems.

In a medium bowl mix the mushroom stems with the Parmesan cheese and stuffing mix, softening with 1 tablespoon olive oil. Stuff the mixture into the mushroom caps. Place the stuffed caps in a 9 x 13 x 2-inch baking dish and pour the remaining olive oil and butter over top. Bake at 350° for 25 minutes.

Makes 24 mushroom caps.

◆ STUFFED CELERY

For a time in the 1950s, children couldn't get through a meal without someone passing them a stuffed celery stick, and adults to this day find that even one bite takes them right out of time. Depending on who else is at the party, that's not necessarily a bad thing.

1   cup shredded Cheddar cheese
½   cup mayonnaise
2   tablespoons chopped pimiento-
      stuffed green olives

6   celery stalks, cut in 4-inch pieces

In a medium bowl combine the Cheddar cheese, mayonnaise, and chopped olives, mixing well. Stuff the celery with cheese mixture.
Makes 12 sticks.

◆ RAISIN-DATE CHEESE BALL

The organized and efficient party-giver will make these cheese balls weeks in advance, label, date, and freeze them for convenient serving at the last moment. The rest of us will notice about 5 o'clock that we're out of bleu cheese and try to fake it with feta. As a matter of fact, feta would work just fine.

3   8-ounce packages cream cheese,
      softened
1   4-ounce package bleu cheese, crum-
      bled
1   cup shredded sharp Cheddar
      cheese

1   8-ounce package chopped dates
1   cup golden raisins
½   cup chopped pecans, toasted

In a large bowl combine the cheeses, dates, and raisins, and divide in half. Shape each portion into a ball and roll in the pecans. Cover and chill.
Serve with shortbread cookies, gingersnaps, and/or apple and pear slices.
Makes two 4-inch balls or 20 servings.

◆ CHEESE-COVERED OLIVES

½ cup butter, softened
1½ cups shredded Monterey Jack
    cheese
¾ cup all-purpose flour
1 cup small pimiento-stuffed green
    olives

¼ cup, plus 2 tablespoons bread-
    crumbs
   Paprika

In a medium bowl cream the butter and Monterey Jack cheese. Add the flour, mixing well. Shape a small amount of dough around each olive, covering it completely. Coat with the breadcrumbs and sprinkle lightly with paprika. Place on an ungreased baking sheet and bake at 350° for 20 to 25 minutes. Serve warm.

Makes 36 olives.

> What kind of clothing did you say I have to wear?
> *Euripides, 407 B.C.*

◆ SESAME BREAD TWISTS

1 8-ounce can refrigerator crescent
    dinner rolls

1 egg
⅓ cup sesame seeds

Unroll the dough and separate into four rectangles. Press two rectangles together end to end, making one long rectangle. Repeat with the second two. Cut each long rectangle lengthwise into six strips.

In a pie plate beat the egg slightly with a fork and set aside. Sprinkle the sesame seeds onto a 15 x 12-inch piece of waxed paper. Twist each strip of dough several times, dip it in the egg, and roll it in the sesame seeds. Place the twisted strips 1 inch apart on a greased baking sheet. Bake at 400° for 8 to 10 minutes or until golden brown.

Makes 12 twists.

◆ HOT VELVEETA DIP

Ah, Velveeta, that grand old warrior—there's really no bad way to fix it.

1   large onion, minced
1   tablespoon olive oil
1   12-ounce can green chilies with
       jalapeños, drained

1   pound Velveeta cheese, cubed
    Paprika

In a skillet sauté the onion in olive oil until translucent, not brown. Add the chilies with peppers and heat thoroughly. Reduce the heat to very low, add the cubes of Velveeta cheese, and stir constantly until melted. Pour into a serving bowl and sprinkle with paprika. Serve hot with crackers or chips.
   Makes 6 servings.

◆ VELVEETA-TOMATO DIP

1   10-ounce can diced tomatoes and
       green chilies, drained

1   pound Velveeta cheese, cubed
    Freshly ground black pepper

In a saucepan stir the tomato-chili mix and Velveeta cheese together over low heat until the Velveeta cheese is melted. Pour into a serving bowl and sprinkle with black pepper. Serve hot with crackers or chips.
   Makes 6 servings.

◆ GUACAMOLE DIP

You can buy avocados the year round, but they're really only good from late June through August. The ones with the dark, gnarled skin are far superior to the smooth, light green variety. Oddly enough for something so rich and oily, avocados are very good for you. Eat as much of this as you want. You'll be doing yourself a favor.

    Salt
1   clove garlic, cut in half
1   large ripe avocado, pitted and
       peeled
¼   teaspoon chili powder

1   teaspoon lemon juice
2   teaspoons minced onion
1   tablespoon chopped tomato
1   tablespoon sliced ripe olives
    Mayonnaise to cover

Sprinkle a bowl with a little salt and rub with the garlic. Discard the garlic. In the bowl mash the avocado and season with the chili powder and lemon juice. Stir in the onion, tomato, and olives. Mix well. Cover with a thin layer of mayonnaise to keep the mixture from darkening. Just before serving, stir well. Serve with chips.
   Makes 1 cup or 4 servings.

 TUNA DIP

1 14-ounce can tuna, drained	½ cup mayonnaise
1 6-ounce can jalapeños, drained	Fresh cilantro, chopped
1 onion, minced	Tortilla chips

In a bowl combine the tuna and jalapeños. Add the onion and mayonnaise. Add the cilantro. Stir well. Serve with chips.

Makes 1 cup or 4 servings.

 CRAB MEAT DIP

1 cup cooked crab meat or imitation crab meat	½ teaspoon Worcestershire sauce
1 8-ounce package cream cheese	1 tablespoon grated onion
1 tablespoon prepared horseradish	Dash white pepper
1 tablespoon heavy cream	Lemon juice to taste

Grease a 1-quart casserole dish. In the dish combine the crab meat, cream cheese, horseradish, heavy cream, Worcestershire sauce, onion, and pepper. Bake at 400° for 15 minutes. Sprinkle with lemon juice. Serve warm with chips.

Makes 2 cups or 10 servings.

◆ CLAM DIP

3 tablespoons butter, melted	½ teaspoon Worcestershire sauce
3 8-ounce packages cream cheese	Dash Tabasco sauce
2 6½-ounce cans minced clams, drained, with juice reserved	
½ teaspoon each chopped chives, salt, ground sage, dried rosemary, instant minced onion	

In a saucepan mix together the butter, cream cheese, and clams, and cook slowly over medium heat. Add the remaining ingredients and thin with reserved clam juice as needed.

Makes 35 servings.

◆ SAUSAGE-CHEESE BALLS

1 pound hot bulk sausage
1 pound sharp Cheddar cheese,
   grated

3 cups biscuit mix

Lightly grease a baking sheet and set aside. In a hot skillet crumble the sausage and cook until lightly browned. Drain off the fat. Reduce the heat to low, add the Cheddar cheese, and stir until melted. Pour into a large mixing bowl and add the biscuit mix. Roll into ¾-inch balls and place on the prepared baking sheet. Bake at 350° for 12 to 15 minutes or until lightly browned. Serve warm.
    Makes 42 balls.

◆ CHICKEN WINGS

There's always a child or two in every family who, once the wishbone and gizzard are snatched up, will start angling for a chicken wing. Children often know more than we give them credit for. Wing meat is the sweetest on the bird, and if you buy all chicken wings and marinate them, you will soon lose interest in breasts and thighs.

½ cup catsup
¼ cup soy sauce
¼ cup honey

¼ cup lemon juice
2 pounds chicken wings

In a large bowl combine the catsup, soy sauce, honey, and lemon juice. Add the chicken and marinate in refrigerator overnight. Spread the wings on a foil-covered baking sheet and bake at 275° for 1 hour.
    Turn twice, basting with marinade. Serve hot.
    Makes 5 servings.

◆ BACON-MUSHROOM TWISTS

Smushed white bread, canned soup, bacon—you might not think it just from the recipe, but these are great appetizers. You could serve them with soup at supper, too.

1 *loaf white sandwich bread, crusts removed*	12 *bacon slices, cut in half*
1 *10¾-ounce can cream of mushroom soup, undiluted*	

With a rolling pin roll the bread slices flat. Spread the soup on top and roll up corner to corner. Wrap each diagonally with a bacon slice. Bake on an ungreased baking sheet at 325° for 30 to 40 minutes. Turn once.
    Makes 24 twists.

◆ SAUSAGE PINWHEELS

This is another test of preplanning and efficiency. Well-prepared cooks have a roll of sausage pinwheels always ready in the freezer. That way, they can slice off a few, pop them in the oven, and be passing around a plate of tasty hors d'oeuvres almost before the guests are out of their coats. It's something to strive for. Or perhaps you could cultivate the friendship of a well-prepared cook.

1 *5½-ounce package biscuit mix*	½ *pound hot bulk sausage*

In a medium bowl mix the biscuit dough according to the directions on the package. Roll out to ¼-inch thick rectangles. Spread the sausage on the pastry. Roll up end to end and freeze. As needed, slice and place on an ungreased baking sheet. Bake at 350° until brown, about 12 to 15 minutes, turning once.
    Makes 36 pinwheels.

◆ SCOTTISH SHORTBREAD

Real shortbread is nothing but butter and sugar with a little flour to hold it together. It pretty much defines the category.

1 cup butter, softened	2½ cups all-purpose flour
½ cup sugar	

In a large bowl cream the butter and sugar. Gradually work in the flour with a wooden spoon. The dough will be very stiff. Shape into a ball and flatten. Wrap and chill for 30 minutes.

On a floured surface roll out the dough to ¼-inch thickness. With a cookie cutter cut into 3-inch rounds and transfer to an ungreased baking sheet. Bake at 300° for 30 minutes or until pale golden.

Remove to a wire rack to cool. Store in an airtight container.

Makes 18 biscuits.

◆ CHEESECAKE BARS

⅔ cup firmly packed light brown sugar	¼ cup sugar
2 cups all-purpose flour	1 egg, beaten
⅔ cup butter, melted	1 cup sour cream
1 8-ounce package cream cheese, softened	½ teaspoon vanilla extract

In a large bowl combine the brown sugar and flour. Stir in the butter and blend. Press the mixture into an ungreased 9 x 13 x 2-inch baking pan and bake at 350° for 15 minutes.

In a separate bowl combine the remaining ingredients and beat until smooth. Pour over the baked layer. Bake for 30 minutes. Cool in the pan before cutting into bars.

Makes 40 bars.

◆ MARSHMALLOW-DEVIL'S FOOD SQUARES

1 cup firmly packed light brown sugar	1 teaspoon vanilla extract
½ cup cocoa	1 cup pecan pieces
2 cups water	Vanilla ice cream
1½ cups miniature marshmallows	
1 18¼-ounce package devil's food cake mix	

Grease a 9 x 13 x 2-inch pan. In the pan blend the sugar, cocoa, and water. Sprinkle with the marshmallows.

In a large bowl prepare the cake mix according to the directions on the package, adding the vanilla. Spoon the batter over the marshmallows and top with the nuts. Bake at 350° for 50 minutes.

Cool slightly in the pan before cutting into squares. Serve bottom-side up with vanilla ice cream.

Makes 12 servings.

◆ STRAWBERRIES WITH CHOCOLATE CREAM

You're at a party and you see people standing around licking chocolate cream off their fingers. It's a sign. You've come to the right place and you'd better stick around.

1 cup whipping cream	2 quarts fresh strawberries, washed
3 tablespoons cocoa	and capped
¼ cup plus 1 tablespoon confectioners' sugar	

In a medium bowl beat the whipping cream until just foamy. In a separate bowl combine the cocoa and confectioners' sugar and beat into the whipping cream until soft peaks form. Serve over the strawberries.

Makes 36 appetizers or 10 desserts.

◆ FROZEN FRUIT JUICE PUNCH

1 6-ounce can frozen orange juice
   concentrate
1 6-ounce can frozen pink lemonade
   concentrate
   Cold water

1 1-pound 14-ounce can pineapple
   juice
1 quart dry ginger ale, chilled
1 6-ounce jar maraschino cherries
   with juice

In a container dilute the concentrates with cold water as directed on the cans. Add the pineapple juice, then the cold ginger ale. Make an ice ring by placing cherries with juice in the bottom of a ring mold, pouring in 1 cup of punch, and freezing.

   Makes 1 gallon or 20 servings.

◆ HOT APPLE PUNCH

1 46-ounce can apple juice or apple
   cider

2 rolls Butter Rum Life Savers

In a saucepan combine the juice and Life Savers. Heat, stirring until the candies are dissolved.

   Makes 10 to 12 servings.

A lively understandable spirit
Once entertained you.
It will come again.
Be still.
Wait.
Theodore Roethke, 1951

◆ ORANGE BLOSSOMS

A delightful and treacherous drink—you might want to confiscate car keys as you hand it around.

1 lemon, thinly sliced	½ cup orange liqueur, chilled
1 cup water	6 oranges, thinly sliced
2 quarts orange juice, chilled	2 quarts champagne, chilled
2 cups vodka, chilled	

In the bottom of a ring mold place the lemon slices. Pour in the water and freeze.

Just before serving, into a 5-quart punch bowl pour the orange juice, vodka, and orange liqueur. Add the orange slices and champagne, stirring lightly. Add the ice ring with lemon slices.

Makes 25 servings.

I never drink...wine.
Bela Lugosi in Dracula, *1931*

◆ RASPBERRY SPARKLE PUNCH

1 10-ounce package frozen raspberries, thawed	2 cups water
1 6-ounce can frozen lemonade concentrate, thawed and undiluted	1 32-ounce bottle lemon-lime carbonated drink, chilled
	Fresh mint sprigs

In a blender or food processor process the raspberries until smooth. Strain, discarding the seeds.

In a container combine the raspberry pulp, lemonade concentrate, and water. Chill.

To serve, combine the raspberry mixture and lemon-lime drink, stirring well. Serve over ice with mint sprigs.

Makes 7 cups.

◆ WINE PUNCH

1 gallon dry red wine
2 limes, sliced
2 lemons, sliced

4 oranges, sliced
1 quart soda water, chilled

In a container combine all the ingredients and serve over ice.
    Makes 25 servings.

◆ SHERRY PUNCH

12 lemons
 3 family-sized tea bags
 1 quart boiling water

1 cup sugar
1 750-ml bottle dry sherry

Squeeze the lemons, reserving the rinds. Brew the tea in the boiling water with the lemon rinds and sugar for 5 minutes. Remove the tea bags and strain.
    When cool, add the lemon juice and sherry. Serve over ice.
    Makes 12 servings.

> This is what we call making an exit.
> Samuel Beckett, 1957

◆ MOCK PINK CHAMPAGNE

½ cup sugar
1½ cups boiling water
 2 cups cranberry juice

½ cup orange juice
 2 7-ounce bottles lemon-lime carbonated drink, chilled

In a container dissolve the sugar in the boiling water. Cool. Stir in the fruit juices and chill.
    Just before serving, add the lemon-lime drink.
    Makes 14 servings.

16

SNACKS

Many's the long night I've dreamed of cheese—toasted mostly.
Robert Louis Stevenson, 1883

Super Bowl Sunday, Saturday night at the movies, the latest medieval murder mystery, twelve miles hard riding on the Natchez Trace.... You live a good life. You work hard. You get a few hours off. You do what you want.

Picture yourself on the trail. You're wearing heavy-tread hiking boots, a space-age Windbreaker you ordered from a national outdoors catalog, khakis. There's a red bandanna knotted jauntily about your forehead, a knobbed walking stick in your hand. It's four in the afternoon. You've got six miles back to base camp. Your blood-sugar level bottomed out in the middle of that last cascade. Your feet feel like lead. You need a reason to go on and that reason is snacks: cheese straws, spiced pecans, caramel corn, blond brownies, raspberry bars, a big sack of chocolate cookies, any one of which will get you down that trail and off that mountain in no time flat.

If, though, you could manage to stay out of the woods, you could settle into some serious snacking. You won't need much—a big-screen TV, a couple of easy chairs, a low table, a few friends, six or eight glorious hours stretching out ahead with no responsibilities and nothing to do but load up the plates: sausage-cheese balls, broccoli dip, black bean dip, hot crab dip, stuffed mushrooms, garlic-buttered popcorn, chili con Velveeta, Cheddar-olive-pecan spread, banana slush, peanut butter squares, chocolate chip bars. It's not a bad way to spend an afternoon or an evening, or two or three.

Time doesn't count with snacks. There's never any age limit. And if you go heavy on the vegetable dip, you won't need any supper.

◆ GORP 1

This is classic gorp and you should eat it while watching The Day the Earth Stood Still. Gort, that well-intentioned robot alien and fine friend, would appreciate the gesture. Everybody on the planet wasn't that hospitable.

1 pound dry-roasted peanuts	1 pound plain M&M candies
1 pound raisins	

Mix together.
Makes 3 pounds.

◆ GORP 2

A more elaborate version of the hiker's little helper—this one has nice roughage for the digestion.

8 cups popped popcorn	½ cup butter, melted
2 cups Cheerios	½ teaspoon seasoned salt
2 cups goldfish crackers	½ teaspoon garlic powder
2 cups Rice Chex	1 tablespoon Worcestershire sauce
1 cup dry-roasted peanuts	

In a large bowl combine the popcorn, Cheerios, goldfish crackers, Rice Chex, and peanuts.

In a separate bowl combine the remaining ingredients and pour over the popcorn mixture, tossing gently to coat. Pour into a large roasting pan and bake at 250° for 1 hour, stirring at 15-minute intervals.

Cool completely. Store in an airtight container.
Makes 15 cups.

> *Mens sano in corpore sano* is a contradiction in terms, the fantasy of a Mr. Have-your-cake-and-eat-it. No sane man can afford to dispense with debilitating pleasures; no ascetic can be considered realiably sane.... Hitler, the French like to remind you, drank tap water and ate unsavory vegetables.
> *A. J. Liebling, 1939, 1962*

◆ SHREDDED WHEAT SNACK

⅓ cup plus 1 tablespoon butter
1½ teaspoons dried oregano
1¼ teaspoons dried basil
½ teaspoon garlic powder

½ teaspoon onion powder
4 cups bite-sized shredded-wheat
    cereal
½ cup dry-roasted peanuts

In a 15 x 10 x 1-inch jelly roll pan melt the butter in the oven. Remove and stir in the seasonings. Add the cereal and nuts, mixing well. Bake at 350° for 15 minutes, stirring at 5-minute intervals.

Let cool in the pan.

Makes 4½ cups.

> Never eat more than you can lift.
> *Miss Piggy, 1975*

◆ NUTTY POPCORN

12 cups popped popcorn, unsalted
1 cup whole almonds, toasted
1 cup pecan halves, toasted
½ cup butter

½ cup firmly packed dark brown
    sugar
½ teaspoon salt

In a large bowl combine the popcorn and nuts and set aside.

In a small saucepan melt the butter. Add the sugar and salt and cook about 30 seconds, stirring constantly. Pour the sugar mixture over the popcorn mixture, stirring until evenly coated. Spread the mixture in an ungreased 15 x 10 x 1-inch jelly roll pan. Bake at 350° for 10 minutes, stirring only once.

Store in an airtight container.

Makes 14 cups.

◆ GARLIC-BUTTERED POPCORN

¼ cup butter	1 tablespoon chopped fresh parsley
1 clove garlic, crushed but intact	3 cups popped popcorn
1 teaspoon salt	

In a small saucepan heat the butter and garlic until the butter is melted. Remove the garlic and stir in the salt and parsley. Pour the butter mixture over the popcorn and toss lightly.

Makes 3 cups.

◆ CARAMEL POPCORN

There are cooks in this country who stir up a triple batch of caramel popcorn on the first day of baseball season, pack it in airtight containers, distribute it around the rec room, and wait for the bar-co-loungers to fill up.

8 quarts popped corn	1 teaspoon salt
2 cups salted peanuts	1 teaspoon baking soda
1 cup butter	1 teaspoon vanilla extract
½ cup light corn syrup	1 teaspoon maple flavoring
1 cup sugar	
1 cup firmly packed dark brown sugar	

In a large bowl combine the popped corn and peanuts and set aside.

In a saucepan combine the butter, corn syrup, sugars, and salt. Bring to a boil, reduce heat, and simmer 5 minutes, stirring occasionally. Remove from the heat and quickly stir in the soda, vanilla, and maple flavoring. Pour over the popcorn mixture and toss well to coat. Spoon the mixture into three ungreased 15 x 10 x 1-inch jelly roll pans. Bake at 250° for 1 hour, stirring occasionally.

Remove from the oven. Stir occasionally while mixture cools.

Makes 8½ quarts.

Nuts!
Anthony Clement McAuliffe, 1944

◆ ROASTED PECANS

Anything you can do with popcorn, you can do also with pecans. Think how nutritious they are—all those minerals, all that roughage. Think how easily people can eat a whole bowl of them. Think what a good person you were to make them in the first place.

1 quart pecan halves	Salt to taste
¼ cup butter	

In a heavy baking pan place the pecans and butter. Bake at 300° until the pecans begin to brown, 5 to 10 minutes. Stir occasionally to keep the mixture from burning. Pour out onto waxed paper and add salt to taste. Cool.

Store in an airtight container.
Makes 1 quart.

◆ SPICED PECANS

1 cup sugar	1 teaspoon ground cinnamon
¼ cup water	3 cups pecan halves
1 tablespoon butter	

In a saucepan mix the sugar, water, butter, and cinnamon. Over medium heat bring to a boil and cook exactly 2 minutes, stirring constantly. Pour in the pecans and stir quickly until the pecans are coated and the syrup is entirely absorbed. Pour out onto waxed paper. Separate and cool.

Store in an airtight container.
Makes 3 cups.

◆ PEPPERED PECANS

½ cup butter	1½ pounds pecan halves (6 cups)
½ cup Worcestershire sauce	Salt and cayenne pepper to taste

In a heavy baking pan melt the butter and add Worcestershire sauce. Mix well. Add the pecans and stir well. Bake at 250°, stirring often, until the pecans have absorbed all the liquid.

Remove from the oven and sprinkle with salt and cayenne. Stir again. Store in an airtight container.

Makes 1½ quarts.

◆ HALFPENNY SNACKS

This is another snack dough you can freeze. Think how embarrassed you'd be if a bunch of people showed up in your rec room and you had nothing to feed them. Then again, feed them too well and there's always the possibility they'll never go home.

½ cup butter, softened	1 cup all-purpose flour
½ pound sharp Cheddar cheese, grated	½ teaspoon salt
	½ 1-ounce package onion soup mix

In a large bowl cream the butter and Cheddar cheese. Add the flour and salt. Add the dry soup mix. Form into a roll, wrap, and chill.

Slice the dough into ¼-inch rounds and bake at 375° on an ungreased baking sheet for 10 to 15 minutes.

Makes 36 biscuits.

◆ RICE KRISPIE-CHEESE WAFERS

Men were men in a world gone by, and women wore nylon stockings and high heels and did lots of things with Rice Krispies.

2 cups grated sharp Cheddar cheese	¼ teaspoon cayenne pepper
2 cups all-purpose flour	½ teaspoon paprika
1 cup butter, softened	½ teaspoon salt
2 cups Rice Krispies cereal	

In a large bowl mix all the ingredients and form into small balls. Place the balls on an ungreased baking sheet and press flat with a fork. Bake at 350° for 10 minutes.

Makes 100 wafers.

◆ CHEESE STRAWS 1

Cheese straws are not just addictively tasty, they're also the quintessential snack. A tastefully arranged plate of cheese straws says to your guests, "I am a pillar of civilized taste and you are lucky to be here." They are lucky. This first version is the kind your grandmother made and shaped with a pastry tube. The second is simpler—all you do is flatten them with a fork.

½ cup butter, room temperature	1¾ cups all-purpose flour
1 pound sharp Cheddar cheese, finely grated, room temperature	½ teaspoon salt
1 egg, beaten	¼ teaspoon cayenne pepper
1 tablespoon ice water	½ teaspoon paprika

In a large bowl cream the butter and Cheddar cheese. Add the egg and water. Beat until smooth. In a separate bowl mix together the flour, salt, cayenne pepper, and paprika and add to the cheese mixture, beating well. Chill dough for 10 minutes.

Pack the dough into a pastry press and squeeze into straw shapes on an ungreased baking sheet. Bake at 350° for 18 to 20 minutes.

Makes 36 straws.

> Time goes by,
> Everything else keeps changing.
> You and I,
> We get continued next week.
> Stephen Sondheim, 1981

◆ CHEESE STRAWS 2

2 cups butter, room temperature	4 cups all-purpose flour
1 pound extra-sharp Cheddar cheese, finely grated, room temperature	1 teaspoon salt
	½ teaspoon cayenne pepper

In a large bowl cream the butter and Cheddar cheese.

In a separate bowl mix the flour, salt, and cayenne pepper and gradually add to the cheese mixture. Form into small balls, place on an ungreased baking sheet, and flatten with a fork. Bake at 350° for 10 to 15 minutes.

Makes 144 small straws.

◆ EASY VEGETABLE DIP

If you and your friends are going to sit around all afternoon and eat, you're going to need lots of dips. Your friends are going to want chips and that's fine. But you should also have a big bowl of vegetables. It's not so much that vegetables are full of vitamins, minerals, and the six natural fibers necessary for proper health. The real reason you need them is that a big chunk of raw cauliflower holds far and away more black bean dip than any puny little corn chip. It's a basic principle of applied physics, which, perhaps, you could explain during a commercial break if anyone's interested.

1 *8-ounce package cream cheese, softened*	¾ *cup tomato juice*
½ *0.7-ounce package Italian salad dressing mix*	*Dash Tabasco sauce*

In a large bowl blend all the ingredients until smooth. Chill.
    Serve with raw vegetables.
    Makes 1½ cups.

◆ VEGETABLES FOR DIPPING:

Artichokes	*Bell peppers*
Broccoli florets	*Mushrooms*
Carrot sticks	*Radishes*
Cauliflower florets	*Spring onions*
Celery sticks	*Yellow squash*
Cherry tomatoes	*Zucchini*
Cucumbers	

◆ BLACK BEAN DIP

2 *10¾-ounce cans black bean soup, undiluted*	¼ *cup Worcestershire sauce*
½ *onion, grated*	*Dash Tabasco sauce*
¼ *teaspoon garlic salt*	*Pinch cayenne pepper*
	Dried chives, chopped

In a saucepan mix the soup, onion, garlic salt, Worcestershire sauce, Tabasco sauce, and cayenne pepper and bring to a boil. Remove immediately from heat. Sprinkle with chives and serve with corn chips.
    Makes 24 servings.

◆ CURRY DIP

1   cup mayonnaise
3   teaspoons curry powder
3   tablespoons catsup
1   tablespoon Worcestershire sauce

1   teaspoon grated onion
Salt and pepper to taste
Dash prepared horseradish

In a medium bowl combine all the ingredients and chill.
   Serve with raw vegetables.
   Makes 1¼ cups.

◆ CHILI CON VELVEETA

Velveeta with the lure of old Mexico—you can almost hear the guitars weeping in the dusty square. This recipe makes a fine dip as well as a base for chili con carne. Just add ground beef to the onion at the beginning, and serve it with sour cream and corn bread.

¼   cup chopped green onion
1   tablespoon butter
1   8-ounce can tomato sauce
1   4-ounce can green chili peppers,
     drained and chopped

1   teaspoon Worcestershire sauce
1   pound Velveeta cheese, cut into
     small cubes
Dash garlic powder

In a skillet sauté the onion in butter until translucent, not brown. Add the tomato sauce, chili peppers, Worcestershire sauce, and Velveeta cheese. Cook over medium heat, stirring constantly until the cheese melts. Stir in the garlic powder.
   Makes 3 cups.

◆ BROCCOLI DIP

1   onion, finely chopped
1   tablespoon butter
1   6-ounce roll garlic cheese
½   10¾-ounce can cream of mushroom
     soup, undiluted

1   8-ounce can chopped mushrooms,
     drained
1   10-ounce package frozen chopped
     broccoli, cooked and drained

In a skillet sauté the onion in butter until translucent. Add the garlic cheese and soup and stir until melted. Add the mushrooms. Add the broccoli.
   Makes 3 cups.

◆ SPINACH SPREAD

1   10-ounce package frozen, chopped
     spinach, thawed and wrung dry
     by hand
1   8-ounce package cream cheese,
     softened

½   8-ounce can whole water chestnuts,
     drained and chopped
Dash garlic powder
Dash Tabasco sauce

In a medium bowl combine the spinach and cream cheese. Add the water chestnuts and season with the garlic powder and Tabasco sauce to taste. Serve on toast or bagels.
    Makes 4 servings.

◆ OLIVE-CHEESE MOLD

1   ¼-ounce envelope unflavored
     gelatin
2   tablespoons cold water
1½ pounds sharp Cheddar cheese,
     grated
1   cup Worcestershire sauce

¾   cup hot water
1   cup chopped pecans
1   2½-ounce jar ripe olives, drained,
     pitted, and chopped
1   teaspoon cayenne pepper

Grease a 1-quart mold and set aside.
    In a small bowl soften the gelatin in cold water. In a separate bowl combine the Cheddar cheese, Worcestershire sauce, hot water, and gelatin, stirring to blend. Add the pecans, olives, and cayenne pepper. Pour into the prepared mold and chill overnight.
    Makes 4 servings.

◆ EASY STUFFED MUSHROOMS

1   3-ounce package cream cheese,
     softened
1   2¼-ounce can deviled ham

24 small mushrooms, brushed and
     stemmed

In a medium bowl combine the cream cheese and ham and stuff into the mushroom caps. Run under the broiler for 3 to 4 minutes until hot.
    Makes 24 caps.

◆ PEANUT BUTTER BARS

You're on a parachute drop behind enemy lines on a dark and starless night. You have a mission. You have a map. You have a pocketful of peanut butter bars. You're set for weeks. These things are power.

1	6-ounce package semisweet chocolate morsels	1	teaspoon vanilla extract
½	cup butter, softened	1¼	cups all-purpose flour
⅔	cup peanut butter	½	teaspoon baking soda
1	cup firmly packed light brown sugar	½	teaspoon salt
1	egg, beaten	1½	cups quick-cooking oats, raw

Grease and flour a 9 x 13 x 2-inch baking pan and set aside.

In the top of a double boiler over hot water melt the chocolate and set aside.

In a large bowl cream the butter and peanut butter. Add the sugar, egg, and vanilla, mixing well.

In a separate bowl combine the flour, soda, and salt and stir into the peanut butter mixture. Stir in the oats. Press three fourths of the peanut butter mixture into the bottom of the prepared pan. Spread the chocolate over the top. Crumble the remaining peanut butter mixture over the chocolate. Bake at 350° for 18 to 20 minutes.

Cool in the pan before cutting into bars.

Makes 24 bars.

◆ RASPBERRY BARS

Okay, so maybe you're just sitting in front of the TV and you don't have a parachute. Maybe you don't even like heights. So what? You're still going to get hungry.

1	cup butter, softened	2	cups all-purpose flour
1	cup sugar	1	cup chopped walnuts
2	egg yolks	½	cup raspberry preserves

Grease and flour a 9-inch square baking pan and set aside.

In a large bowl cream the butter and sugar, beating until fluffy. Add the egg yolks and blend well. Add the flour. Stir in the walnuts. Spread one third of the batter on the bottom of the prepared pan. Drop the preserves by spoonfuls over the batter and spread evenly to the edges. Completely cover the preserves with the remaining batter. Bake at 325° for 50 minutes or until golden.

Cool in the pan before cutting into bars.

Makes 12 bars.

◆ CHOCOLATE CHIP BARS

⅔ cup shortening
1 1-pound box light brown sugar
3 eggs, beaten
2¾ cups all-purpose flour
2½ teaspoons baking powder

½ teaspoon salt
1 12-ounce package semisweet chocolate morsels
1 cup chopped walnuts

Grease and flour a 9 x 13 x 2-inch baking pan and set aside.

In a large bowl cream the shortening and sugar and add the eggs, beating until smooth.

In a separate bowl combine the dry ingredients and add to the creamed mixture. Stir in the chocolate morsels and nuts. Spread the batter in the prepared pan and bake at 350° for 25 minutes. Cool in the pan before cutting into bars.

Makes 36 bars.

◆ DARK BLOND BROWNIES

Dark Blond Brownie sounds like the title of a foreign film. Maybe there's one on television. Maybe you could reach the channel changer.

⅔ cup butter, melted
1 cup firmly packed light brown sugar
1 cup firmly packed dark brown sugar
2 eggs, beaten
1 teaspoon vanilla extract

2 cups all-purpose flour
1 teaspoon baking powder
½ teaspoon baking soda
½ teaspoon salt
½ cup chopped pecans
1 cup milk chocolate morsels

Grease and flour a 9 x 13 x 2-inch baking pan and set aside.

In a large bowl combine the butter, sugars, eggs, and vanilla, beating well.

In a separate bowl combine flour, baking powder, baking soda, and salt and add to the sugar mixture. Stir in the nuts. Spread the batter in the prepared pan and sprinkle with the chocolate morsels. Bake at 350° for 25 minutes. Cool in the pan before cutting into bars.

Makes 24 bars.

◆ PEANUT BUTTER BROWNIES

In case you've forgotten, peanut butter is very nutritious. So are peanuts. It's practically your duty to eat them. The rest of this stuff is just along for the ride.

2	*eggs, beaten*	1½	*teaspoons vanilla extract*
¾	*cup sugar*	1	*cup all-purpose flour*
⅓	*cup firmly packed light brown sugar*	1½	*teaspoons baking powder*
¼	*cup peanut butter*	1½	*teaspoons salt*
2	*tablespoons shortening*	½	*cup chopped peanuts*

Grease and flour a 9 x 13 x 2-inch baking pan and set aside.

In a large bowl cream the eggs, sugars, peanut butter, shortening, and vanilla until fluffy. Add the flour, baking powder, and salt, stirring only until moistened. Stir in the peanuts. Spread in the prepared pan and bake at 325° for 25 minutes.

Cool in the pan before cutting into bars.

Makes 24 bars.

◆ RAISIN-NUT BARS

1	*cup firmly packed light brown sugar*	¼	*teaspoon ground cloves*
⅓	*cup shortening*	1	*teaspoon salt*
2	*cups dark raisins*	2	*teaspoons ground cinnamon*
1¼	*cups water*	½	*teaspoon ground nutmeg*
2	*cups all-purpose flour*	1	*cup chopped pecans or walnuts*
1	*teaspoon baking powder*		

Grease and flour a 9-inch square pan and set aside.

In a large saucepan combine the sugar, shortening, raisins, and water and bring to a boil. Boil for 3 minutes; then cool.

In a medium bowl combine the flour, baking powder, cloves, salt, cinnamon, and nutmeg and add to the raisin mixture. Add the nuts. Pour the batter into the prepared pan and bake at 325° for 50 minutes. Cool in the pan before cutting into squares.

Makes 12 squares.

> With rue my heart is laden
> For golden friends I had,
> For many a rose-lipt maiden
> And many a lightfoot lad.
> A. E. Housman, 1896

◆ CRANBERRY CREAM

2 cups cranberry juice cocktail,
   chilled
2 cups vanilla ice cream, softened

2 cups cherry soda, chilled
1½ teaspoons lemon juice
   Dash salt

In a blender combine all the ingredients. Blend at high speed for 30 seconds. Serve cold.
   Makes 12 servings.

◆ BANANA SLUSH

Bananas are full of potassium and potassium helps prevent leg cramps. If you're going to sit all afternoon without moving in front of a television set, sooner or later the blood is going to pool in your legs and you're going to need a banana.

3 medium bananas, mashed
1 cup sugar
1 20-ounce can crushed pineapple,
   undrained

Juice of 2 lemons
2 cups frozen orange juice concentrate, undiluted
2 cups ginger ale

In a blender combine the bananas and sugar and blend well. Stir in the pineapple, lemon juice, orange juice concentrate, and ginger ale and freeze until firm. Thaw slightly to serve.
   Makes 6 servings.

◆ BANANA SHAKE

1 cup vanilla yogurt
1 ripe banana
½ cup sugar

1 cup orange juice
12 ice cubes

In a blender place the yogurt, banana, sugar, and juice. Blend for 30 seconds. Continue processing and drop in the ice cubes one at a time until the desired thickness is reached.
   Makes 4 servings.

17

COMMUNITY

Oh, we'll all fry together, when we fry.
Tom Lehrer, 1965

Twenty-one pounds of macaroni. Twenty-one gallons of boiling water. Twenty-four pounds of shredded cheese. Three pounds of melted butter. Six pounds of breadcrumbs. Six gallons of milk. One and a half cups of Worcestershire sauce. Five hundred people. One common bond... Fundraisers, school suppers, political rallies, lunches for the homeless, church breakfasts, natural disasters, civic celebrations—they all depend on food. Pass around a hundred bowls of Texas chili with green onions and sour cream and you've got a following. Throw in twenty pounds of chocolate pudding and you might just wind up president.

Good food brings people together and keeps them there. There's nothing quite as redeeming to a damp church basement at seven in the morning as the smell of eighty-four eggs and eighteen pounds of sausage baking in a cheese-cream sauce. Fried catfish, hush puppies, three-bean salad, Apple Brown Betty, a dozen pumpkin pies lined up on the trestle tables next to the sandbag trucks. You might not be able to stop a flood with three hundred servings of candied sweet potatoes, but you can save a town.

Feeding the multitudes is more than a matter of simple multiplication. It takes inspiration, hard work, an understanding of seasonings. It's a gift, and if you have it your neighbors are blessed indeed.

◆ BISCUITS FOR A CROWD

Natural disasters require homemade biscuits. If you ever find yourself called upon to feed heroes, this is the first thing you fix.

13½ cups biscuit mix   3¾ cups milk

In a very large bowl mix all the ingredients to make a soft dough. Turn out on a floured surface and knead 10 times. Roll to ½-inch thickness and cut with a 2½-inch biscuit cutter. Place the biscuits close together on ungreased baking sheets. Bake at 450° for 8 to 10 minutes.
    Makes 50 biscuits.

Oh, good. For a moment I thought we were in trouble.
Paul Newman in Butch Cassidy and the Sundance Kid, *1969*

◆ CORN BREAD FOR FIFTY

You can't raise money for a church or school without a chili supper. And you can't have chili without corn bread.

12 eggs, lightly beaten   9 cups self-rising yellow cornmeal
 6 cups milk   6 cups all-purpose flour
1½ cups vegetable oil   1½ cups sugar

Grease two 12 x 20 x 2-inch pans and set in the oven to heat. In a very large bowl combine all the ingredients in the order given and pour into the hot pans. Bake at 450° for 30 to 35 minutes or until light brown.
    Makes 50 servings.

◆ HUSHPUPPIES FOR A CROWD

Hushpuppies for a hundred are exactly the same as hushpuppies for two. You just make more of them and there are more people waiting around for them to come out of the skillet. On a warm summer night on the front lawn of the local elementary school, a paper plate of fried catfish with hushpuppies, coleslaw, and baked beans is as clear a symbol of this nation's grandeur as you'll ever need.

2 cups white cornmeal	1 teaspoon black pepper
2 cups all-purpose flour	1 medium onion, chopped
3 tablespoons baking powder	3 cups milk (scant)
2 teaspoons salt	Vegetable oil for frying

In a large bowl sift the cornmeal, flour, baking powder, salt, and pepper together. Add the onion. Add the milk.

Heat 1½ inches of oil in a large skillet to 375°. Drop the batter by half spoonfuls into the oil and fry until lightly browned. Drain on paper towels.

Makes 72 hushpuppies.

◆ OVEN-FRIED CHICKEN FOR FIFTY

If you're cooking for fifty or a hundred or two hundred, and you don't have time or space to actually fry the chicken, this is a perfect alternative. It can bake on its own while you peel and mash a hundred potatoes.

4 cups all-purpose flour	2 teaspoons black pepper
4 cups nonfat dry milk powder	50 chicken quarters or 100 breasts and
2 tablespoons salt	thighs
1 tablespoon paprika	1 pound butter, melted

Grease several baking sheets and set aside.

In a large bowl mix the flour, milk, and seasonings. Dredge the chicken with the seasoned flour and place in a single layer on the prepared baking sheets. Brush the chicken with the melted butter. Bake at 350° for 1 hour or until the chicken is brown and the juices run clear.

Makes 50 servings.

> In the East, we believe we are born with happiness and one of life's important tasks...is to protect it.
> Le Ly Hayslip, 1989

◆ POT ROAST FOR A CROWD

18 pounds boneless beef inside-round roast	1 teaspoon black pepper
1½ tablespoons salt	2 quarts water
	3 bay leaves

Season the meat with the salt and pepper. Place in a roasting pan and brown at 450° for 30 minutes.

When the meat is brown, add the water and bay leaves and reduce the heat to 300°. Cover and cook slowly about 4 hours until tender. Add water as necessary.

When the meat is done, remove from the pan and let stand 30 minutes before slicing.

Makes 50 servings.

◆ MEAT LOAF FOR FIFTY

The lure of the meat loaf is the saving grace of many a community dinner. It's economical, easy to fix, and people will cross town in heavy traffic just for a taste of it.

10 pounds ground beef	1 #3 can stewed tomatoes, drained
2 pounds ground pork	2 tablespoons salt
3 cups breadcrumbs	1 teaspoon black pepper
1 quart milk	⅛ teaspoon cayenne pepper
12 eggs, beaten	Catsup
1 large onion, minced	Light brown sugar
1 large green bell pepper, diced	

Grease five 5 x 9-inch loaf pans and set aside.

In a very large bowl mix the beef, pork, breadcrumbs, milk, eggs, onion, pepper, tomatoes, salt, and peppers until just blended. Press into the prepared loaf pans. Top with the catsup and sprinkle with brown sugar. Bake at 325° for 1 hour and 30 minutes.

Makes 50 servings.

◆ SHEPHERD'S PIE FOR FIFTY

12	pounds ground beef or chuck	1	cup Worcestershire sauce
3	large onions, chopped	3½	pounds frozen mixed carrots and
1	large bulb garlic, peeled and		peas
	chopped	6	cups prepared instant mashed pota-
1	cup olive oil		toes
2	teaspoons black pepper	2	cups grated yellow cheese

Grease two 12 x 20 x 2-inch baking pans and set aside.

In a skillet brown the meat, onions, and garlic in olive oil a third at a time, setting aside the browned portions as you go. Season the meat mixture with the pepper and Worcestershire sauce and mix in the carrots and peas. Divide between the prepared baking pans and cover with the mashed potatoes and yellow cheese. Bake at 300° for 2 hours.

Makes 50 servings.

> Since I lost the brindle cat
> The rats come right up
> And peer into the pot.
> *Han-shan, 8th century*

◆ BEEF STEW FOR FIFTY

15	pounds stew beef, cubed	4	pounds potatoes, cubed
2	quarts water, divided	3	pounds carrots, diced
3	tablespoons salt	1	pound onions, diced
2	teaspoons black pepper	5	stalks celery with leaves, diced
¾	cup Worcestershire sauce	4	10-ounce packages frozen green
3	cups all-purpose flour		peas
1	quart warm water		

In a kettle brown the beef. Add the water and seasonings. Cover and simmer for 2 hours, adding more water as necessary.

In a large bowl mix the flour with 1 quart warm water and stir until smooth. Add to the meat and cook until thickened.

In a pot cook the fresh vegetables in 1 inch of water until tender and add to the meat. Simmer covered until needed. The frozen peas should be added at the last.

Makes 50 servings.

◆ BAKED HASH FOR A CROWD

10 pounds cooked beef, chopped
8 pounds potatoes, cooked and diced
4 large onions, coarsely chopped

¼ cup salt
1 teaspoon black pepper
2 quarts canned beef gravy

Grease two 12 x 20 x 2-inch pans and set aside.

In a very large bowl mix the beef and vegetables. Add the seasonings and gravy. Mix to blend. Place in the prepared pans. Bake at 350° for 1 hour.

Makes 48 servings.

◆ CHILI CON CARNE FOR A CROWD

Chili suppers give communities their sense of identity—chili suppers and the eight-hundred-pound butter cow they build at the state fair grounds every August. You should probably stick with chili.

10 pounds ground beef
2 large onions, chopped
1 clove garlic, minced
3 quarts canned tomatoes with juice, diced
1 quart tomato purée
2 quarts water

¾ cup chili powder
1½ tablespoons ground cumin
3 tablespoons salt
½ teaspoon pepper
⅓ cup sugar
1 #10 plus 3 1-pound cans red kidney beans

In a large skillet cook the beef, onion, and garlic.

In a large bowl mix the tomatoes, purée, water, and seasonings and add to the beef. Cook until blended. Add the beans to the meat mixture. Cover and simmer for 1 hour. Add water if the chili becomes too thick.

Makes 3 gallons or 50 servings.

◆ GLAZED BAKED HAM FOR FIFTY

You may think you couldn't fix supper for your church fellowship, but you could. Glazing a ham for fifty is no more work than glazing one for five—you just use more cloves.

1   15-pound ham, boneless and fully
      cooked
3   tablespoons whole cloves

GLAZE:
1   cup firmly packed dark brown
      sugar
2   tablespoons cornstarch
¼   cup dark corn syrup
2   tablespoons orange juice

Place ham fat-side up on a rack in a roasting pan and bake uncovered at 325° for 2 hours.

Remove the ham from the oven and drain off the drippings. Score ¼-inch deep in diamond pattern and stud with the whole cloves.

In a medium bowl combine the ingredients for the glaze and spoon over the ham. Repeat until the glaze is of a desired thickness. Return the ham to the oven and bake 30 minutes more.

Makes 50 servings.

◆ DEVILED PORK CHOPS

1½   quarts chili sauce
3   cups water
2   teaspoons dry mustard
3   tablespoons Worcestershire sauce

3   tablespoons lemon juice
1   tablespoon grated onion
17   pounds pork chops, cut 3 per pound

Grease several baking sheets and set aside.

In a medium bowl combine all the ingredients except the pork chops to make a sauce. Dip each chop into the sauce and place in a single layer on the prepared baking sheets. Bake at 350° for 1 hour and 30 minutes, basting occasionally with the remaining sauce.

Makes 50 servings.

> Once again, we've saved civilization as we know it.
> *William Shatner in Star Trek VI, 1991*

◆ CHEESE-STUFFED FRANKFURTERS FOR FIFTY

10	pounds frankfurters		100	slices (4 to 5 pounds) bacon
3	pounds yellow cheese		100	frankfurter buns
1	quart sweet pickle relish			

Grease several baking sheets and set aside. Split the frankfurters lengthwise but do not cut completely through. Cut the yellow cheese into strips about 3½ inches long. Place the cheese and ½ teaspoon relish in each frankfurter. Wrap one slice of bacon around each frankfurter and secure with a wooden pick. Place on the prepared baking sheets and bake at 350° for 30 minutes. Remove the picks and serve in buns.

Makes 50 servings.

◆ SALMON LOAF FOR FIFTY

3¾	cups milk		1	tablespoon dried dill weed
1⅓	pounds soft bread cubes, trimmed of crusts		2	teaspoons paprika
18	eggs, beaten		1	teaspoon white pepper
10	pounds canned salmon, drained		1	medium onion, chopped
2	tablespoons capers		½	cup lemon juice

Grease five 5 x 9-inch loaf pans and set aside.

In a very large bowl mix the milk and bread cubes. Add the eggs. Add the salmon, capers, dill weed, paprika, pepper, onion, and lemon juice and mix lightly. Divide the salmon mixture among the prepared loaf pans. Bake at 325° for 1 hour to 1 hour and 30 minutes.

Makes 50 servings.

"O Oysters," said the Carpenter,
"You've had a pleasant run!
Shall we be trotting home again?"
But answer came there none—
And this was scarcely odd, because
They'd eaten every one.

Lewis Carroll, 1871

◆ SCALLOPED OYSTERS FOR FIFTY

If you live inland, you mainly see oysters at Christmas inside a turkey. If you live on the coast in a community of fishermen, scalloped oysters are a glorious way of life.

2 pounds Ritz cracker crumbs	6 quarts oysters, drained, with liquor reserved
1 pound butter, melted	
1½ teaspoons salt	1 quart half-and-half
½ teaspoon paprika	3 cups oyster liquor
½ teaspoon white pepper	

Grease two 12 x 20 x 2-inch baking pans and set aside.

In a large bowl mix the crumbs, butter, and seasonings. Spread one third over bottoms of the prepared pans. Cover with half the drained oysters. Repeat the layering.

In a separate bowl mix the half-and-half with the oyster liquor and pour over the oysters. Cover with the remaining crumbs. Bake at 400° for 30 minutes.

Makes 50 servings.

◆ LEMON FISH FOR FIFTY

1 pound shortening, melted	50 5-ounce frozen fish fillets
1 tablespoon salt	3½ cups all-purpose flour
1 teaspoon white pepper	¾ cup half-and-half
½ cup lemon juice	¼ cup butter, cut in small bits

Grease two 20 x 12 x 2-inch baking pans and set aside.

In a large bowl mix the shortening, salt, pepper, and lemon juice. Dip each frozen fillet into the seasoned fat, then dredge with the flour. Place the fillets close together in a single layer in the prepared pans. Pour the half-and-half over the fish and dot with the butter. Bake at 375° for 20 to 25 minutes or until the fish flakes easily with a fork.

Makes 50 servings.

◆ CREAMED TUNA FOR FIFTY

Creamed tuna on corn bread sounds like something out of a happy childhood. If you have to volunteer at a homeless center to rediscover it, let it be your reward for kindness rendered.

¾ cup butter	1 4-ounce jar plus 1 2-ounce jar
1½ cups all-purpose flour	pimientos, chopped and drained
1 tablespoon salt	6 tablespoons Worcestershire sauce
1 gallon milk	¼ teaspoon cayenne pepper
1 large green bell pepper, chopped	7 12-ounce cans tuna, flaked
1 large onion, chopped	9 hard-cooked eggs, chopped

In a large skillet melt the butter over medium heat. Add the flour and salt, stirring with a wire whisk until smooth. Cook 5 minutes. Add the milk gradually, stirring constantly. Cook until thickened. Add the green pepper, onion, pimiento, and seasonings. Add the tuna and eggs. Reheat to serving temperature. Serve over corn bread.
    Makes 50 servings.

◆ SCRAMBLED EGGS

Seventy-five eggs? The first time you scramble eggs for a long line of sleepy people leaning up against painted cinder block with Styrofoam cups of tepid coffee in their hands, you'll be amazed at your own strength. Seventy-five eggs? You could handle three hundred.

75 eggs	2 tablespoons salt
1½ quarts milk	1 cup butter

In a large bowl beat the eggs. Add the milk and salt. In a large frying pan melt the butter. Pour in the egg mixture. Cook over low heat, stirring occasionally until the eggs are of desired consistency.
    Makes 50 servings.

 CREAMED EGGS

There's hardly a man alive who would pass up a breakfast meeting if he knew he was going to get creamed eggs.

1	pound butter	1	teaspoon black pepper
2	cups all-purpose flour	1	gallon milk
1½	teaspoons salt	75	hard-cooked eggs, quartered

In a large saucepan melt the butter over medium heat. Add the flour, salt, and pepper, and stir until smooth. Cook for 5 minutes, stirring constantly with a wire whisk. Add the milk gradually, stirring constantly. Cook until thickened. When ready to serve, pour the hot sauce over the eggs and mix carefully. Serve on toast or biscuits.

Makes 50 servings.

◆ EGG-AND-SAUSAGE FOR A CROWD

If you have any hopes of getting off the food committee in this lifetime, do not make this egg-sausage casserole for the annual community prayer breakfast.

2	pounds 8 ounces white bread, trimmed of crusts and cubed	3	quarts milk
9	pounds bulk sausage	42	eggs, beaten
2	pounds 8 ounces yellow cheese, shredded	1½	tablespoons dry mustard

Grease two 12 x 20 x 2-inch baking pans and cover the bottoms with the bread cubes.

In a skillet brown the sausage and drain. Spread the sausage and yellow cheese over the bread cubes.

In a large bowl combine the milk, eggs, and mustard. Pour over the sausage mixture. Bake uncovered at 325° for 1 hour or until set.

Makes 48 servings.

◆ DEVILED EGGS FOR A CROWD

You might think stuffing a hundred deviled eggs would be a day-long proposition. But sit down with a bunch of volunteers in the basement of a community center, and you'll have those eggs outside on the trestle tables before the sand trucks get back from the levee.

50 hard-cooked eggs, halved, with yolks removed	2 teaspoons dry mustard
½ cup milk	1 teaspoon sugar
1½ cups mayonnaise	½ cup cider vinegar
1 tablespoon salt	Paprika

Arrange the egg-white halves in rows on trays.

In a large bowl mash the yolks and add the milk, stirring until blended. Add the mayonnaise, salt, dry mustard, sugar, and vinegar and mix until smooth. Refill the whites with the mashed yolks. Sprinkle with paprika.

Makes 40 to 50 servings.

◆ PORK AND BEANS FOR A CROWD

1 pound bacon, diced	¼ cup cider vinegar
1 large onion, chopped	½ cup firmly packed light brown sugar
2 #10 cans pork and beans	1 tablespoon prepared mustard
1 cup catsup	

In a skillet fry the diced bacon until soft. Add the onions and cook until translucent, not brown. Pour off the fat.

In a very large bowl add the bacon and onions to the beans. Stir in the catsup, vinegar, brown sugar, and mustard. Bake in a 12 x 20 x 4-inch pan at 350° for 2 hours.

Makes 50 servings.

◆ CANDIED SWEET POTATOES FOR FIFTY

3 #10 cans sweet potatoes, drained	2 cups water
2¾ cups firmly packed dark brown sugar	1 cup butter
1 cup pecan pieces	½ teaspoon salt

Grease two 12 x 20 x 2-inch baking pans. Arrange the potatoes in the pans.

In a large saucepan mix the sugar, nuts, water, butter, and salt, and heat to boiling. Pour over the potatoes. Bake at 400° for 20 to 30 minutes.

Makes 50 servings.

◆ RICE PILAF FOR FIFTY

6 large onions, finely chopped	1 bay leaf
1 cup butter, melted	1 tablespoon dried parsley
3 pounds white rice, uncooked	3 49½-ounce cans chicken broth,
1 teaspoon salt	heated just to boiling
1 teaspoon white pepper	

Grease a 12 x 20 x 2-inch pan and set aside.

In a skillet sauté the onions in the butter until translucent, not brown. Add the uncooked rice and stir over medium heat until the rice turns a milky color. Place the rice in the prepared pan and add the seasonings and hot broth. Stir. Cover tightly with foil. Bake at 350° for 45 minutes.

Remove the bay leaf. Stir before serving.

Makes 50 servings.

◆ MACARONI AND CHEESE FOR A CROWD

It is every bit as easy to please a crowd with macaroni and cheese as it is to please a child.

3½ pounds uncooked macaroni	1 tablespoon dry mustard
3½ gallons boiling water	¼ cup Worcestershire sauce
2 tablespoons salt	1 gallon milk
2 tablespoons vegetable oil	4 pounds Cheddar cheese, shredded
1½ cups butter	1 pound breadcrumbs
2 cups all-purpose flour	¾ cup butter, melted
2 tablespoons salt	

Grease two 12 x 20 x 2-inch pans and set aside.

In a large pot cook the macaroni in 3½ gallons of salted water. Drain and coat with the vegetable oil. In a saucepan melt 1½ cups of butter. Stir in the flour, salt, mustard, and Worcestershire sauce and cook 5 minutes, stirring constantly with a wire whisk. Add the milk gradually, stirring constantly, until thickened. Add the Cheddar cheese and stir until melted. Pour over the macaroni and mix carefully. Place in the prepared pans.

In a large bowl mix the crumbs and melted butter and sprinkle over the macaroni and cheese. Bake at 350° for 35 minutes.

Makes 48 servings.

◆ THREE-BEAN SALAD FOR FIFTY

Remember those aisles in grocery stores and discount houses with row after row of #10 cans? Remember how you always wondered what on earth anyone would do with that many beans? Well, this is what they do. It's the same three-bean salad you make for Sunday dinner—only bigger.

1 #10 can French-style green beans, drained	3 cups cider vinegar
1 #10 can wax beans, drained	3¾ cups sugar
3 1-pound cans red kidney beans, drained and rinsed	¼ cup soy sauce
6 large onions, thinly sliced	¼ cup celery salt
1 large green bell pepper, diced	1 tablespoon celery seed
	2 teaspoons black pepper
	1 cup vegetable oil

In a large bowl mix together the beans. Add the onions and green bell pepper.

In a separate bowl combine the vinegar, sugar, soy sauce, and seasonings and pour over the beans. Cover and marinate overnight in refrigerator.

Just before serving drain the vegetables well. Add the oil and toss lightly.

Makes 50 servings.

◆ CUCUMBER SALAD FOR FIFTY

5 pounds cucumbers, scored and thinly sliced	3 cups mayonnaise
2 large onions, thinly sliced	1½ teaspoons salt
3 cups sour cream	3 tablespoons sugar
	¾ cup cider vinegar

In a large bowl mix the cucumbers and onions.

In a separate bowl blend the remaining ingredients and pour over the cucumbers and onions. Cover and refrigerate 3 hours.

Makes 50 servings.

◆ COLE SLAW FOR FIFTY

2 cups mayonnaise
2 cups half-and-half
½ cup cider vinegar
⅔ cup sugar

1½ tablespoons salt
½ teaspoon white pepper
7 pounds cabbage, shredded

In a large bowl combine the dressing ingredients and add to the cabbage. Mix lightly. Cover and refrigerate 3 hours.

Makes 50 servings.

◆ MACARONI SALAD FOR FIFTY

2 pounds uncooked macaroni
2 gallons boiling water
3 tablespoons salt
1 tablespoon vegetable oil
14 hard-cooked eggs, chopped
1½ pounds yellow cheese, shredded
2 cups sweet pickle relish
1 bunch celery with leaves, finely chopped

1 large onion, finely chopped
1 4-ounce jar pimientos, drained and chopped
1 tablespoon salt
¾ teaspoon white pepper
3 cups mayonnaise

In a large pot cook the macaroni in boiling, salted water. Drain and coat with the oil. Add the remaining ingredients. Mix lightly. Cover and chill for 3 hours.

Makes 50 servings.

◆ PEACH CRISP FOR A CROWD

Fruit crisps are simple desserts on any scale. You dump any kind of fruit into a baking dish and cover it with a crumbled mixture of sugar, oats, flour, and butter. You could make dessert for five hundred in minutes. It's all a matter of pans.

1⅔ cups sugar
⅓ cup lemon juice
15 pounds fresh, frozen, or canned peaches, drained
2½ cups butter, softened

3 cups all-purpose flour
2 teaspoons ground ginger
4½ cups regular rolled oats, raw
4 cups firmly packed dark brown sugar

Grease two 12 x 20 x 2-inch pans and set aside.

In a very large bowl mix the sugar and lemon juice with the fruit. Arrange in the prepared pans.

In a separate bowl combine the remaining ingredients until crumbly. Spread evenly over the fruit. Bake at 350° for 45 to 50 minutes.

Serve with whipped topping or ice cream.

Makes 64 servings.

◆ APPLE BROWN BETTY FOR A CROWD

12 pounds fresh apples, pared, cored, and sliced, or 10 pounds canned apples, drained	3 teaspoons ground cinnamon
4 quarts cake crumbs or breadcrumbs	1 teaspoon ground nutmeg
3 cups firmly packed light brown sugar	2 quarts apple juice
	2 tablespoons lemon juice
	1 cup butter, melted

Grease two 12 x 20 x 2-inch pans. Layer the apples and crumbs alternately in two layers of each in each pan.

In a large bowl mix the sugar, spices, apple juice, and lemon juice and pour half the mixture over each pan. Pour half the melted butter over each pan. Bake at 350° for 1 hour.

Makes 64 servings.

◆ RUSSIAN CREAM FOR FIFTY

Imagine Russian cream at a homeless shelter.

6 ¼-ounce envelopes unflavored gelatin	5 8-ounce cartons sour cream
1¼ quarts cold water	2½ tablespoons vanilla extract
1½ quarts half-and-half	5 pounds frozen raspberries, partially thawed
4½ cups sugar	

In a large bowl sprinkle the gelatin over the cold water and let stand 10 minutes.

In a double boiler over hot water combine the half-and-half and sugar and heat until warm. Add the softened gelatin, stirring until the gelatin and sugar are dissolved. Do not boil. Remove from the heat and cool. When the mixture begins to thicken, fold in the sour cream and vanilla, which have been beaten together. Chill for 3 hours.

Serve in ½-cup servings topped with raspberries.

Makes 50 servings.

◆ PUMPKIN PIE FOR A CROWD

14 eggs, beaten
3 #2½ cans pumpkin, drained
4 cups sugar
1 ¼ cups firmly packed dark brown
    sugar
1½ teaspoons pumpkin pie spice

1½ teaspoons ground ginger
1½ teaspoons ground cinnamon
1 tablespoon salt
2¾ quarts milk, hot
7 9-inch prepared pastry shells,
    unbaked

In a large bowl combine the eggs and pumpkin.

In a separate bowl combine the sugars and seasonings and add to the pumpkin mixture. Add the hot milk and mix lightly. Pour into the unbaked pie shells. Bake at 450° for 15 minutes.

Reduce the heat to 350° and bake for 30 minutes more.

Makes 56 servings.

◆ PECAN PIE FOR A CROWD

A big slice of pecan pie straight from the hands of a volunteer cook will restore even the weariest firefighter.

11½ cups sugar
10 tablespoons butter
1 tablespoon salt
30 eggs, well beaten
1¼ quarts white corn syrup

3 tablespoons vanilla extract
2 pounds pecan pieces
7 9-inch prepared pastry shells,
    unbaked

In a large bowl cream the sugar, butter, and salt until fluffy. Add the eggs, beating well. Add the corn syrup and vanilla and blend thoroughly. Divide the pecans evenly between the pie shells. Pour the egg-sugar mixture evenly over the pecans. Bake at 350° for 40 minutes or until filling has set.

Cool before cutting.

Makes 56 servings.

◆ CHOCOLATE PUDDING FOR FIFTY

5¼ cups sugar
1½ cups all-purpose flour
9 tablespoons cornstarch
1 teaspoon salt

2¼ cups cocoa
1 gallon milk
1 cup butter
2 tablespoons vanilla extract

In a large bowl combine the sugar, flour, cornstarch, salt, and cocoa. Into a large pot pour the milk. Gradually add the dry ingredients while stirring briskly with a wire whisk. Heat just to boiling, reduce heat, and cook until thickened, about 20 minutes, stirring occasionally. Remove from heat. Add the butter and vanilla and blend. Cover with plastic wrap while cooling to prevent film from forming on top.

Makes 50 servings.

◆ ICED TEA FOR FIFTY

9 quarts water
1 cup tea leaves loosely tied in
   cheesecloth or 40 small tea bags

3 cups sugar
7 lemons, cut in eighths

In a large pot bring the water to a boil and immediately add the tea. Cover and let steep for 3 to 5 minutes. Remove the tea leaves. Add the sugar and stir to dissolve. Serve over ice with lemon wedges.

Makes 50 servings.

◆ COFFEE FOR FIFTY

2 39-ounce cans ground coffee
3 cups sugar

1 quart milk or cream

Brew coffee in percolator or drip pot according to the directions on the package.
   Serve with sugar and milk or cream.
   Makes 50 servings.

18

GIFTS

*Oh, as a matter of fact, I had just been saying to myself at
that very moment, for the wings of a dove.*
P. G. Wodehouse, 1919

It's the tenth of December. The air is heavy with the threat of snow.
The interstate has been gridlocked since the day after
Thanksgiving. Stores are packed. Already you've been flattened
twice by star-struck four-year-olds headed for the video department. Even if you got to the mall, even if you found a parking spot,
even if you managed to get inside without getting mugged, they'd
be out of your sizes. It's going to be one of those holiday seasons.
You can tell.

But take heart. These are not disasters. These are signs. What
they're saying is, "Get out your cookbook, make your list, get on
down to your neighborhood grocery." It's seven in the morning.
You've got the place to yourself. You load up your cart with gift-
friendly ingredients. Elvis is singing "Blue Christmas" on the oldies
station on the way home. In a matter of hours your kitchen counters are stacked with neat packages of cranberry-nut bread, nutty
granola, black pepper-cheese logs, spicy nut bars, jars of champagne jelly, Christmas jam, India relish, Russian tea mix, instant
hot chocolate. There are whiskey balls on the table, orange
coconut balls in the freezer, peanut butter squares, sugar cookies,
and marshmallow fudge.

Your holiday spirit is back. Your house smells great. Your gifts
are ready. And all your friends are going to be very, very happy.

◆ SPICED TEA MIX

Hot spiced tea on a cold winter night is the gift of a true and thoughtful friend.

1   18-ounce jar orange-flavored instant
     breakfast drink
1   cup sugar
½   cup presweetened lemonade mix
½   cup instant tea

1   3-ounce package apricot-flavored
     gelatin
2½ teaspoons ground cinnamon
1   teaspoon ground cloves

In a large bowl combine all the ingredients, mixing well. Store in airtight containers.
    To serve, use 1½ tablespoons per 1 cup boiling water.
    Makes 10 half-pint gift jars.

◆ CAPPUCCINO MIX

You can go out for a cup of cappuccino, but if it's late and the weather is really rotten, you can open that jar of instant your neighbor gave you for Christmas.

1   cup powdered instant nondairy
     creamer
1   cup chocolate milk mix
⅔   cup instant coffee granules

½   cup sugar
½   teaspoon ground cinnamon
¼   teaspoon ground nutmeg

In a medium bowl combine all the ingredients, mixing well. Store in an airtight container.
    To serve, use 1 heaping tablespoon per 1 cup boiling water.
    Makes 4 half-pint gift jars.

◆ INSTANT RUSSIAN TEA

2½ cups sugar
2   cups instant orange-drink powder
½   cup instant tea
2   5-ounce packages lemonade mix
     with sugar

2   tablespoons ground cinnamon
1   tablespoon ground cloves

In a large bowl combine all the ingredients, mixing well. Store in an airtight container.
    To serve, use 2 teaspoons mix per 1 cup of boiling water.
    Makes 6 half-pint gift jars.

◆ INSTANT HOT CHOCOLATE

1   2-pound box instant chocolate milk
      mix
1   1-pound box confectioners' sugar

1   11-ounce jar nondairy coffee
      creamer
1   8-quart box powdered milk

In a large bowl combine all the ingredients, mixing well. Store in an airtight container.
   To serve, use 2 heaping tablespoons per 1 cup boiling water.
   Makes 12 half-pint gift jars.

◆ BARBECUED PECANS

Pecans only get better the more you do to them. You can order them in by the truckload from groves in Georgia, barbecue to your heart's content, fill your entire gift list,
and never have to leave your house.

2   tablespoons butter, melted
¼   cup Worcestershire sauce
1   tablespoon catsup

2   dashes Tabasco sauce
4   cups pecan halves
     Salt to taste

In a large bowl combine the melted butter, Worcestershire sauce, catsup, and
Tabasco sauce, stirring well. Add the pecans and stir to coat. Spread evenly in a 15 x
10 x 1-inch jelly roll pan. Bake at 400° for 13 to 15 minutes, stirring every 5 minutes.
   Place the pecans on paper towels and sprinkle with salt. Cool completely before
storing in airtight containers.
   Makes 4 half-pint gift jars.

> ### What do you want? Flowers?
> *Sharon Stone in* Basic Instinct, *1992*

◆ CARAMEL CRUNCH

8 cups popped popcorn	½ cup sugar
1½ cups whole almonds, peanuts, cashews, and/or pecan halves	⅔ cup butter
	⅓ cup light corn syrup
16 ounces dried fruit bits	½ teaspoon baking soda
1 cup firmly packed light brown sugar	½ teaspoon vanilla extract

In a large bowl combine the popcorn, nuts, and fruit and place on a baking sheet. Set aside.

In a large saucepan combine the sugars, butter, and corn syrup. Cook over medium heat to boiling, stirring often. Continue to cook about 15 minutes, stirring occasionally, until mixture is golden brown.

Remove from the heat and stir in the soda and vanilla. Pour over the popcorn mixture, stirring gently to coat. Bake at 300° for 15 minutes. Stir and bake 5 minutes more. Transfer to foil and cool completely. Break up and store in airtight containers.

Makes 10 cups.

◆ MARSHMALLOW POPCORN BALLS

1 1-pound bag large marshmallows	6 quarts popcorn, popped
⅓ cup butter	Vegetable oil cooking spray

In a saucepan combine the marshmallows and butter. Cook over low heat until the marshmallows are melted, stirring occasionally.

In a large pan place the popped popcorn. Add the hot marshmallow mixture, tossing to coat. Coat hands with cooking spray. Shape the mixture into balls and place on waxed paper to cool. Wrap the popcorn balls individually in colored cellophane or plastic wrap.

Makes 16 balls.

◆ HOLIDAY MUNCHIES

It's difficult sometimes to match the gift with the recipient, but anyone on your list with a houseful of ravenous guests can use a bowl of munchies.

1	6-ounce package seasoned croutons	1	12-ounce can mixed nuts
1	6-ounce package fish-shaped crackers	¾	cup butter, melted
		1	teaspoon hickory-flavored salt
1	6½-ounce package pretzel twists	¼	teaspoon garlic powder

In a large roasting pan combine the croutons, crackers, pretzels, and nuts and stir well.

In a medium bowl combine the butter, salt, and garlic powder, and drizzle over the nut mixture, stirring well. Bake at 250° for 1 hour, stirring every 15 minutes.

Makes 10 cups.

◆ NUTTY GRANOLA

Some families spend the holidays in reclining chairs in front of the television, moving only the occasional languid hand to reach the channel changer. Some families hike their boots off. Granola fits them both.

3	cups regular rolled oats, raw	¼	cup vegetable oil
1	cup pecan halves	2	tablespoons water
1	2¼-ounce package sliced almonds	¾	teaspoon vanilla extract
½	cup flaked coconut	¼	teaspoon salt
¼	cup salted sunflower kernels	1	8-ounce container dried fruit mix, diced
¼	cup plus 2 tablespoons honey		

In a large bowl combine the oats, pecans, almonds, coconut, and sunflower kernels.

In a separate bowl combine the honey, oil, water, vanilla, and salt, and pour over the oats mixture, stirring well. Spread the mixture evenly in a 15 x 10 x 1-inch jelly roll pan. Bake at 350° for 25 minutes or until golden brown, stirring every five minutes. Cool.

Stir in the dried fruit. Store in airtight containers.

Makes 5 cups.

◆ OLIVE-CHEESE BALL

Make a cheese ball. Freeze it. Take it to your favorite teacher.

1 8-ounce package cream cheese, softened	⅔ cup pitted and chopped ripe olives, drained
1 8-ounce package bleu cheese	1 tablespoon chopped fresh chives
¼ cup butter, softened	⅓ cup chopped walnuts

In a large bowl blend the cheeses and butter. Stir in the olives and chives. Chill slightly.

Form a ball and chill well. Roll in nuts. May be frozen.

Makes 1 ball.

We don't need...no stinking badges.
Alfonso Bedoya in The Treasure of the Sierra Madre, *1948*

◆ BLACK PEPPER-CHEESE LOGS

1 8-ounce package cream cheese, softened	1 teaspoon chopped fresh chives
1 tablespoon milk	2 tablespoons dried parsley
1 clove garlic, crushed	Coarsely ground black pepper

In a medium bowl combine all the ingredients except the pepper. Shape into two 5-inch logs. Roll in the pepper. Cover and chill. May be frozen.

Makes 2 logs.

◆ PEPPER-ONION RELISH

If you can find something special that only you make and give, your friends will look forward to it year after year. A good relish works that way, or a good chutney. The organized and efficient cook makes her gifts in late summer when the peppers come in and enjoys her own holidays, duty free. The rest of us should try to remember at least to stock up on canning jars when the shelves fill up in July.

2 *quarts chopped green bell pepper*	1 *hot red pepper*
2 *quarts chopped sweet red pepper*	1½ *cups cider vinegar*
1½ *cups chopped onions*	¾ *cup sugar*
2 *teaspoons mixed whole pickling spices*	2 *teaspoons salt*

In a large bowl combine the peppers and onions. Add enough boiling water to cover. Let stand 5 minutes. Drain.

Cover again with boiling water. Let stand 10 minutes and drain.

Tie the spices and hot pepper in a cheesecloth bag and in a Dutch oven combine with the vinegar, sugar, and salt. Bring to a boil, reduce heat, and simmer uncovered 15 minutes.

Add the vegetables and simmer 10 minutes.

Remove the spice bag and bring mixture to a boil. Quickly spoon the relish into hot, sterilized jars, leaving ¼ inch of head space. Wipe the jar rims with a cloth dipped in boiling water, cover at once with metal lids, and screw the bands tight. Process in a boiling water bath 5 minutes.

Note: Sterilize the jars by boiling the jars, lids, and bands covered for 5 minutes. Lift out the jars with sterilized clamps, fill, and cover with lids and bands lifted out also with sterilized clamps. For a boiling water bath, use a kettle deep enough to accommodate the jars on a rack that keeps them off the bottom. Fill and seal the jars, place on a rack, and cover completely with boiling water.

Makes 9 half-pint jars.

◆ INDIA RELISH

3 quarts peeled and chopped toma-
    toes
3 cups chopped celery
2 cups chopped onions
3 tablespoons salt
4 cups cider vinegar
3 cups firmly packed light brown
    sugar

⅓ cup whole mustard seeds
2 hot red peppers, seeded and
    chopped (handle with rubber
    gloves)
1 teaspoon ground cinnamon
¾ teaspoon ground allspice
¾ teaspoon ground cloves

In a large Dutch oven combine the tomatoes, celery, onions, and salt, stirring gently. Let stand 2 minutes. Add the remaining ingredients and bring to a boil. Reduce the heat and simmer uncovered for 2 hours or until thickened, stirring occasionally.

Quickly spoon the hot relish into hot sterilized jars, leaving ¼ inch of head space. Wipe the jar rims with a cloth dipped in boiling water, cover at once with sterilized metal lids, and screw the bands tight. Process in a boiling water bath for 15 minutes.

Makes 4 pints.

◆ CHAMPAGNE JELLY

There are elderly ladies in large families whose reputation for eccentricity is predicated almost entirely upon champagne jelly. Every year you think they won't show up with it, and every year they do. Once they've gone home, however, you get to eat the jelly.

3 cups sugar
2 cups pink champagne

1 3-ounce package liquid pectin

In a large Dutch oven combine the sugar and champagne. Cook over medium heat, stirring until the sugar dissolves. Do not boil. Remove from the heat and stir in the pectin. Skim off the foam with a metal spoon and discard. Quickly pour the hot jelly into sterilized jars, leaving ¼ inch of head room. Wipe the rims with a cloth dipped in boiling water, cover at once with sterilized metal lids, and screw the bands tight. Process in a boiling water bath 5 minutes. Let stand 8 hours for the jelly to set up.

Makes 5 half-pint jars.

◆ CHRISTMAS JAM

1   cup chopped fresh cranberries   2   cups sugar
1   10-ounce package frozen strawber-
    ries, thawed

In a saucepan combine the berries and bring to a boil. Add the sugar and boil for 8 to 10 minutes or until thickened. Pour into sterilized jelly glasses and seal with melted paraffin.

Makes five 4-ounce jars.

◆ STEAMED BROWN BREAD

The very thought of steaming bread in a soup can is beyond some people's imagination. Other people do it every Christmas and their fortunate friends eat fresh brown bread and cream cheese every morning for a week.

$1\frac{1}{2}$ cups white cornmeal   2   teaspoons baking soda
$1\frac{1}{2}$ cups whole wheat flour   1   cup dark molasses
1   cup all-purpose flour   2   cups dark raisins
1   teaspoon salt   2   cups buttermilk

In a large bowl mix the dry ingredients thoroughly. Add the molasses, raisins, and buttermilk. Spray one 1-quart mold and two to three $10\frac{3}{4}$-ounce soup cans with vegetable cooking spray. Fill two-thirds full of batter. Tie aluminum foil tightly around the tops. Place the mold and cans on racks in Dutch ovens. Fill the Dutch ovens with water halfway up the sides of the mold and cans. Heat to boiling, reduce, cover, and simmer for 2 hours and 30 minutes. Add water as needed.

Carefully remove the mold and cans from the Dutch ovens. Remove the foil. If the bread is still wet, bake at 250° for 15 to 30 minutes. Turn out the bread to cool on a wire rack.

Makes one 1-quart mold and 2 to 3 soup cans.

◆ CRANBERRY-NUT BREAD

Cranberries are so symbolic of Christmas you would think you could buy them only in December, but that's not true. By December, the bogs are frozen and bare and cranberries have been in the stores for months. It is true, however, that you can make cranberry-nut bread only at Christmas.

2 cups all-purpose flour	¾ cup orange juice
1 cup sugar	1 tablespoon orange rind, grated
1½ teaspoons baking powder	1 egg, well beaten
½ teaspoon baking soda	½ cup chopped pecans or walnuts
1 teaspoon salt	2 cups coarsely chopped fresh cranberries
¼ cup shortening	

Grease and flour a 9 x 5-inch loaf pan and set aside.

In a large bowl combine the flour, sugar, baking powder, soda, and salt. Cut in the shortening with a pastry blender until the mixture resembles coarse meal.

In a separate bowl combine the orange juice, rind, and egg. Pour all at once into the dry ingredients, mixing with a fork just enough to moisten. Carefully fold in the nuts and cranberries. Spoon into the prepared loaf pan, spreading the corners and sides slightly higher than the center. Bake at 350° for 1 hour or until the crust is golden brown and a wooden pick inserted in the center comes out clean.

Remove from the pan and cool before slicing.

Makes 1 loaf.

Saintliness is also a temptation.
Jean Anouilh, 1959

◆ SUGAR COOKIES

½ cup butter	½ cup confectioners' sugar
½ cup sugar	½ teaspoon cream of tartar
1 egg, beaten	½ teaspoon baking soda
½ cup vegetable oil	2 cups all-purpose flour

Grease a baking sheet and set aside.

In a large bowl cream the butter and sugar until fluffy. Add the remaining ingredients in the order listed. Stir until blended. Spoon by teaspoonfuls onto the prepared baking sheet. Dip the bottom of a glass into sugar and press the cookies lightly. Bake at 350° for 7 minutes. Do not overbake.

Remove and cool on wire rack. Store in airtight containers.

Makes 36 cookies.

◆ WHOLE WHEAT CRITTERS

These sweet crackers are not made with whole wheat because it's good for the digestion. They're made with whole wheat because the combination is delightful. It's only serendipitous that you cut them out in the shapes of your friends' favorite pets.

2 cups whole wheat flour	1/3 cup honey
1 cup all-purpose flour	1 teaspoon vanilla extract
1 teaspoon baking powder	1/2 cup milk
1/2 cup butter	2 tablespoons sugar
1/2 cup firmly packed light brown sugar	1/2 teaspoon ground nutmeg

In a medium bowl combine the flours and baking powder.

In a separate bowl cream the butter for 30 seconds. Add the brown sugar, honey, and vanilla and beat until fluffy. Add the dry ingredients and milk alternately to the butter mixture, beating after each addition. Divide the dough in half, cover, and chill several hours or overnight. On a floured surface, roll half the dough to 1/8-inch thickness. Using large cutters, cut into shapes of dogs, cats, ducks, etc. Reroll the dough as needed. Place on ungreased baking sheets and prick sparingly with a fork.

In a small bowl combine the sugar and nutmeg and sprinkle over the crackers. Repeat the process with the remaining dough. Bake at 350° for 12 to 14 minutes.

Remove immediately from the baking sheets and cool on a wire rack.

Makes about 36 crackers.

◆ MARSHMALLOW BROWNIES

1/2 cup butter	FROSTING:
1 cup sugar	1/4 cup butter
1/4 cup cocoa	1/4 cup evaporated milk
2 eggs	1/4 cup cocoa
3/4 cup all-purpose flour	1 cup confectioners' sugar
1 cup chopped pecans	
1 teaspoon vanilla extract	
1/2 pound miniature marshmallows	

Grease an 8-inch square pan and set aside.

In a large bowl cream the butter, sugar, and cocoa. Add the eggs one at a time, beating well after each addition. Stir in the flour, nuts, and vanilla. Spread the batter evenly in the prepared pan. Bake at 350° for 20 minutes.

Remove from the oven and while hot cover the top with a single layer of miniature marshmallows. Return to the oven for 3 minutes or until light golden in color. Remove from the oven and cool in the pan on a wire rack.

For the frosting, combine all the ingredients and beat until smooth. Spread over the cool brownies. Cut into squares.

Makes 12 brownies.

◆ SPICY NUT BARS

½ 18¼-ounce package spice cake mix
1 egg, beaten
½ cup cooking oil
1 cup quick-cooking oats, raw

½ cup dark raisins
½ cup chopped pecans
½ cup plain yogurt

Grease an 8-inch square pan and set aside.

In a large bowl combine all the ingredients and spread in the prepared pan. Bake at 375° for 15 minutes.

Cool in the pan before cutting into bars. Store in an airtight container.

Makes 12 bars.

◆ EASY NUT FUDGE

There are people who eat fudge only at Christmas, and then only if someone else makes it for them. It was a lucky day when they met you.

1 1-pound box confectioners' sugar
½ cup cocoa
¼ teaspoon salt
¼ cup milk

¼ cup plus 2 tablespoons butter
1 tablespoon vanilla extract
¾ cup chopped pecans, divided

Grease a 9 x 5-inch loaf pan and set aside.

In the top of a double boiler over hot water combine all the ingredients except the pecans. Bring the water to a boil, reduce the heat, and cook, stirring constantly, until the mixture is smooth. Remove from the heat and stir in ½ cup of pecans. Quickly spread into the prepared loaf pan and sprinkle with the remaining pecans.

Chill until firm and cut into 1-inch squares. Store in refrigerator.

Makes 42 bars.

◆ CHERRY NUT FUDGE

3⅔ cups confectioners' sugar
½ cup cocoa
½ cup butter
3 tablespoons milk

1 tablespoon vanilla extract
½ cup chopped candied cherries
½ cup chopped pecans

Grease an 8-inch square pan and set aside.

In a large bowl combine the confectioners' sugar and cocoa and set aside. In a saucepan over low heat combine the butter and milk and stir until butter is melted. Remove from the heat and stir in the cocoa mixture. Add the vanilla, cherries, and pecans. Pour the mixture into the prepared pan. Chill until firm. Cut into 1-inch squares.

Makes 66 bars.

◆ EASY PEANUT BUTTER FUDGE

½	cup butter	½	pound confectioners' sugar
4	large graham crackers, crushed	1	6-ounce package semisweet choco-late morsels
1	cup peanut butter		

Grease an 8-inch square pan and set aside.

In a large saucepan slowly melt the butter over low heat. Remove from the heat and blend in the cracker crumbs, peanut butter, and confectioners' sugar. Press into the prepared pan.

In the top of a double boiler over hot water, melt the chocolate and spread on the peanut butter mixture. Cool in the pan before cutting into 1-inch squares.

Makes 60 bars.

◆ POTATO CANDY

1	medium Irish potato	½	cup peanut butter
1	1-pound box confectioners' sugar		

Peel and boil the potato and in a large bowl mash it with a fork. While hot, add the confectioners' sugar to make a stiff dough. Roll out on waxed paper sprinkled with confectioners' sugar. Spread a thin layer of peanut butter over the top. Roll into a log 1 inch in diameter. Cut into ¼-inch slices.

Makes 48.

◆ DATE BALLS

Small, dense balls of dried fruit, crumbs, butter, and nuts rolled in confectioners' sugar are a holiday tradition. Sometimes they're flavored with fruit juice, sometimes whiskey, sometimes rum. Every home needs a bowl of them on the table after dinner. Every family needs a friend to make them.

¾	cup butter	1	cup chopped pecans
1	cup sugar	2	cups Rice Krispies
1	8-ounce package chopped dates		Confectioners' sugar in bag

In a saucepan melt the butter over medium heat. Add the sugar and stir until blended. Add the dates and cook for 5 to 6 minutes until soft. Cook no more than 10 minutes.

Remove from heat and add the pecans and Rice Krispies. Drop by teaspoonfuls onto waxed paper. Roll into balls and drop into a bag with confectioners' sugar. Shake to coat. Store in airtight containers in the refrigerator.

Makes 84 balls.

◆ ORANGE-COCONUT BALLS

2 cups finely crushed graham cracker crumbs	1 cup sweetened flaked coconut
1 cup confectioners' sugar	¾ cup frozen orange juice concentrate, thawed and undiluted

In a medium bowl mix the crumbs, confectioners' sugar, and coconut until well blended. Add the orange juice and stir until the dough is stiff. Form into small balls and roll in confectioners' sugar. Chill overnight before serving.

Store in airtight containers in the refrigerator.

Makes 36 balls.

◆ WHISKEY BALLS

These are called "whiskey balls," but you can substitute rum.

2 cups vanilla wafer crumbs	3½ tablespoons light corn syrup
2 tablespoons cocoa	½ cup whiskey
1 cup chopped walnuts	Confectioners' sugar

In a medium bowl blend the crumbs and cocoa and add the walnuts, corn syrup, and whiskey. Roll into small balls and let set for 15 minutes.

Roll the balls in confectioners' sugar and place on an ungreased baking sheet. Let stand for 1 hour.

May be stored in jars for up to 2 weeks.

Makes 60 balls.

PANTRY LIST

Most recipes in this cookbook can be prepared with the following staples. Everything you'll need for every recipe is not here—notably perishables—but you can cook for months on what is here, and you can always substitute if you lack an exact ingredient. Hard cheeses keep well in the fridge, but if you use a lot of sour cream, half-and-half, or yogurt, you'll have to remember to pick it up on the way home.

CANNED GOODS

Beans (green, red kidney, lima, lentils)
Beef broth
Black bean soup
Celery soup, cream of
Cheddar cheese soup
Chicken broth
Chicken soup, cream of
Coconut
Corn (creamed and whole kernel)
Fruits
Milk (evaporated and sweetened condensed)
Mushroom soup, cream of
Mushrooms
Olives (pimiento-stuffed green and ripe)
Onion rings, French-fried
Peppers (green chili and jalapeño)
Pickle relish
Pie filling
Pimientos
Salmon
Tomato sauce
Tomato soup
Tomatoes
Tuna
Water chestnuts

CHEESE

Bleu
Cheddar
Feta
Monterey Jack
Parmesan
Swiss
Romano
Velveeta

DRIED GOODS

Baking powder
Baking soda
Biscuit mix
Breadcrumbs
Cake mixes (yellow, lemon, devil's food)
Cocoa
Cornmeal
Flour
Gelatin (unflavored and flavored)
Oatmeal
Onion soup mix
Pasta (angel hair, macaroni, noodles, spaghetti, shells)
Rice
Sugar (white, light and dark brown, confectioners')
Yeast, active dry

FROZEN GOODS

Broccoli, chopped
Fish sticks
Mixed vegetables
Peas
Shrimp
Spinach, chopped
Whipped topping

OILS

Butter
Olive oil
Shortening
Vegetable oil
Cooking oil spray (Almost all greasing of pans or skillets
can be done with cooking oil spray.)

SEASONINGS

Almond extract
Amaretto
Basil
Bay leaves
Brandy
Catsup
Celery seed

Chili powder
Cinnamon (ground and stick)
Cloves, whole
Cointreau
Cognac
Curry powder
Dill weed
Garlic powder
Ginger, ground
Italian seasoning
Mayonnaise
Mustard (prepared and dry)
Nutmeg, ground
Onion, instant minced
Oregano
Paprika
Parsley flakes
Pepper (white, black, and cayenne)
Salt
Sherry, dry
Soy sauce
Tabasco sauce
Tarragon
Thyme
Vanilla extract
Vinegar, cider
Wine (dry red and dry white)
Worcestershire sauce

INDEX

W

Z